Anna's Friends

Lessons learned from a short, beautiful life.

JOHN C. STUIVE & KATHLEEN A. FEENEY

Rogue River
BOOKS

BELMONT ✳ MICHIGAN

ISBN 0-9718076-3-9

Library of Congress Control Number: 2002091836

Printed in the United States by
Color House Graphics,
    3505 Eastern Avenue S.E.
    Grand Rapids, Michigan, 49508
    616.241.1916

Scanning by PhotoLith, Inc.
    948 Scribner N.W.
    Grand Rapids, Michigan, 49504
    616.459.3586

Cover Design by Myrick Design Studio
    9082 E. Long Lake Drive
    Scotts, Michigan, 49088
    616.217.6282

Front Cover Photography by Bass Photography
    6231 West River Drive N.E.
    Belmont, Michigan, 49306
    616.363.7486

Dedication

This book is dedicated to all of Anna's Friends. You know who you are.

Acknowledgments

Thanks to everyone who encouraged us to put pen to paper and tell Anna's story. Thanks to Bruce Boutet, Neil Kimball, Olan Mills, Michelle Wise, Sears Portrait Studio, and Paul De Boode for giving us images of Anna that we will always treasure. Thanks to Pam Eicher for her text design guidance and to Wanda Myrick for her cover design. Thanks to all of our editors for your time and thoughtful consideration. Thanks to Sheri Volkhardt for her transcription talents and to Mike Volkhardt for showing us that there was indeed light at the end of the tunnel and then for carrying us to the light. Thanks to everyone at PhotoLith for all of the finishing touches. Thanks to Paul and Amy Wellman, Mike and Ann Feeney, Brian and Crystal Feeney, Perry and Darla Pabst, Marc and Julianna Feeney, and Trudy Rysdam for their incomprehensible generosity. Finally, we offer special thanks to our parents, siblings, and extended families, and all of Anna's Friends. You fed us, you took care of us, you held us, and you comforted us. We can never repay your kindness.

Credits

The words and photographs that grace these pages are principally the work of the authors; nonetheless, in some instances you will also see the works of others which we have reproduced here with their permission. A special thank you to these contributors.

Photographs, Drawings and such.

Photographs by Brian Bass: front cover, p. 15 bottom right, pp. 167-170, pp. 314-315, pp. 318-319, p. 336.

Photographs by Bruce Boutet: p. 20 bottom, p. 21 bottom, p. 22 top right, p. 23 top row, p. 146 bottom center. Copyright © 1999 Bruce Boutet Photography, 6080 E. Fulton Street, Ada, Michigan 49301, 616.682.1160.

Photographs by Paul De Boode: p. 17 center left, p. 21 top center and right, p. 43 bottom, p. 114 top, pp. 164-166, p. 196 bottom left, pp. 197-199, p. 202 middle right center, p. 259 bottom, p. 262 bottom center left and bottom center right. Copyright © 1999-2000 Paul's Photography, 8183 Lamplight Drive, Jenison, Michigan 49428, 616.457.4926.

Photographs by Michelle Wise: p. 9, p. 202 bottom left, p. 206, p. 215 bottom, p. 216, p. 284, p. 306, p. 322, back cover. Copyright © 2000 Wise Photography, 65 E. Bridge Street, Rockford, Michigan 49341 616.866.6081.

Photographs by Rita Allen of Olan Mills Portrait Studios: p. 28 center right, p. 29 center left, p. 112, p. 139, p. 143, p. 145, p. 147 top and bottom, p. 150, p. 179 center, p. 202 bottom center. Copyright © 1999 Olan Mills Portrait Studios.

Photographs by Sears Portrait Studios: p. 173, p. 208. Copyright © 2000 Sears Portrait Studios.

Photographs by Neil Kimball: p. 30 bottom left, p. 56 bottom, p. 144, p. 146 bottom left, p. 148 bottom center, p. 202 top left center and bottom right.

A photograph by Sister Rosemary Smith: p. 292. A photograph by James McMahon: p. 67. Photographs by Bonnie Piers: p. 201, p. 220. Photographs by Dawn Wichmann: p. 154. Photographs by Jerry Nagelkirk: p. 226. Photograph of James Cromwell and Babe: p. 161. Copyright © 1995 Universal City Studios, Inc. The photograph of Esther Morris, our nation's first female judge, appears at the top of page 198 courtesy of the Wyoming State Archives, Department of State Parks and Cultural Resources. The photograph of Sarah Wertman, our state's first female lawyer, appears at page 198 courtesy of the Bentley Historical Library, University of Michigan. The photograph of Joan and Scott Pawlowski on page 65 appears courtesy of Joan Pawlowski. The photographs at pages 181, by Rex D. Larsen and T.J. Hamilton, respectively, appear courtesy of the Grand Rapids Press. The photograph at page 256 appears courtesy of Lauran Bittinger.

The logo of the Mitochondrial and Metabolic Disease Center appears at page 41 and 334 courtesy of Dr. Robert Naviaux. The photograph of Neocate appears at page 54 courtesy of SHS North America. The photographs and logos at page 61 appear courtesy of Baxa Corp., we especially thank Marian Robinson and Neva Chatterson for their assistance and friendship. The illustrations of Anna's button and feeding tube appear at page 128 courtesy of Kimberley Clark/Ballard Medical, and we especially thank Mark Foster for his assistance and encouragement.

The logo of DeVos Children's Hospital appears at pages 175 and 212 courtesy of that institution, special thanks to Martha Slager. The logo of Children's Miracle Network appears at page 174 courtesy of that institution. The photograph of Anja Downe appears at page 174 courtesy of Anja and EZ 105.7, now Star 105.7. The logo of the United Mitochondrial Disease Foundation appears at pages 209 and 334 courtesy of that institution. The photograph and map of Festival 2000 appear at page 210 courtesy of the Grand Rapids Arts Council. The photograph of Old Kent Park, now Fifth Third Ballpark, and the logo of the West Michigan White-caps appear at page 224 courtesy of the West Michigan Whitecaps. The photograph and logo at page 250 appear courtesy of the Grand Traverse Resort.

The drawing of Anna at page 84 appears courtesy of Ryan Kimball. The drawing at page 185 and the painting at page 187 appear courtesy of Jim Wisnewski.

Words.

The poems of Melanie Vugteveen that appear at pages 138, 150 and 291 are reprinted here with her permission. The interview with Anja Downe of EZ 105.7, now Star 105.7, appears at pages 176-177 courtesy of that radio station. The video transcript at pages 184-187 appears courtesy of Jim Wisnewski. The interview with Brian Sterling of WOOD TV8 appears courtesy of that television station. The poem reproduced at page 321 appears courtesy of its author Sister Felicia Bertaina.

The lyrics to "If I Had Words" by J. Hodge, reproduced at page 161-162, appear courtesy of Rak Publishing Ltd., special thanks to John Massa of Music & Media International for his assistance and kindness. The lyrics to Lullabye (Goodnight My Angel) by Billy Joel, reproduced at page 312, appear courtesy of Impulsive Music. Lullabye (Goodnight, My Angel) Coypright © Impulsive Music. All rights reserved. Used by permission.

Table of Contents

In the beginning . . .
Wherein you will be introduced to Anna and the first six months of her life through pictures.

The Day Things Changed
Wherein you will learn that Anna has Leigh's Syndrome, a rare metabolic disease.

The List
Wherein you will discover how we learned to live with a terminally ill child and how we communicated with all of Anna's Friends.

The Trip
Wherein you will travel with us to the University of California, San Diego Medical Center to learn more about Anna and her illness.

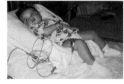

The Surgery
Wherein you will spend the holidays with Anna and keep her company during her preparation for and recovery from surgery.

Preface

Death is part of life. Even children die. That, too, is just part of life. When children are diagnosed with a terminal illness, however, it is the exception rather than the rule. Perhaps because it is the exception, we tend to shy away from it. We catalog the fact of terminal illness, equate it with death, and move on. But, terminal illness does not equal death. There is a lot of living that goes on after the diagnosis of a terminal illness.

In some respects living with a terminally ill child is the hardest possible life. But you might be surprised to learn that living with a terminally ill child can also be the richest possible life. Imagine living each day as if it is your last, just relishing the here and now.

Of course, if you are inclined to shy away from terminal illness, you will not see the beauty of that life. In fact, if you shy away you will be abandoning a family in need. So, do not shy away. Whether you are a medical professional, a colleague, a friend, a family member, or even a neighbor, you have a role to play in that child's life and in that family's life.

Those are the two things we hope you will take from Anna's story. First, that life, no matter how brief, is precious and beautiful. And second, that by not turning away, but instead participating in the life of a terminally ill child, you will see the beauty and your own life will be enriched.

Introduction

This is Anna Evaleen Stuive. Anna was born on March 9, 1999 at 1:16 a.m. When Anna was about six months old she was diagnosed with a rare and terminal disease, Leigh's syndrome. At 3:00 a.m. on November 23, 2000, Thanksgiving morning, Anna died.

We are Kathleen Feeney and John Stuive, Anna's parents. Anna was a wonderful gift from God. She taught us many lessons. Our journey with Anna changed us so profoundly that we felt compelled to share that journey with you.

After Anna died we tried many times to write her story. Knowing how the journey ended, however, seemed to color our description of almost every step. To permit you to see the journey as we did, you will read most of Anna's story as we wrote it while she was still with us. Between e-mails, letters, photos, and interviews you can trace almost every step.

The words we spoke and wrote while Anna was with us reveal many of the lessons that Anna taught us. But, there are a few gaps in the record and hindsight has helped us see a couple of things more clearly. Accordingly, we will fill those gaps in this margin throughout the book.

We hope Anna will give you as much joy and inspiration as she gave us.

It may help you to know a few things about Kathleen and me before you get started. Kathleen is the daughter of Verne and Dee Feeney. Her ethnic heritage is Polish, Irish and French Canadian. She grew up in Farmington Hills, Michigan and Bryan, Ohio with her older brothers Patrick and Brian. Perhaps because of her brothers' influence, Kathleen is an athlete as well as a scholar. She is particularly skilled at basketball and swimming.

Kathleen earned her undergraduate degree at Michigan State University. She attended law school at the University of Illinois, graduating in 1987. She then joined the law firm of Foster, Swift, Collins & Smith in Lansing, Michigan. She worked there three years before fate drew her to Grand Rapids, Michigan and the law firm of Mika, Meyers, Beckett & Jones. That is where she met me.

I am the son of John and Johanna Stuive. My ethnic heritage is Dutch; my folks came over on the boat. I grew up in Grand Rapids, Michigan. I have two sisters, Lauran, who is two years my senior, and Lisa, who is two years my junior. Although I like to consider myself a scholar, I am no athlete.

I earned my undergraduate degree at Calvin College. I went to law school at the University of Michigan, graduating in 1988 (yes, I am younger than Kathleen). After graduation, I went to work for the law firm of Mika, Meyers, Beckett & Jones. I met Kathleen when she was interviewing with the firm.

When Kathleen joined the firm, we were the only single attorneys. Thus, we were naturally thrown together at firm functions. We started dating, but we kept that a secret at work. We kept our secret well. When we eventually informed our colleagues that we were engaged, many thought it was a joke. You see, Kathleen and I are so different that they could not imagine us together. Once they saw us together for a while, they could not imagine us apart.

Despite our differences, we were married during November of 1992. That was our first step in forming a family. It took us a while to take the second step. But, after five and one-half years of marriage, we decided it was time. About a year later, Anna Evaleen Stuive came into our lives.

I thought I would write a marginal note here so you could see how they will work throughout the book. Kathleen is a very motivated individual. She was selected as the Outstanding Woman Law Graduate of her class. A few years later she was selected as Michigan's Outstanding Young Lawyer. I, on the other hand, am not so motivated. I have never been selected as anything. Nonetheless, Kathleen considers me a good, moral, and God-fearing human being. That is good enough for me.

Chapter 1
In the Beginning

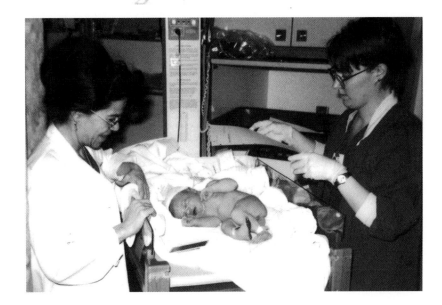

Anna's story begins on March 9, 1999, at 1:16 a.m. At least that was the first time we met her face-to-face. We did not start writing about Anna until six months later, so we will introduce you to Anna and show you the first six months of her life with pictures.

MARCH 1999

7

Anna was the picture of a healthy baby girl. >

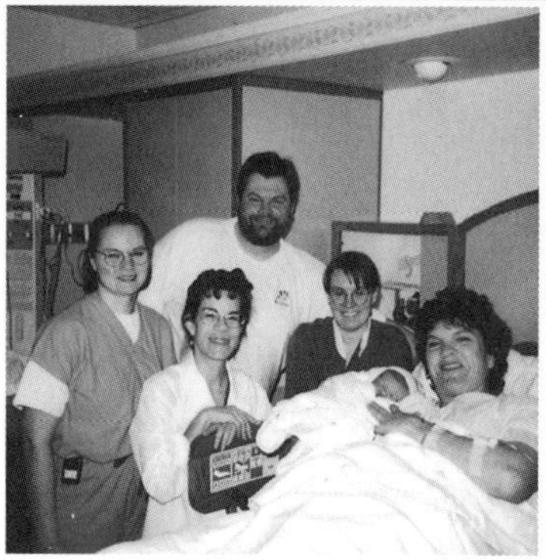

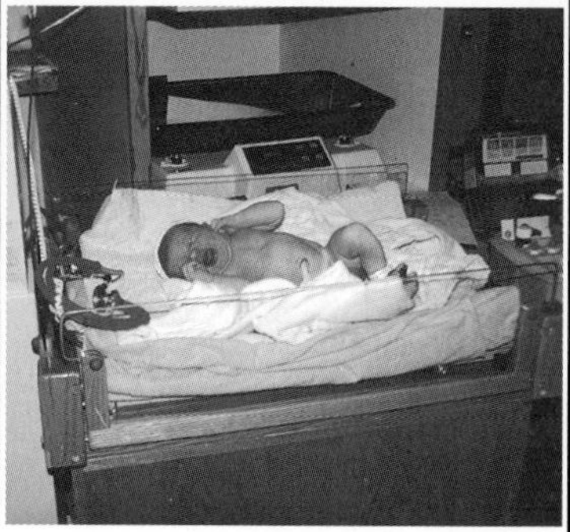

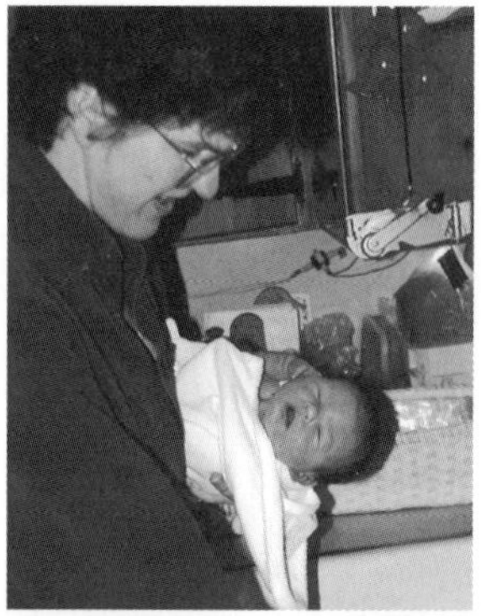

15

< We had a lot of new things to learn: baths, diapers, etc..

Anna received a lot of gifts, Some bigger than she. >

22

< Anna soon met her Grammie and her Great Aunt Shirley.

After a couple of weeks I had to go back to work. >

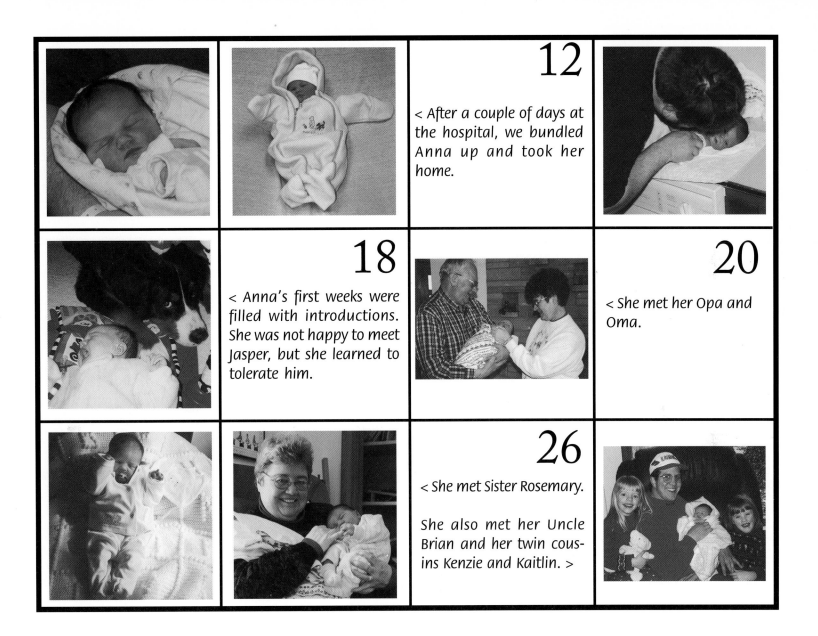

12

< After a couple of days at the hospital, we bundled Anna up and took her home.

18

< Anna's first weeks were filled with introductions. She was not happy to meet Jasper, but she learned to tolerate him.

20

< She met her Opa and Oma.

26

< She met Sister Rosemary.

She also met her Uncle Brian and her twin cousins Kenzie and Kaitlin. >

APRIL 1999

28

Anna met her Uncle Patrick. >

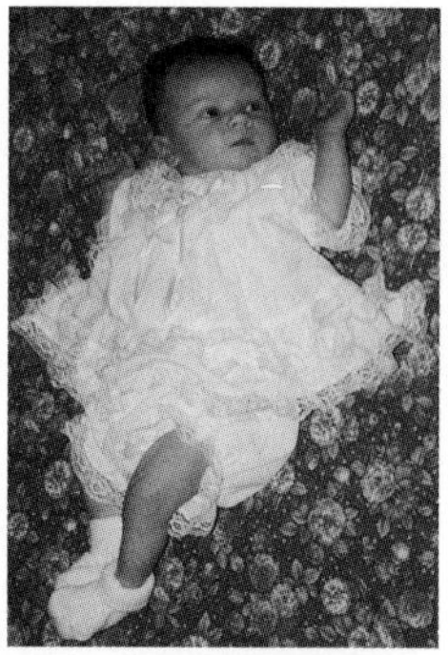

5

< Anna got all dressed up for her first Easter.

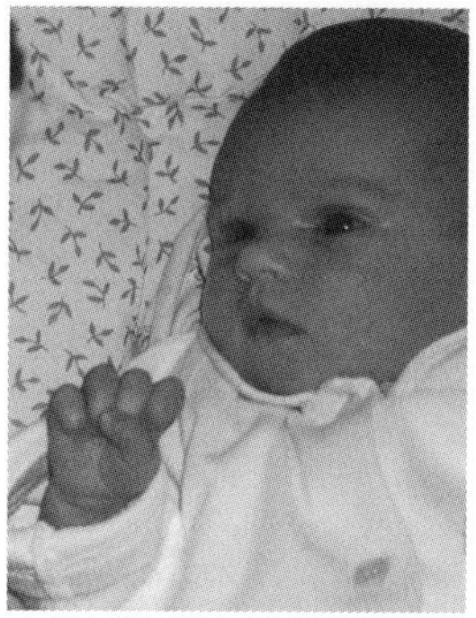

12

Although Anna smiled a lot, she also cried a lot. >

< Kathleen had a very special Mother's Day.

31

Anna smiled for the first time when her friend Glow Worm lit up. >

2

Once she started smiling, she smiled a lot. >

8

< For Anna's first public outing she went to see the butterflies at Fredrick Meijer Gardens.

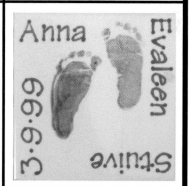

Anna made Mother's Day tiles for her grandmas with her footprints.

14

16

< Anna went for her first outdoor walk at Riverside Park.

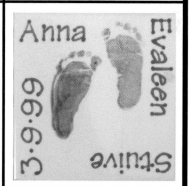

Anna   Evaleen
3.9.99   Stuive

A	18		20
P			< Anna was always fond of her green bunny.
R			
I		26	27
L		< Anna went to the Tulip Festival in Holland, Michigan.	
1		Anna loved her new hairdo. >	
9	2		4
9	Anna was named after her maternal grandmothers: Anna Masek and Evalene Feeney. >		
9			

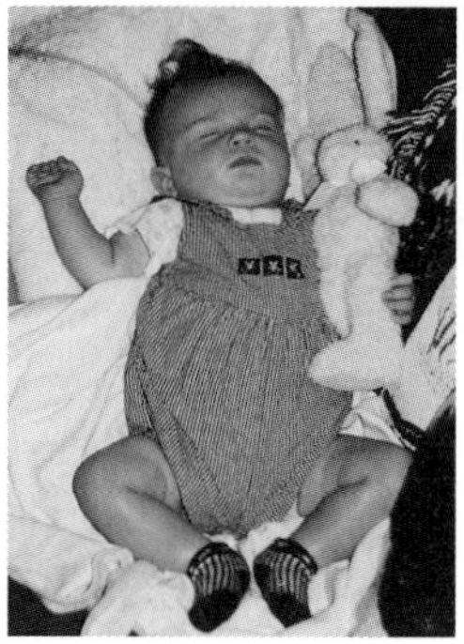

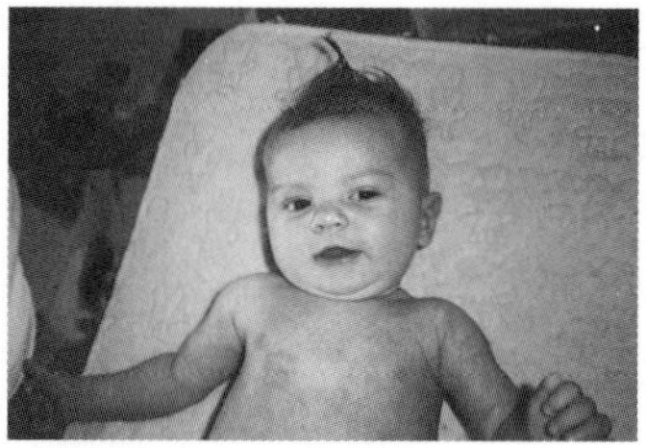

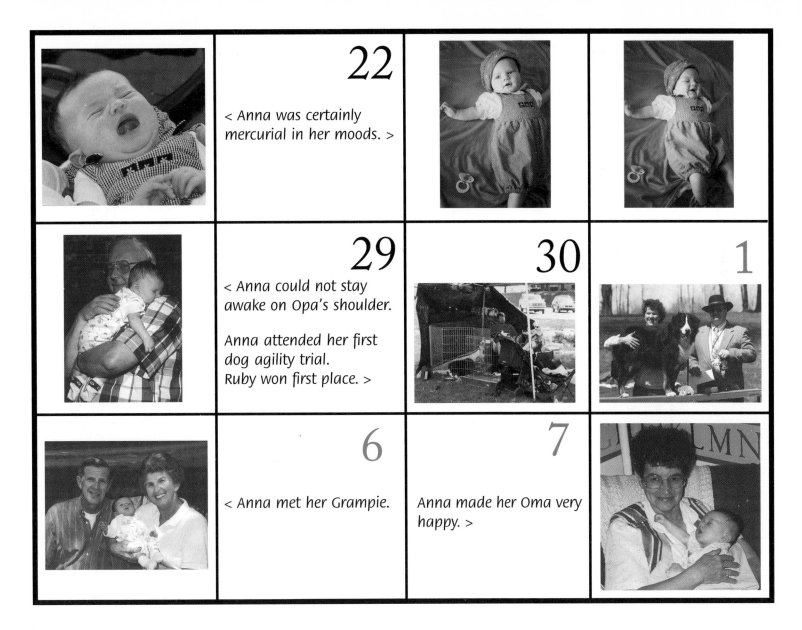

22

< Anna was certainly mercurial in her moods. >

29

< Anna could not stay awake on Opa's shoulder.

Anna attended her first dog agility trial.
Ruby won first place. >

30

1

6

< Anna met her Grampie.

7

Anna made her Oma very happy. >

MAY 1999

10 < Anna slept in Aunt Lauran's arms.

16

18 < Anna's Dad was very proud of her.

24 Anna liked to sneak naps with her Mom. >

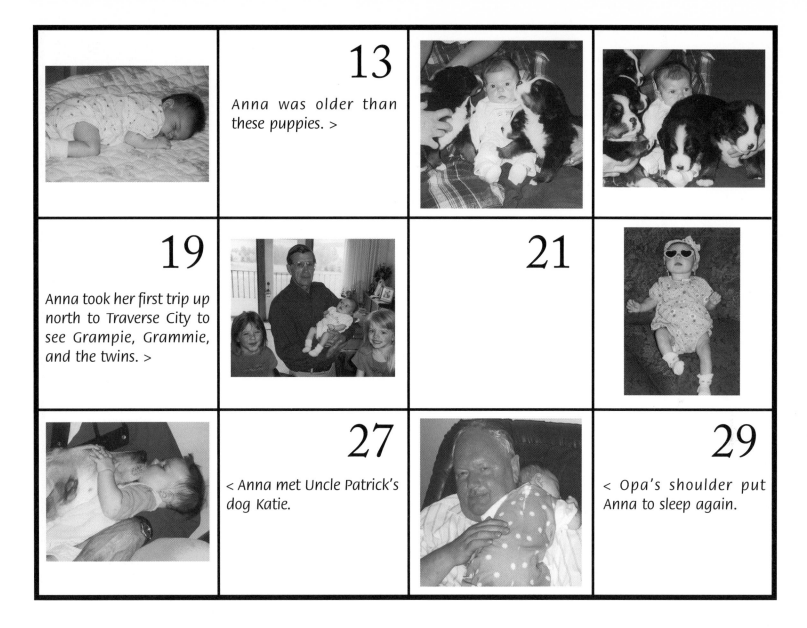

13

Anna was older than these puppies. >

19

Anna took her first trip up north to Traverse City to see Grampie, Grammie, and the twins. >

21

27

< Anna met Uncle Patrick's dog Katie.

29

< Opa's shoulder put Anna to sleep again.

JUNE 1999

31

< Anna met her Uncle Ron.

Mom went back to work and took Anna with her. >

< Anna was baptized. ^ We threw a big party for her.

13

Anna posed for her first studio photo session. >

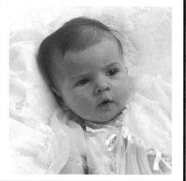

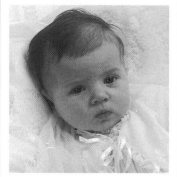

3

Anna met her Aunt Lisa and, when she woke up, posed with the whole Stuive family in the back-yard. >

9

11

Anna made faces at her cousin Kaitlin.

19

JUNE / JULY

21

< Anna loved ribbons.

27

29

< Grammie thought that Anna was cute, adorable and huggable.

5

< Anna went to Leland to see Opa and Oma on vacation.

Then, Anna met Great Uncle Harry and Great Aunt Shirley again. >

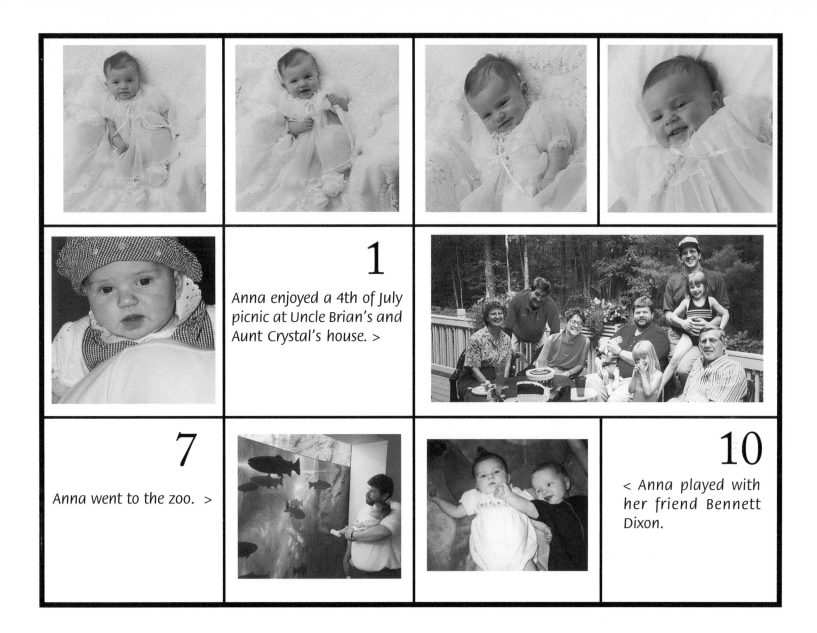

1

Anna enjoyed a 4th of July picnic at Uncle Brian's and Aunt Crystal's house. >

7

Anna went to the zoo. >

10

< Anna played with her friend Bennett Dixon.

11

Anna sang as she bathed. >

13

19

Anna went swimming for the first time. >

25

27

< Anna could wear hats with style; not everyone can. >

15

On Fridays, Anna stayed with her friend Brianna Volkhardt. >

23

Anna was comforted by Jamie and Cameron Pirochta. >

29

Anna played with her cousins. >

31

AUGUST 1999

2

< Anna went to another dog show and Ruby won again.

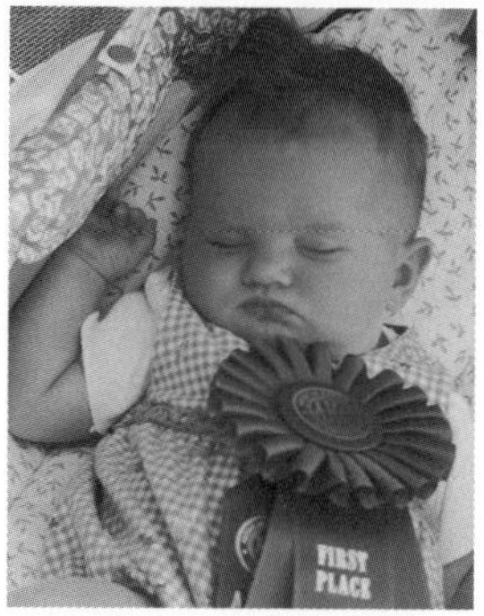

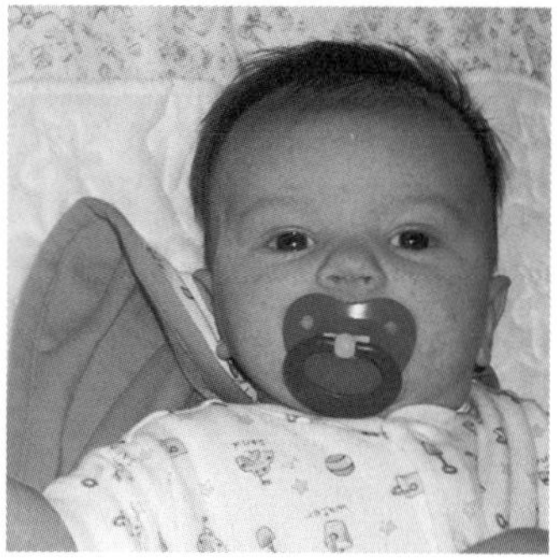

9

< Anna thought Nuks were very important.

15

Anna also looked good with the roses from Grammie's garden. >

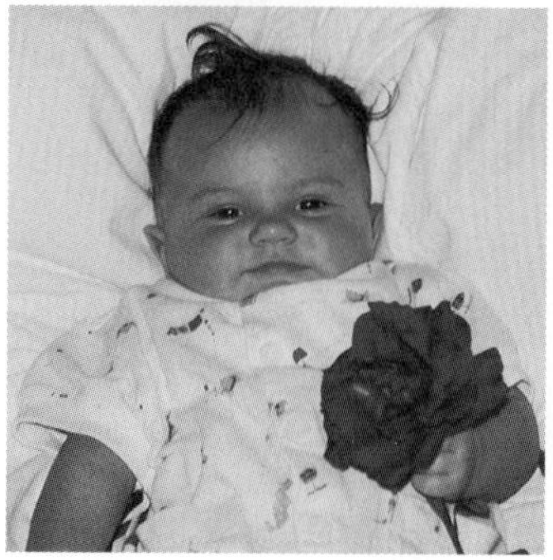

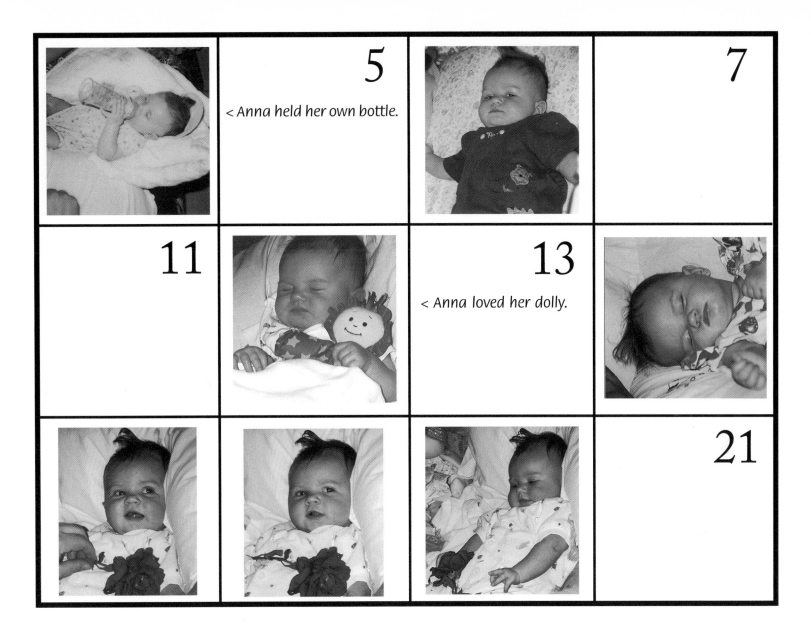

5

< Anna held her own bottle.

7

11

13

< Anna loved her dolly.

21

A U G U S T / S E P T E M B E R	22	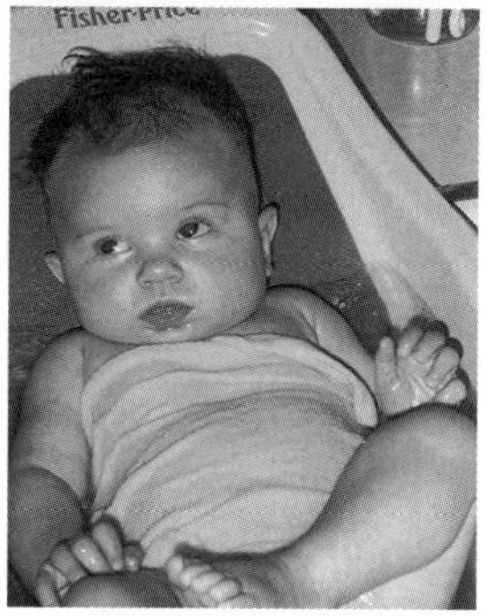	24 < At first, Anna thought baths were silly.
		30 < Sometimes we tickled Anna mercilessly.	
	5 Anna was skeptical when we took this picture. >		7

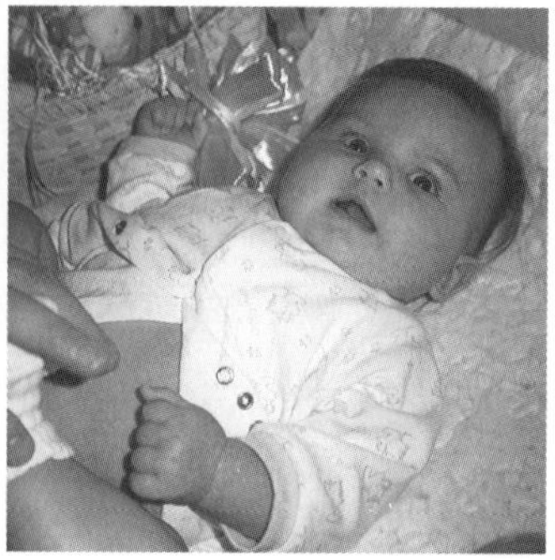

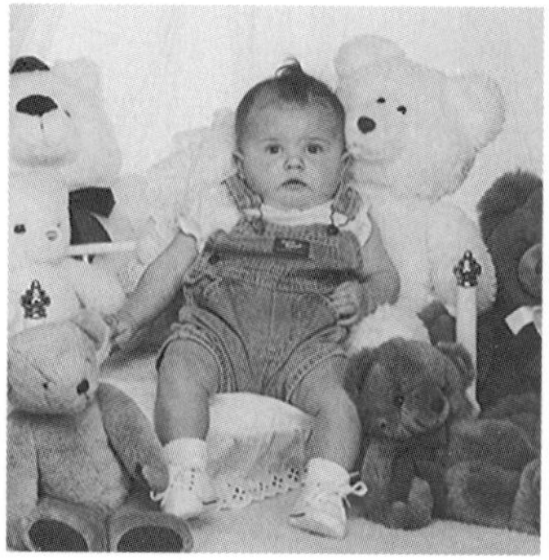

26

< Anna was surprised when we took this picture.

28

< Grampie put Anna to sleep too.

1

< Anna's second studio session was also successful. >

3

Mom tried to get Anna to do a song and dance routine. >

9

< Anna went to Chelsea to see Kathleen's Uncle Mike and Aunt Ann and to see where Kathleen's grandparents were buried.

11

SEPTEMBER

14

< Opa and Anna would talk for hours.

20

< Anna was willing to substitute her thumb for a Nuk.

Anna would get all bundled up for stroller rides. >

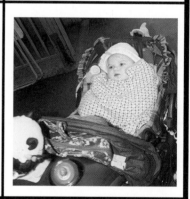

16

Anna enjoyed her third dog agility trial, but this time Ruby did not win. >

S
E
P
T
E
M
B
E
R

23

and then everything changed.

Chapter 2
The Day Things Changed

In mid-September Anna started to wake up in the middle of the night. That was unusual because she had always slept through the night. She would stiffen, throw her arms out to the side, and hoot. It would only last a few seconds. Our pediatrician scheduled an MRI. We went in on September 23, 1999.

That day we learned that Anna suffered from a rare mitochondrial disease: Leigh's Syndrome. That was the first day of a new life for all of us. Later we wrote a letter to Anna's family and friends to explain what was going on with Anna. That letter is a good place to start with the written part of Anna's story, but it left out some important lessons we learned those first few days in the hospital. We will fill in that gap after the letter.

Dear Family and Friends:

We are coming to you at this difficult time asking for your support and prayers. Our beautiful baby girl, Anna Evaleen, has recently been diagnosed with Leigh's Syndrome, a progressive, irreversible, terminal metabolic disease. There is no treatment for Leigh's Syndrome. Thus, we are left with an uncertain future and a very limited amount of time with Anna. Please bear with us as we share our story.

IN THE BEGINNING

Anna was born on March 9, 1999 without complication. At 8 pounds 11 ounces and 20.5 inches long, she was a big, healthy baby. After a few weeks at home, Anna tipped the scales at over 10 pounds. At 6 weeks of age, however, she began to experience severe stomach cramps while breastfeeding. We saw the pediatrician regarding this problem when she was 7 weeks old, and he identified her condition as "failure to thrive." She weighed less than 10 pounds at that time. It was not unusual for her to nurse for two minutes and cry for five; she would refuse to eat at times. Anna became noticeably skinny. While her head size and height were normal for her age, her weight lagged behind all expectations.

At the suggestion of our pediatrician, Kathleen radically changed her diet, eliminating all dairy products and eating only brown rice and bagels to rule out the possibility that Anna's problems were due to some food allergy. On Mother's Day, when Anna was 9 weeks old, we took her to the emergency room because she seemed dehydrated and extremely agitated. An x-ray of her stomach revealed that all of her bowel loops were filled with gas. Every time she ate, the gas would move through her system, causing her more discomfort.

The decision was made to start her on Prosobee formula (soy based and lactose free). Anna's condition improved on the Prosobee but she became horribly constipated. Working with the pediatrician and gastroenterologist, we arrived at a "cocktail" of Prosobee, breast milk, and Karo syrup. This combination suited her well as she gained weight quickly. Soon, her weight gain caught up with her height and head growth, and she was the picture of a healthy baby girl!

We did not write about the events of September 23 until we wrote this letter a couple of months later. The letter does a pretty good job of summarizing Anna's first six months, at least from a medical perspective, and it touches upon the events of September 23 as well. We hope the letter will serve as a good introduction to the way things changed.

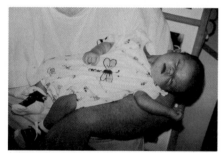

Looking back it was easy to see that Anna was skinny. As new parents, however, we did not have a standard that would permit us to make that determination. The comments of others helped us to see a possible problem.

While we were exploring Anna's stomach problems, the pediatric gastroen-terologist told us that it was unusual that Anna took 45 minutes or more to finish a four-ounce bottle, and he thought she may have some suck and swallow problems. So we decided to have a video fluoroscopy performed on Anna at the end of June. The video fluoroscopy confirmed his suspicions. Anna would suck 8-12 times but only swallow once. As she held the thin liquid in the back of her throat, it would drip down her esophagus and often get aspirated into her lungs. The speech therapist who performed the video evaluation recommended that we thicken her formula with barley cereal, which would make her swallow more often. Every day, we added barley cereal to Anna's cocktail, which Anna happily sucked down in 10-15 minutes. We were thrilled and felt as though we finally had turned the corner with her. She flourished physically and appeared to be meeting her developmental milestones.

For a couple of months, everything proceeded normally, although we noticed that Anna was not trying to roll over and that her neck and torso were a bit floppy. We believed that she may have been developing a bit more slowly than average due to the fact that she had two significant weight loss periods while she was very young, and no one could tell us how her period of failing to thrive would affect her developmentally.

We began to run out of breast milk at the end of August. We replaced the breast milk with Maltsupex, and Anna appeared to tolerate the change well. But we noticed that Anna's feeding rate started to slow again. We scheduled another video fluoroscopy for August 31. The speech therapist saw the same problems that she pinpointed in the first examination. The therapist recommended even thicker liquids and suggested that we consult with a neurologist.

On September 7, Anna went to our pediatrician for her 6-month shots and examination. After examining her overall weak muscle tone and failure to meet several developmental milestones, the pediatrician also recommended that we speak to a neurologist. We made an appointment "as soon as possible" (in mid-November) with the pediatric neurologist and we waited.

Anna gained weight steadily over the summer.

Then, on September 13, everything changed. Anna, who had slept through the night since the second night home and all during her stomach problems, began waking up at least twice a night, typically between 1:20 and 1:40 a.m. and then between 3:00 and 5:00 a.m. She would wake out of a sound sleep half screaming, half hooting, with her arms outstretched at her sides and her body as stiff as a board. When you picked her up and began to rub her back, she would stop screaming and begin to gasp, burp, and often spit up, which indicated to us that she was suffering from reflux or possibly was having some odd reaction to the Maltsupex.

On September 15, Kathleen called the pediatrician to discuss these "night terrors" and to schedule an appointment for him to see Anna. The next day the pediatrician prescribed Propulsid, which would move the food from Anna's stomach into her intestines more quickly, thereby reducing the possibility of reflux and throwing up at night. The Propulsid medication prevented her from spitting up but did not resolve the "night terrors." We tried sitting her up in a chair or in her bed to sleep, but to no avail. The night terrors continued. On Sunday, September 19, Anna had 5 episodes, including two during the day (a first). We called the pediatrician and received a prescription for Zantac. Again, we were focused on her stomach (or from the neck down) and we hoped that this would help. It did not.

On Wednesday, September 22, the pediatrician called; he had managed to get Anna an MRI appointment for the next morning. We happily prepared her for the event, expecting that we would merely be eliminating the remote possibility of neurological impairment and then moving on. On that morning at 9:35 am, Anna was given a full dose of chloral hydrate to knock her out for the MRI; the full dose was necessary because she refused to fall asleep (probably because she had not eaten since 11pm the day before). After the test concluded around 10:30 a.m. Kathleen remained with Anna in radiology waiting for her to wake up. Although she was supposed to wake after an hour or two, Anna would only stir briefly and then fall back to sleep. By 3:00 p.m., the radiologist, who, unbeknownst to us, had not yet reviewed the MRI films, spoke with our pediatrician and decided to admit Anna so she could be hydrated by IV. His promise that she would then get a "full work-up" appealed to us.

The diagnosis

At 4:30 pm, the pediatric neurologist examined the still-sleeping Anna and then the MRI films. According to the neurologist, the MRI revealed gross abnormalities in Anna's brain, brain stem and basal ganglia. The neurologist explained that this appeared to be an indicator of Leigh's Syndrome, a rare metabolic disease that had detrimentally affected Anna's brain. Specifically, Anna's brain was smaller than it should be, there was fluid around the brain, there were deep fissures in the brain itself, and portions of the brain stem had already degenerated. She said that the effects were irreversible, degenerative, and progressive, and that this disease would greatly shorten Anna's life.

Everything that happened after that time is a large blur. Anna did not wake up from the chloral hydrate until 7:00 pm that evening—almost 10 hours after it was administered. Anna was admitted to the hospital and a battery of tests were performed.

During our second night in the hospital, the pediatric pulmonologist saw Anna's "night terrors" and diagnosed them as seizures. We immediately got Anna started on phenobarbitol but the seizures continued. It took us 8 days—until the day we left the hospital—to get her seizures under control. They have yet to reappear, thankfully.

Anna never cried despite having electrodes taped to and removed from her chest repeatedly in order to monitor her heart and respiration as well as for the ECHO of her heart and for her EKG. She had myriad blood and urine tests, a lumbar puncture, an EEG, a skin biopsy, a sleep study, a 24-hour pH probe, a 12-hour apnea monitor, and an IV drip. The tests confirmed the initial diagnosis of Leigh's Syndrome.

The day before we left the hospital, the neurologist was able to pinpoint the problem that caused Anna's Leigh's Syndrome: a genetic point mutation in Anna's mitochondrial DNA commonly referred to as "NARP."

Anna and her pediatric neurologist, Dr. Liza Squires, then the director of pediatric neurology at DeVos Children's Hospital, and Liza's husband Matt Venema.

LEIGH'S AND NARP

NARP is an acronym that stands for the symptoms observed in adults with this illness: Neurogenic (muscular) weakness, Ataxia (misfiring of the muscles creating jerky movements), and Retinitis Pigmentosis (degeneration of the retina). At nucleotide 8993 of Anna's mitochondrial DNA (the ATP 6 gene), there is a T to G mutation, meaning that the T amino acid that is supposed to be there has been replaced with a G amino acid. The mutation can be spontaneous or inherited. Based on tests of Kathleen's blood showing that she has the mutation in some of her mitochondria, it appears that Anna inherited the mutation.

Due to this mutation, Anna's mitochondria cannot process the energy that they should from the foods she eats and the air she breathes (remember in biology—the mitochondria is the powerhouse of the cell). No one has been able to adequately explain to us exactly how the mutation affects Anna's cells, but we know Anna's cells do not work properly. Apparently this failure has caused the damage in Anna's brain. Eventually, Anna's other vital organs will suffer damage as well.

Anna's doctors have told us that the disease will progress, but they cannot tell us how or when. Part of the reason Anna's doctors cannot tell us much is that Leigh's syndrome is very rare. NARP as the cause of Leigh's is even more rare. The nature of mitochondrial diseases generally presents another complicating factor. The same mutation can produce very different symptoms and similar symptoms can be produced by very different mutations. Thus, even a definitive diagnosis of NARP leaves many unanswered questions.

Right now, the mutation is not affecting Kathleen at all and she is in good health. Merely as a precaution, Kathleen is pursuing many of the vitamin therapies prescribed for Anna. There is, however, one immediate impact of the disease in Kathleen: all of our children will be at 100% risk for this illness.

Anna during her first hospital stay.

There are no known effective treatments for NARP or Leigh's, but we are trying some antioxidant therapy on the recommendation of Anna's physicians. Among the many items that make up her current "cocktail" are large doses of Vitamin C, Vitamin E, and Coenzyme Q. Hopefully, these vitamins will help her cells eliminate toxins. Anna is also taking a prescription version of carnitine. This too will hopefully assist Anna's cells in producing energy from the foods she eats.

In addition to the antioxidants and the carnitine, we are also treating some of Anna's symptoms with other vitamins and prescription drugs. For example, Anna is taking Phenobarbital to address her seizures. Anna is also taking medications to reduce the severe reflux revealed by the studies at the hospital. The doctors consider this to be a dangerous problem because Anna is at risk to aspirate anything that comes back up because of the reflux.

Our first line of attack on the reflux problem consists of the Propulsid and Zantac Anna has been taking since before she went into the hospital. The only difference is that Anna is taking these medications in higher doses now. Because these drugs have not entirely resolved Anna's reflux, we are attempting to address the reflux in other ways.

There are different possible causes of the reflux. Because the reflux may be a product of food allergies, we are slowly weaning Anna from Prosobee and introducing a formula called Neocate. Once Anna is completely switched over, we will repeat the pH study to see if the reflux continues.

Another possible cause of the reflux is muscle weakness from the disease. Anna is hypotonic, which means that she has weak muscle tone. The bottom of the esophagus uses muscles to keep the food from coming back up from the stomach. If Anna's esophageal muscles are weak, it could result in reflux. If this is the problem, it can be corrected surgically.

The surgical procedure is called a "Nissen" or fundoplication. The top part of the stomach is stretched around either side of the esophagus and then sewn together. This will keep pressure on the bottom of the esophagus to prevent reflux. If, or more accurately when, the Nissen is performed the surgeon will put in a gastric

Reflux occurs when the contents of the stomach come up through the esophagus.

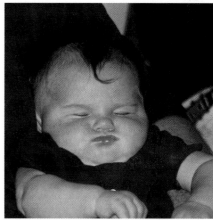

Anna was able to sleep comfortably, even in the hospital, so long as she was in someone's arms.

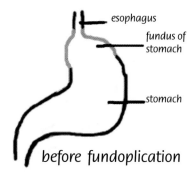

before fundoplication

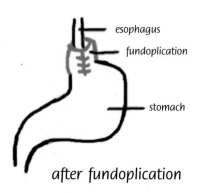

after fundoplication

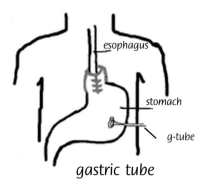

gastric tube

tube that will permit us to feed Anna directly into her stomach. The Nissen and G-tube often go hand-in-hand. Given Anna's poor suck and swallow reflex, doctors believe that she may lose that reflex over time and will be unable to take nutrition by mouth. At that point, we will feed her through the G-tube. We hope to never need it, but it is a precaution that we feel we must take. Given Anna's delicate medical condition, even a slight cold would set her back greatly and would make her lose her appetite. With the G-tube, we will be able to continue her feedings and medication cycles without interruption.

Because the Nissen/G-tube procedure is major surgery, we have some reluctance about going forward with it. Nonetheless, all of our doctors and many parents with children in similar circumstance have strongly recommended the procedure. They have also been unanimous in recommending that we proceed sooner rather than later so that Anna will be in the best possible health for the surgery. Based on these recommendations, we have tentatively scheduled the surgery for the end of January, 2000.

Another symptom that we have been tracking and trying to treat is elevated lactic acid levels. Anna's cellular dysfunction results in the creation of certain toxic byproducts, including lactic acid. When Anna was admitted to hospital the lactic acid levels in her blood and her cerebrospinal fluid were dangerously high. To treat this problem, Anna's neurologist prescribed thiamine. Within three days of starting on thiamine treatments, Anna's lactic acid levels returned to a normal range. This was a good sign as some forms of the disease are reactive to thiamine—but that does not mean that the effects of the disease are reversible or will be slowed.

Since we left the hospital, Anna has endured several blood tests and another spinal tap to evaluate her lactic acid levels. The most recent results suggest that we cannot yet draw any conclusions as to whether the thiamine treatments are effective. We will try to reach a more conclusive determination regarding the value of thiamine when we visit the Mitochondrial and Metabolic Disease Center associated with the University of California, San Diego Medical School.

A leader in the field of metabolic disease reasearch, the MMDC is a diagnostic center for Leigh's and other metabolic and mitochondrial diseases. The doctors at the Center have seen many children with the diagnosis of Leigh's syndrome, and some NARP patients as well. The MMDC is also testing the effects of dichloroacetate, or DCA, a drug not yet approved by the FDA. The MMDC doctors believe that DCA can control lactic acidosis in Leigh's patients.

Although we have a confirmed diagnosis, and Anna appears to be responding to the thiamine treatments, we intend to travel to the Center in December. They are interested in testing whether Anna is actually reacting to the thiamine. We are interested in talking to doctors that have so much experience with the disease and we are interested in the DCA if the thiamine is proven ineffective. If she receives the DCA treatments, we will need to return to the MMDC every six months for observation and more testing. Again, although we hope that these efforts may delay the degenerative process, we have no idea whether they will do so.

Anna today

If you were looking at Anna right now, you would never know that she has a terminal disease. You would probably not even realize that she has fallen a little behind in her development. She tips the scales at over twenty pounds and measures over 28 inches in length. For her age, her weight and length put her in the ninetieth percentile. Since Anna has been home from the hospital, she has returned to her routine of sleeping through the night. Despite the Phenobarbitol she receives for the seizures, she is awake and alert for most of the day; the only difference we perceive is that she sleeps very soundly now; so she no longer cat naps. From our perspective, Anna is no different today than she was two months ago when she was just our little girl.

We have enclosed a prayer card and a brochure with some pictures of Anna. Although we are biased, we think you would have to agree that she has every appearance of a beautiful healthy baby girl. Only upon close examination will you realize that Anna cannot hold herself up. Her muscles are simply too weak. Only after you have spent some time with her will you realize that Anna neither smiles nor cries. She seems to have lost these skills. Only after you have tried to feed her will you realize that sucking and swallowing are laborious tasks for Anna. Right now these deficits are not so noticeable. As she ages and grows and as the disease progresses, the deficits will become more glaring. We are working hard with speech

MMDC
≡ U C S D ≡

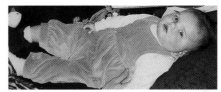

Anna was always very tall.

therapists, physical therapists, and occupational therapists to help Anna develop and use all of her abilities. We do not know, however, whether our efforts will be successful because of the progressive, degenerative nature of the disease. Nevertheless, we must proceed as much for ourselves as for her.

OUR GOALS FOR ANNA

Although we know little about Anna's future, what we have read about the disease and what the doctors have told us lead us to believe that it is unlikely that Anna will be with us for more than another year or two. Anna has no awareness that her life should be any different or any longer than it will be. We plan to do everything we can to enrich her short life. It is our principal goal that Anna know she is loved. Along the way, we want her to happily discover and experience as many sights, sounds, smells, tastes, and textures as she possibly can. We are committed to making her life full of love, excitement, color, new experiences, and new sensations.

WE ARE NOT ALONE

We continue to thank God for all of our family, friends, and colleagues who have come to our rescue. The outpouring of love and selfless acts of kindness are often more than we can take with a dry eye. To say that this is the most difficult time of our lives would be an understatement, but it has made us realize that we are not in this struggle alone. Rather, we find that the web of support that holds us up and catches us when we stumble is one hundred times bigger than we could have ever imagined. The outpouring of concern and love has been and continues to be overwhelming and a source of strength for us. Each person who has donated time or money, written to us, called us, brought food, come to visit, or prayed for us is God returning to us and reminding us that He is with us throughout this ordeal.

YOU CAN HELP

The question we have heard most often is "How can we help?" First, you can pray for Anna and for everyone who is close to her. The gift of faith that our parents gave to us has proven the most powerful gift in coping with Anna's illness. We know that God has a plan for Anna and for us, but that plan is just not clear to us right now. Sometimes, it is hard to know what to pray for. We are praying first for the miracle of healing. If that is not part of the plan, we are praying for strength, wisdom, comfort and peace. Please join us in that prayer. We have enclosed a prayer card with Anna's picture to help you remember.

There have been so many other ways that people have helped us. Staying focused on Anna has left little time for many other things. Kathleen has been off work since Anna was diagnosed. Although we hope to soon settle into a routine that will permit Kathleen to return to work, that is not a certainty. It will depend in large part on Anna. John has already returned to working half days. We have been assisted in our ability to spend time with Anna by John's colleagues, who have generously donated their vacation time to him. We have both already exhausted the available vacation and sick time otherwise available to us.

Numerous friends and family members have brought meals. We are still enjoying that benefit as we receive our supper from others three days a week. If you are interested in getting into the rotation, contact Sheri Leisman. She has coordinated that effort since Anna left the hospital.

We had a group from our old law firm that took care of the leaves in the yard this fall. Sometimes it is difficult to marshal enough energy to deal with this type of task. That effort was greatly appreciated. Similarly, we have enjoyed the assistance of many with regard to Ruby and Jasper. Our vet took them in for more than a week when Anna was hospitalized. We already have volunteer hosts for our trip to San Diego. If you can help with dog lodging at some future date or if you can even take them for a walk sometime, please let us know.

We are learning that many of the expenses associated with Anna's care are not covered by insurance. To address any shortfalls, we have set up a foundation to pay the extraordinary costs of Anna's medical care. We have been amazed at the financial generosity of the many people who have already contributed to the foundation. We have enclosed a brochure regarding the foundation if you would like to help in this way.

John's co-workers donated hundreds of hours of their vacation time to him. Because of their generosity and his boss's understanding he was able to continue to work about half-time for several months.

This is Anna with Dr. Kirsten Marshall and her husband Frank. The Marshalls took care of Ruby and Jasper when Anna was in the hospital in September of 1999. They took care of Jasper again when Anna was in the hospital in December of 1999, and January, February, and August of 2000.

We have also received many offers to watch Anna for a while so that we can get away. Right now, however, we want to spend every minute we can with her. As time passes, we may need that respite and we appreciate the offers.

Finally, you can help us by just thinking about us now and then. If you would like to receive updates regarding Anna's progress, please become a member of the Anna's Friends mailing list. We have enclosed a flier regarding the mailing list. It's a great way to keep abreast of what's happening with us and Anna.

In Closing

We are doing as well as one could possibly expect. As painful as this has been, we have been continuously uplifted by the thoughts, deeds, and prayers of others. We want to express our heartfelt gratitude for every gift you have given us. Please feel free to call us if you would like to talk about any of this. We periodically update our answering machine greeting with information about Anna. Feel free to call just to get the updates.

We thank you all for sharing our joy and our grief. May God bless all of us with his love and mercy.

Much love,

Anna's family—John, Kathleen, Anna, Ruby and Jasper

P.S.   We do not know if we will have time to express all of our holiday wishes to you in a separate writing this year. So, we wish you all a blessed Thanksgiving, a Merry Christmas, and a Happy New Year.

For several months we received dozens of hang-ups every week because people were calling just to get an "Anna update" from our answering machine. At least once a week, we would change our message greeting to tell the world how Anna was doing. We truly regret that we did not save all of our recorded greetings. They, too, would tell a story.

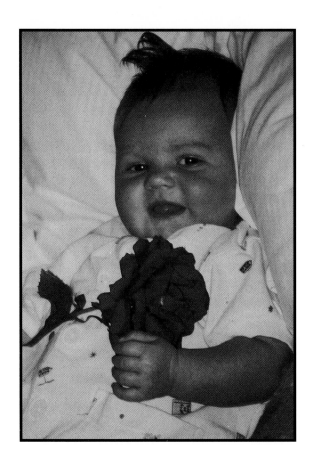

We sent several items along with our first letter: a brochure about the foundation, a pamphlet about the mailing list, and a prayer card. This is what the laminated prayer card looked like. It had our favorite picture of Anna on one side and some basic information on the reverse. During the first six months after Anna's diagnosis we distributed literally thousands of Anna's prayer cards.

My name is Anna Evaleen Stuive.
I have a rare, progressive,
irreversible and terminal disease
called Leigh's syndrome.
**Please pray for me
and my family.**
For updates on my condition,
send an e-mail to
**AnnasFriends-
subscribe@onelist.com**
or contribute to my care by
sending a check to
The Anna's Friends Foundation
6132 Rogue Lane NE
Belmont, MI 49306.
For more information call
616-361-9478
Thank You

Our first letter provided an accurate synopsis of Anna's condition and the road ahead. But, the letter did not adequately tell the story of the first days in the hospital as we struggled to come to grips with Anna's diagnosis. Because the early struggles taught us much, they warrant closer scrutiny.

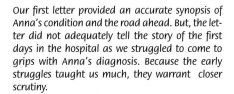

This is the Butterworth Campus of Spectrum Health. The tallest tower includes the DeVos Children's Hospital. From this view, we can pick out all of the rooms where Anna stayed.

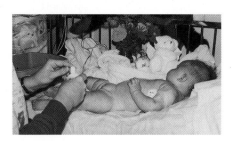

It is utterly devastating to hear that your beautiful child will not live a long, healthy life but instead will endure a steady decline to an imminent death. Mere words cannot convey the impact of that blow. Kathleen was alone with Anna at the hospital when she got the news. I was at home when she telephoned to tell me. It was divine providence that my parents showed up at our house precisely at that moment. They took me to the hospital to join Kathleen. We listened to Dr. Squires describe Anna's condition for quite a while. We were still reeling as we bumbled through the admissions process and carried Anna to her room.

We both felt the need to let others know what had happened to Anna and to us, but what do you say? Kathleen had taken copious notes as Dr. Squires explained what we were facing but we could not seem to get our arms around the concepts well enough to share them with others. We, who made our living with the written and spoken word, were completely speechless. Our radiology sedation nurse, Laura Wagner, rescued us. She wrote out a nine-point script:

1. There are abnormal areas in Anna's brain which showed up on the MRI.

2. These abnormalities are indicative of a metabolic disorder.

3. There are many different kinds of metabolic disorders. Dr. Squires thinks it may be a disorder called Leigh's syndrome.

4. More testing will be required in order to determine exactly what type of disorder this is.

5. Some of the tests, especially the skin biopsy, are complicated and can take a long time to get results.

6. The skin biopsy will help to definitively diagnose the disorder.

7. Metabolic disorders can result in growth and developmental problems which can be severe.

8. This type of disease is an internal disease at a cellular level. There is nothing that can be given or done to correct this disorder.

9. Therapy is directed at doing all the supportive things which can add to her quality of life and comfort. Everything will be done to maximize her growth and developmental potential.

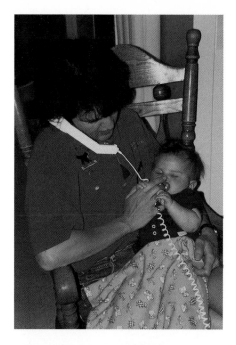

So, we called people. We asked them to bear with us while we read them something. We read the nine-point script, and when we got to the end we said goodbye. That was all we could do.

After we got the first few phone calls out of the way and the nurses made Anna comfortable, we were alone. Then the tears began to flow. We cried together in the dark. As we look back, it is easy to downplay our fears in those first few days. You see, now we know that we had more time with her. Then, we did not know. We did not know whether she would die that night or the next day or the next. No one could tell us.

Our reactions to the fear were very different. I wanted to circle the wagons, hold Anna close, and shut out the rest of the world. Kathleen, on the other hand, wanted to bring in the rest of the world. She felt a burning desire to tell everyone so they could pray for us and comfort us. It proved difficult to reconcile these two ways of coping and that added significant tension to an already stressful situation.

Fortunately, we learned a couple of things almost immediately that helped reduce that tension. The first was to hold Anna. Anna could convey peace. I am not kidding, she could. No matter how wound up you might be, if you just sat and held her for a few minutes you would find peace. Not peace that you brought to yourself; it was peace she gave you. She could give you peace like a comedian could make you laugh. At first I thought this was just my imagination, but over time many others told us the same thing. What a gift.

The second thing we learned was the simple fact that there is no right way to react to a terminal diagnosis. We had to try to respect our different reactions as much as we could. The worst thing to say was that the other person was wrong.

We learned those lessons and lots of other things about dealing with terminal illness from the pediatric hospice team from Hospice of Michigan. The first week-

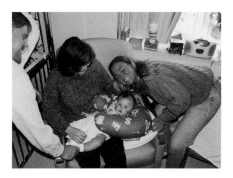

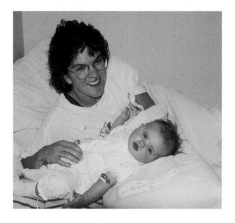

end in the hospital following Anna's diagnosis we spent hours talking to members of the pediatric hospice team.

Hospice does not typically intervene so early in a case. It is not that such intervention is inappropriate. Hospice means palliative end-of-life care. That was certainly fitting. The hospice benefit, however, exists in a larger context of medical care provision that includes hospitals and doctors and insurance companies. In that larger context, hospice is a particular model for the way medical services are provided and paid for at the end of life. Although we desperately needed hospice's expertise and counsel, we were not at a point in Anna's illness that the hospice model of providing and paying for services was appropriate. They stepped in anyway because Anna's Aunt Lauran was part of the pediatric hospice team.

The perspective that hospice was able to provide was critical because it took into account the whole patient as well as the family. That is very different from the fragmentation that necessarily follows from consulting with a variety of specialists, each focusing on a different body system in the patient. For example, it is not likely that Anna's pulmonologists or gastroenterologists, who are all wonderful doctors, could take the time to sit with Kathleen and me, together or separately, and talk with us about respecting the ways that we dealt differently with Anna's terminal illness. That does not mean that the specialists were not doing their job; it just means that there were additional needs that the hospice team was able and willing to meet. We needed everyone's help.

We learned a lot in the hospital about how Anna's disease was presently affecting her. We learned little, however, about what the future was going to look like. The specialists could tell us her current status and how the disease might impact her in the future, but they could not tell us when or how "it" would happen. The hospice team could tell us what the end of life would look like and the types of decisions we would likely face, but they could not tell us when that would occur either. The only question we wanted answered was a simple one: when? That was the only answer they could not provide.

Before we were discharged from the hospital, we organized a care conference with Anna's pediatrician, her neurologist, her pulmonologist, her gastroenterologist, her physical therapist, and the pediatric hospice team. Once we had them all together, Kathleen sat in front of the door so no one could leave until we got answers. It did not make a difference. In the end, we learned that "when" was nowhere nearly as important as we thought it was. "When" makes very little difference as to how you should spend today. But at the time it seemed to be critically important to us.

In those first days we learned about a phenomenon we called "hospital time." Looking back we tend to see it as a whirl of activity, but most of the time was spent waiting: waiting for a test, waiting for a test result, waiting to talk to one specialist or another. Hospital time starts early in the morning and it tails off at about 7:00 p.m. In the hospital, time actually stops on the weekend. The one immutable characteristic of hospital time is that it is wholly outside of your control.

We were not very good at letting things be out of our control. We took steps to establish a zone that was ours even in the hospital. We covered the walls of Anna's room with pictures. We rearranged the furniture to suit our needs. We even brought in our own inflatable bed. We kept music playing constantly. Anna only had a few CD's, so we just played them again and again. We cannot hear those songs now without being instantly transported back to the hospital.

We filled the place with visitors at all hours. Sometimes the doctors would just walk by because they did not think they could get into Anna's room. That is what we called it: "Anna's room." Because we had so many visitors we would often not be the ones closest to the phone when it rang. To let the callers know they had reached the right room even if they did not recognize the voice, we directed every-

In the hospital we were completely isolated. We could not see beyond ourselves. In the park we could see the world going on around us as if nothing had changed. It was comforting. This is the view from the park on the hill.

one to answer "Anna's room." We held onto that even after we got out of the hospital; our house became "Anna's house." It helped keep things in perspective.

One Saturday evening we ran away from the hospital. We bundled up Anna and took her, IV pole and all, to a little park by the hospital. Downtown Grand Rapids is situated in the Grand River valley. The hospital sits on a hill that rims the valley. The park has a commanding view of downtown, the river, and the hill on the opposite side of the valley. We needed some time away from the hospital. We left a note in Anna's room that said where we were. That evening Anna held court on a park bench overlooking downtown. We had many visitors. You could tell people were relieved to be somewhere other than a hospital room. For three hours we sat and talked about everything and nothing in the golden light of the sunset. As darkness fell we trudged back to the hospital.

After more than a week, all the tests were completed and the diagnosis was confirmed. It was time to go home. Being discharged seemed anticlimactic. It was like they were done with us. Knowing the diagnosis, of course, was a lot better than not knowing. Those first days in the hospital were most valuable, however, for teaching us how to focus on Anna. Even if it had seemed like it before, from then on there could be no question; everything was about her.

Chapter 3
The List

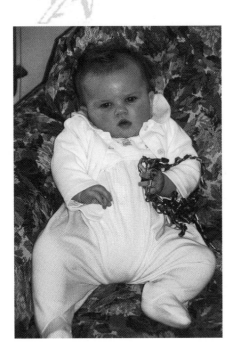

Once we returned home from the hospital, we had to figure out how to help Anna live her life. The first step was to find out everything we could about Leigh's Syndrome. We believed the more we knew, the more we could help Anna. We spent a lot of time reading and a lot of time consulting with specialists.

We also wanted to let our friends and family know how Anna was doing. We tried to do that by telephone, but we spent an awful lot of time on the telephone repeating the same story over and over. We complained about that to our friends Nancy Torstenson and Marianne Becktel. The result was the Anna's Friends mailing list.

A mailing list allows e-mail messages sent to one address (the mailing list address) to be distributed to a group of people. The Anna's Friends list permitted us to write about Anna's condition only once, yet we could reach scores of people with that one message.

The list started out as a means for us to save time and, thus, to spend more time with Anna. By the time we last posted to the list on March 10, 2001, the list had accomplished that and more. It gave us a community of support right at our fingertips. It taught us that sharing the burdens of caring for Anna made providing that care a little easier.

We will show you a significant part of Anna's life through our posts to the Anna's Friends mailing list.

Pictured to the right are Bob and Marianne Becktel (and pack) and Bob and Nancy Torstenson (and pack) and their kids Sean and Trisha. Over the past decade we have been brought together many times because of our common love of Bernese Mountain Dogs. We generally refer to these folks as our "dog friends." Among all of us, that is considered pretty high praise.

These are the people who started the Anna's Friends mailing list. We can never thank them enough for giving us that lifeline.

Although Anna's Friends was a mailing list, it was also a webpage of sorts. If you navigated to www.onelist.com/community/annasfriends, it looked something like this. >

OneList Groups: AnnasFriends

◆Home
Message
Chat
Files
Photos
Bookmarks
Database
Polls
Members
Calendar
Promote

─────────

★ =Owner
☆ =Moderator
✪ =Online

Description   Category: Support

This group is started out of love and support for our friends John and Kathleen as we follow the developments in their daughter Anna's struggle with Leigh's disease. We hope it will make it easier for John and Kathleen to share information with us, and also provide an ongoing means of showing all three of them how much we care.

Most Recent Messages

	Jan	Feb	Mar	Apr	May	Jun	Jul	Aug	Sep	Oct	Nov	Dec
2001	7	10	6									
2000	21	29	15	6	7	14	9	6	9	28	25	11
1999									1	37	97	32

Group Email Addresses

Post message: AnnasFriends@onelist.com
Subscribe: AnnasFriends-subscribe@onelist.com
Unsubscribe: AnnasFriends-unsubscribe@onelist.com
List owner: AnnasFriends-owner@onelist.com

Group Info

Members: 181
Founded: 9/29/99
Lang.: English

Group Settings

* Not listed in directory
* Open membership
* Unmoderated
* All members may post
* Archives for members only
* Email attachments

Sunday, October 3, 1999, 7:11 p.m.
From: Anna's Dad
Subject: Anna today

It is Sunday night, our first full day home from the hospital and from being up north to fill in Kathleen's family. It feels very good to be home. Anna is doing well. I know that sounds weird given her disease, but you really would never have the slightest clue that anything was wrong if you were looking at her. She is fat and sassy (like Kathleen). In fact, with her medications for the seizures and the reflux, she is much better coming home from the hospital than she was going in. We are going to try to schedule the surgery (to control the reflux and put in a feeding tube) for the week of October tenth. We need a quiet week at home without doctors and nurses first. We thank you for your thoughts, prayers, and concerns. We thank you for this forum. We will use it to update you as frequently as we can.

    Love,
Anna's Dad

Monday, October 4, 1999, 8:50 p.m.
From: Anna's Dad
Subject: Anna today, Monday

Hello again. Another banner day for Anna. We scheduled her surgery for October the 18th. That gives us a couple of weeks to prepare. I wish I could send a current photo with this message (Can I Bob?). We wish you could see how happy she is and how healthy she looks right now. Kathleen and I are holding up ok. We are trying to straighten things up at work so that Kath can take some time off and I can ease off for a while as well. The support we have received from family, friends, co-workers and fellow church members is overwhelming. Thank you again for your thoughts and prayers.

    Love,
Anna's Dad

When Anna was diagnosed, Kathleen's mother was recovering from hip surgery. Thus, her folks could not come down to Grand Rapids and Kathleen did not want to give them the complete news about Anna over the telephone. We kept them informed by telephone about the seizures, but we did not explain the full extent of Anna's disease. As soon as we were out of the hospital, we traveled north to Kathleen's parents' home in Traverse City to let her family know about Anna's condition.

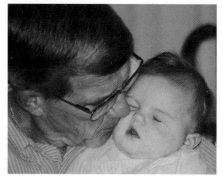

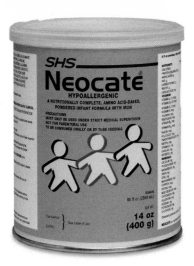

Eventually, we found the Neocate.

The Zantac and Propulsid were directed at Anna's reflux problems. The Phenobarbitol was directed at helping Anna with her seizures. The remaining items (Thiamine, Vitamin E, Coenzyme Q, Vitamin C, and Carnitine) are commonly prescribed for children with metabolic illnesses. These items are supposed to assist metabolism at a cellular level. They do not fix the problem, but they might help. At this stage we would have done anything if a doctor told us it might help.

Well, yesterday we saw the neurologist and today we saw the pediatrician. Based on what the neurologist told us, we have decided to postpone Anna's surgery. We have learned there is a possibility that Anna's problem with reflux (the problem that prompted the surgery recommendation in the first place) might be the product of a food allergy. Accordingly, we are going to put off the surgery until we have had a chance to see if Anna's reflux will respond to feeding an elemental formula.

The formula prescribed is Neocate. If anyone has seen or heard of it, let us know. We have not found it locally yet.

We have also started Anna on a more aggressive antioxidant and vitamin regimen. In addition to her Thiamine, Anna will now also take Vitamin E, Coenzyme Q, Vitamin C, and Carnitine. Added to her Propulcid, Zantac, and Phenobarbital, her primary diet is now pills.

Anna is still doing very well. She is now up to 19 pounds 7 ounces fully dressed. She runs errands with us every day. She seems very happy.

Many people have asked us if they can help with meals. The provision of meals is being coordinated by Sheri Leisman. Thank you again for your thoughts and prayers.

Anna's Dad

Well, it has been a week since we returned home from the hospital. It is amazing how much can change in a week. Anna is still sleeping through the night, although she is trying to move her bedtime later and later (much to our chagrin). She is doing well but is distrustful of any pureed food now because we keep putting more and more crushed vitamins into it! Smart kid. We are still searching for the Neocate formula. We just received her apnea monitor, which we may use at night. More than likely, we will put off using it until later. Not much else to report except that it has not been our greatest day, but we are bound to have ups and downs along the way. We are enjoying the wonderful food that our friends bring to us each night! Maybe we will put a cookbook together from all the recipes people provide to us when everything is said and done. Anna sends kisses to everyone!

Love,
Anna's Mom

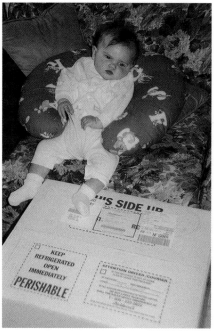

This is Anna with a meal a friend sent from Balducci's of Greenwich Village. Over the course of the following fourteen months, we were fortunate enough to receive many delicious meals from our friends. At first, it was difficult to accept because we had always been able to take care of ourselves. Charity was something we gave, not something we received. But we learned that it freed up more time for us to spend with Anna. And it gave our friends a chance to spend some quality time with Anna, too, when they came to deliver the meals. Even now, months after she returned to heaven, we are still trying to get back into the swing of cooking for ourselves.

Anna is snoozing and the Lions are losing. Sorry, poetic license. Anna is still doing well. We located the magic formula, Neocate, at Meijer. Given the expense, we are going forward one can at a time. Although we are gradually increasing the Neocate versus her Prosobee, it will be a while before she is totally switched over. So far so good.

Anna's friend Neil Kimball visited today for the purpose of taking some photographs of Anna. We will post the best of them. We are working up some prayer cards that include a photo of Anna. If you would like one, just e-mail your real mailing address and we will send you one. We have spent some time on the internet reviewing the site for the Mitochondrial and Metabolic Disease Center at the University of California-San Diego. We are convinced that a trip to see them will be worthwhile. The only question now is timing. If any of you know anything about the Center, please let us know.

Thank you,
Anna's Dad

This is Neil and his son Daniel with Anna. Neil's pictures of Anna are featured throughout the book, but here are a few samples.

I only have a few minutes (between Anna's Propulsid dose and her final meal of the day) in which to update all of you, so I must be brief. Anna looked smashing in her MSU cheerleader outfit on Saturday and was quite thrilled with the outcome of the game, although she did a good job comforting Dad!

We made contact with the Mitochondrial and Metabolic Disease Center at San Diego and things look good for us to go there for a 9 day visit in November. The doctors have to make the necessary referrals but then we will receive the green light and plans will be made. Anna will be in-house at the University of California San Diego Medical Facility for 4 days and will be watched for the following five days but will not have to stay at the hospital. We will let you know when we get a firm date.

She is still doing great and is growing in leaps and bounds. Anna is going to be evaluated on Tuesday by experts at Ken-O-Sha, a local organization that offers a variety of services and assistance for developmentally disabled children and their parents. Just one more step in the right direction. We are almost ready to mail out prayer cards to everyone on our Christmas card list. Feel free to share the information with your friends. We need all the help and prayers we can get.

Anna sends kisses to everyone.

Love,

Anna's Mom

If you met Kathleen and me, it would not take you very long to figure out that we are very different people. Perhaps the most troubling difference, however, is that I am a University of Michigan fan while Kathleen is a Michigan State University fan. Anna always had an extensive wardrobe from each school. When the schools competed against each other in any athletic contest, Anna would wear the colors of one school in the first half and the other in the second half. Unfortunately, when the schools met on the football field in 1999, Michigan State emerged the victor.

Thursday, October 14, 1999, 9:36 p.m.
From: Anna's Mom
Subject: Thursday's Happenings

While we were in the hospital in September, several friends found the MMDC on the Internet. They immediately notified us and we confirmed with our doctors that it was the place to go for the diagnosis and treatment of mitochondrial illnesses. You can find them on the web at biochemgen.ucsd.edu/mmdc.

It has been a hectic few days but we are making headway in the scheduling department. We now have a date with the folks at the Mitochondrial and Metabolic Disease Center at the University of California, San Diego. We will be flying out on December 5th and staying 9 days. Anna will be an in-patient for the first four or five days and then we will do out-patient activities for the remainder of the visit. The Center graciously provides its "guests" with passes to the San Diego Zoo and other attractions, so we will try to turn this trip into a vacation of sorts.

We believe that the doctors at the MMDC will be able to give us some idea of what we are facing, whether Anna is doing better than average or worse than average. Our doctors here, while wonderful, refuse to even speculate regarding her prognosis or the progress of the disease. Thus, we eagerly await this trip despite the type of news we may receive.

Because of the trip, we have had to reschedule many appointments with Anna's doctors. We have also moved her stomach surgery to January 2000. It will take a while for us to prepare ourselves for the event, as we are not in "that place" where we really want to do this. The surgery is very important. When Leigh's kids get sick, they do not want to eat. When they do not eat, you cannot give them their medication. So, we have to keep Anna healthy until the surgery in January.

Other than that, we have been in touch with the local school group that works with developmentally disabled children. We were not sure what to expect and we are still trying to figure out how best to use this resource.

Anna is in her swing and just got done with a wonderful physical therapy session. Her neck seems to be getting stronger and we are optimistic that she will continue to improve! Anna also had a great time visiting with her Grammie and Grampie and Uncle Patrick in Traverse City on Wednesday. She is a great traveler! Time to feed the princess.

Love to all,
Anna's Mom

We received our packet of information from the Mitochondrial and Metabolic Disease Center (MMDC) in San Diego on Saturday. To our surprise, we discovered that there are two families in Ann Arbor whose children have different metabolic diseases than Anna's but who have published articles regarding their experiences. One article mentioned a physical therapist in Waterford, Michigan who did hydrotherapy with one of the children in order to strengthen her muscles.

Hypotonic children (those with weak muscle tone), such as Anna, benefit from working in water because they can feel the water against their skin, it helps them to orient their bodies, and they do not have to fight gravity as much in the water. I have been wanting to take her swimming for a long time. Perhaps we will drive to Ann Arbor for some lessons. We have already placed a call to the therapist.

We also discovered that she will be taking part in a multitude of tests while at the MMDC. First, however, we need to determine whether the tests are for diagnostic purposes, whether they are required for the medication protocols, or whether they are just standard tests performed on every child coming into the facility. (By the way, the MMDC only takes two new children each Monday, which is one reason why we have to wait until December 6th.) We are meeting with our neurologist on Tuesday and will try to get as many questions answered as possible.

It has not been the greatest weekend. We are learning it is difficult to spend any amount of time with other babies as they only remind us of what Anna is unable to do. We thought we had these feelings under control, but we were wrong. There will probably be a lot of these weekends but we are glad that this one is over.

We will be mailing out prayer cards as soon as we finish a few other things. The Anna's Friends Foundation will soon be an officially formed trust, thanks to our wonderful friends at Mika, Meyers, Beckett & Jones. There is a lot more to say but we are tired, so we will say good night to all our friends. Anna sends her love.

Always,
Anna's Mom

Although Anna always enjoyed her bath, she only went swimming once, during August of 1999.

For the most part, even though you have a child with a terminal disease, you still go through your day-to-day activities without thinking about that constantly. Every once in a while, however, something triggers that thought and then you can think of nothing else. That weekend, we were in the cry room at mass with a couple of other families with kids. There was another boy there who was about Anna's age. He was very active. It was a hard reminder of all the things Anna could not do. We kept crying all day.

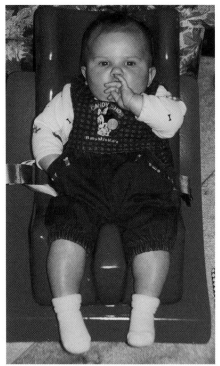

Here, Anna is sitting in her first Tumbleform chair. The chair had a velcro backing. It could be attached to the sloping curve of the base in different spots so that Anna could sit in a reclined or upright position. The stronger her trunk and shoulder muscles got, the more upright she could sit. It was an indispensable aid for her and for us.

As Anna sits in her Tumbleform chair playing with her mylar balloons we are contemplating the fact that schedules are meant to be changed and that we should never write in Anna's day-timer with a pen! After our visit with the pediatric neurologist, we are now rethinking whether a trip to the MMDC in San Diego is worthwhile. Because Anna has already been affirmatively diagnosed with NARP causing Leigh's Syndrome, much of the MMDC's work is done.

Also, her lactic acid levels appear to be responding to her thiamine therapy—something that the MMDC said was virtually impossible. We are taking steps to confirm this. If it is true, Anna may be making medical history (i.e., she is "reportable" in medical journals). Because the MMDC studies the effects of another drug, DCA, in lowering lactic acid levels, our participation in their studies may be unnecessary. It may still be helpful for us to go out and get a "second opinion," but we are still trying to decide how to proceed. What fun.

Anna has not been eating well for the past three days, probably because she does not like the taste of the Neocate. So we put more Prosobee in her formula today and she has been chowing like crazy! We also noted that her rate of drool has increased dramatically over the past few days, so we think that she is gearing up to show off her teeth! We will keep all of you on tooth alert.

We had hoped that Anna could do aquatherapy (based on an article we read regarding the benefits of water therapy for hypotonic or low muscle tone children), but the doc says that the risk of infection is too great. So we will have to limit it to our own bath tub. Maybe we will put in a hot tub! We may still go to Ann Arbor to work with the woman who has had experience with hypotonic children and water therapy and then modify our exercise regimen.

Take care and keep those prayers coming.

Love,

Anna's Mom

Thursday, October 21, 1999, 10:52 p.m.
From: Anna's Dad
Subject: Thursday-just a baby

Thursday night. We are celebrating a recent minor triumph. We finally got our hands on some 3ml syringes that are designed for dosing oral medications for kids. We would tell you where we got them, but then we would have to kill you.

On the developing news front, Anna is cutting her first tooth. The last few days Anna had slowed down with her feedings, taking less and taking longer to do it. Ever vigilant, we were sure she was losing her ability to suck and swallow and started thinking about feeding tubes. I guess we forgot that Anna is still a baby first and a patient second. When we looked in her mouth, we became plain old parents again. Lesson learned. We believe we will be announcing her second tooth soon.

Anna had another blood test to determine her blood lactic acid level on Wednesday. This time, the test followed a twelve hour fast. We are trying to figure out whether fasting might affect her lactic acid level. Anna will soon have another lumbar puncture to see if her lactic acid levels in her cerebrospinal fluid are also within normal limits. Other than that, there are no tests on the horizon and no new doctor's appointments. Hopefully, we will be able to settle into some kind of routine. Regular weekly sessions with the physical therapist will probably be the first step.

Thanks for your support.
Anna's Dad

John developed a personal relationship with Neva, a representative from Baxa, a medical supply company. Baxa sells, among other things, oral syringes. Over time, we accumulated an entire dresser filled with 3ml to 2 ounce syringes. We used the syringes to dose and store Anna's liquid medications for the week. That way, we did not have to carry bottles of liquid medications with us. Anna was on the go a lot between doctor's appointments and therapy, so we packaged her medications in one-day pill packs and Baxa syringes. We also obtained multi-colored syringe caps so we could distinguish one clear liquid medication from another. Neva made our lives so much easier. All it took was a telephone call to the right person at the right company.

Exacta-Med Oral Dispensers

Self-righting Luer Tip Caps

Adapta-Cap

This is Anna in her second Tumbleform chair. Anna loved balloons, especially mylar balloons because they reflected light so nicely. She was not very strong, but she could certainly handle balloons. We still have hundreds of Anna's balloons and our own helium tank. We always had about ten or fifteen inflated at a time just hanging around the house. Sometimes at night while you were sleeping, something would brush by your face. On occasion it was Jasper, but most of the time it was just one of Anna's balloons taking a walk through the house. We are pretty confident that there are balloons in heaven.

It is a blustery day. After a brisk morning walk with Anna and the dogs, we visited friends. It felt pretty good to be social. After that we spent a quiet day at home working on the materials for an upcoming mailing. Hopefully next week, we will be sending out a letter detailing Anna's health history and our plans for the coming months, a brochure about the Anna's Friends Foundation Trust, and some info about this list.

We got the results from Wednesday's blood test. As you may recall, that test followed a twelve hour fast. The test revealed high lactic acid levels. We are proceeding on the assumption that the high lactic acid levels are a product of the fast and not just a "natural" increase in Anna's lactic acid levels. The doctor has suggested that we include corn starch in Anna's last bottle of the day. This should put something in her system that her body can work on all night long. Other than that, we are trying to make sure Anna gets fed at least every four or five hours. We will repeat the fasting test next week to see if the corn starch makes a difference. We will keep you posted.

The news of the elevated lactic acid level put the December trip to San Diego at the forefront of our minds. If the thiamine is not controlling her lactic acid level, that trip and the treatments available there will take on a greater significance.

Anna's occupational therapist gave us a larger tumble-form chair so Anna could sit in an upright supported position and reach for things hanging in front of her. This should help improve Anna's muscle tone and coordination. We were surprised to see her actively reach for toys and play in her seat for over an hour today. Based on her cooing and babbling, we think she thoroughly enjoyed the experience.

Thanks again for your support.

Anna's Dad

Another Anna day is drawing to a close. Today's central point was a blood test to determine Anna's lactic acid level. By way of background, when Anna was first admitted to the hospital, her lactic acid levels were 7+. Levels are dangerously high when they exceed 3. Last week Monday, Anna tested at 1.9, well within normal ranges (.5 to 2.7). Then, last week Wednesday, we tested Anna following a twelve hour fast. She tested in the 3.3 range.

That level caused us significant concern, but the only time Anna "fasted" was while she slept. To try to avoid lactic acid build up during that time period, Anna's neurologist suggested we give Anna corn starch in her last bottle. Apparently, the body takes more time to work through corn starch than the other things Anna eats. Today's test results came in at the high end of normal, 2.7, but that is still within a normal range. Anna will have a lumbar puncture next week to check the lactic acid levels in her cerebrospinal fluid.

Today we also had the distinct pleasure of experiencing a massive government bureaucracy. Someone had suggested that we apply for social security disability for Anna. Today we tried. We walked in and took a number. Forty-five minutes later our number was called. We approached the counter and were given forms. We spent an hour filling out the forms. We then came back to the counter with the forms. They told us to wait until we were called. Half an hour later, we sat down with the interviewer. Two minutes later, our claim was denied because we make too much money. Yes, we laughed too. If you ever have a day to kill, go to your local social security administration office and find out how fortunate you really are.

Thank you all for your support and prayers.

Anna's Dad

Over the course of a relatively short life, Anna had her blood drawn almost one hundred times. Her favorite phlebotamist was Tim who is legendary in Western Michigan for his ability to draw blood from very young infants and children on the first poke. Tim taught us to appreciate the level of skill his job required. It was certainly not a level of skill shared by all who attempted to draw Anna's blood.

Thursday, October 28, 1999, 9:15 p.m.
From: Anna's Mom
Subject: Thursday-more teeth?

We have now determined that Anna's "ya-ya-ya-ya" or "aaaaahhhhh" means "rub my Nuk on my gums where my other tooth may be trying to come through and where the first one has already seen the light of day."

It has been a busy week. Our printing press, i.e., computer and printer, has been going non-stop as we are preparing for our mailing. We plan to send out prayer cards, a brochure regarding the Anna's Friends Foundation, and a letter explaining what we have been through these past seven months. It is a large under-taking but it will be worth it. On a basic level, this is one of the few concrete things we can do for Anna other than loving her like crazy and making sure she gets all of her medications. Perhaps things will settle down a bit when this project is done.

We have discovered that no one makes the gear necessary to transport a hy-potonic (low muscle tone) child with little head/neck control in a back pack. We do a lot of hiking with the dogs and would like to take Anna with us, but the small baby packs are too small and the toddler packs fail to provide enough support. So, our friends secured a Hensinger neck brace for Anna that works great at keeping her head steady, and we are going to buy her a baby's personal flotation device that will hopefully provide her with the trunk support she needs. Then, hopefully Kid Kelty will have a backpack that will work for her. We will keep you posted.

Anna had her first physical therapy and occupational therapy sessions at the hospital this week. She has a lot of exercises to do but does not seem to mind them (actually, we do them for her and she squawks at us). We will start going every week now. Here is hoping for some improvements in her physical abilities.

Friends are coming this weekend to rake the millions of leaves in our large yard, so there is much to prepare. Anna, who is dancing on Dad's lap right now, sends hugs and kisses to all and is excited to be a daffodil for Halloween!

Take care and thanks for the prayers.

Love,

Anna's Mom

As Dad and Anna watch the end of Monday Night Football, I wanted to send a message to tell everyone that Anna had a wonderful Halloween! She was the cutest orange-cup narcissus that you would ever want to see! Even Anne Geddes would have been proud to photograph Anna in her costume. We will be wearing it to see the geneticist and the neurologist on Tuesday.

I just got off the phone with a woman in Chicago whose son was diagnosed at 1.5 years of age with NARP. He is now 5 and is not doing well, but his mother is very hopeful. She could not say enough nice things about the people at the MMDC in San Diego. Our resolve to go there in December is even stronger now that we have spoken with her. We hope to travel to their home and look at all the equipment that their son can no longer use and that Anna might like to try. We had a long, very productive conversation—the first of many, I am sure. She is going to get us signed up on the "Mito list," which is a mailing list of sorts for parents of children with mitochondrial illnesses. It will be up to us to sift out the good from the bad, but we are anxious to see what is going on in the Mito world.

I also have the name of one other woman in New Jersey whose daughter has Leigh's Syndrome. We will call her soon. I also spoke to a woman who does great work with hypotonic children via water therapy. Our neurologist does not want Anna going into public pools (due to the risk of infection), but we could probably do the therapy with her at home in our tub or in a jacuzzi (which we would need to purchase). We will keep you informed.

We are almost ready to send out our mailing. It will be a great load off our minds once it is sent out. Look for it in your mailboxes.

Take care. Anna sends hugs and kisses.

Love,
Anna's Mom

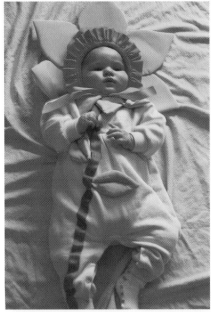

Anna in her Halloween finery, created especially for her by Kristie Byrnes.

This is Scott from Chicago with his mother, Joan. He had the same form of Leigh's Syndrome as Anna.

Wednesday, November 3, 1999, 9:26 p.m.
From: Anna's Mom
Subject: Wednesday-therapy, therapy, therapy

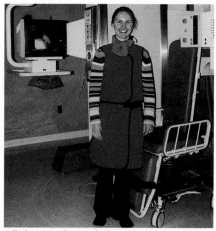

Juli Rice, Anna's speech therapist, by the machine used to perform video fluoroscopies.

Although Anna regularly went to the hospital for physical therapy and occupational therapy, we also did the exercises at home.

It has been a busy last few days. On Tuesday, we saw the genetics expert and confirmed that medical science has no way of determining which of my eggs contain higher/lower percentages of mutated mitochondrial DNA. Thus, any future plans for family will be nontraditional or at least less traditional. So be it.

This morning, Anna had speech therapy. She learned to say "Constantinople." Just kidding. Our speech therapist watched her eat and drink and advised us that it would be wise to schedule another (our third) video fluoroscopy. During this procedure, Anna drinks formula mixed with barium and we x-ray her to see if she is aspirating the liquid into her lungs. She has been sounding pretty "gurgly" while she is eating, which means that she is getting liquid down by her vocal cords and, unfortunately, into her lungs. Because aspiration is a major threat for her (it could develop into pneumonia, which would be a very bad thing), we need to keep this condition monitored.

On the eating front, Anna has been eating faster during the last day or two. Now, rather than taking an hour or more to finish a bottle, she is eating in 15-30 minutes. Let us hope that this is a permanent trend.

Right after speech therapy, Anna headed across the hall at the hospital and did an hour of physical therapy. The exercises we are doing with her seem to be paying off as Anna's therapist noticed that Anna is using her neck muscles more (although she is still very weak) and that she is using her legs more. It was a very positive experience but it really wore her out. Because she did so well and worked so hard, Mom treated Anna to a new knit hat at the hospital gift shop! (It was quite cold here today—she needed it!)

We are firming up travel plans now for our adventure to San Diego. We will be leaving on December 5th. We were told that many people who do not use their frequent flier miles OR who do not accumulate enough miles for a free ticket can donate the miles to a good cause, like, well, the Anna's Friends Foundation (which was formally instituted as a not-for-profit trust on October 1, 1999). Is anyone familiar with this process? Just wondered. Please advise.

It is time to wake the sleeping baby, who benefitted from some professional infant massage this evening. We need to get up early tomorrow to get Anna fed before she has the spinal tap at 9:00 a.m. on Thursday. This is only her second lumbar puncture. It is necessary because we need to know the lactic acid levels in her cerebrospinal fluid. Then we have an appointment with the neurologist. Let us hope for an uneventful afternoon.

Oh, we will pick up the daffodil's/orange-cup narcissus' photos tomorrow and will post them as soon as possible. G'night to all from the snoozie Miss Anna!

Love,

Anna's Mom

The Foundation was the result of another helping hand from our friends at Mika, Meyers, Beckett & Jones. The members of the firm and their spouses are pictured here. The picture was taken at the firm Christmas party in December of 1999. Kathleen and I are at the far right. These are the same folks who came to rake our leaves. Kathleen and I met while we were working as associates in the firm. Because of that, the firm took a special interest in us as a couple and as a family. Shortly after we were married, Kathleen left the firm to work for the Michigan Court of Appeals. I left the firm three and one-half years later to take a position with the United States District Court for the Western District of Michigan. Even after we left, we stayed and continue to stay in close contact with our friends at the firm.

Thursday, November 4, 1999, 7:31 p.m.
From: Anna's Dad
Subject: Thursday-lactic acid

It took a lot of coaxing, but Dr. Squires let us stay with Anna for the lumbar puncture procedure. That was important to us because Anna's first lumbar puncture was particularly troubling for her. After the first procedure, she spent the rest of the day whining and grabbing big clumps of her hair, as if she were trying to pull it out. This was difficult for us to watch and it took hours to get her to stop.

We surmised that Anna was suffering from a headache because she had been moved too soon after the first lumbar puncture. We were determined that things would be different this time. So, we insisted on staying with her and keeping her still for 30 minutes after the procedure. It made a difference.

Over her short life, Anna had four lumbar punctures. For two of them we were able to stay with her and keep her still for a time afterwards. She never had a problem with either of those. For the other two, however, they moved her almost immediately. Both times she struggled afterwards. The doctors who moved her afterwards insisted that she would not experience the headaches we described. We learned that there is a lot that the medical profession assumes about infants and pain. Sometimes they are wrong. We are grateful for the doctors who let us do it our way.

Over the course of months of treatments and procedures we developed many of our own theories as to the right way to do things. We tested these theories, accepting some and disproving and rejecting others. Either way we learned something new every step of the way.

For the third day running, we got up early to go to the hospital. Tuesday, the geneticist, Wednesday, the speech therapist and the physical therapist, Thursday, the lumbar puncture.

Anna tolerated the test well. Actually, she let us know in her own way that she was none too happy about the needle. About twenty minutes afterward, however, she forgave us and drifted off to sleep. It did not take too much longer than that to get the results.

Anna's lactic acid levels were high in her blood and her cerebrospinal fluid. These results were disappointing. When Anna's lactic acid levels were tested during her initial hospital stay, they were very high. After a few days on thiamine, her blood tests showed that her lactic acid levels were within normal limits. Subsequent testing also demonstrated lactic acid levels within normal limits. Although Anna tested high following a twelve hour fast, we thought we beat back the problem by giving her corn starch in her last bottle. The test after the corn starch was normal. So, we are left with the question why are today's results so high and what does it mean for the future.

There are several possibilities as to why Anna's lactic acid levels were so high today. It could be that her body is subject to some particular stress (such as an oncoming cold or perhaps even her teething) which caused an unusual result. It could also be that Anna's lactic acid levels were never really controlled by the thiamine and that the shifts in her lactic acid levels to date have simply been the "normal" waxing and waning in a NARP/Leigh's patient. It could also be that a recent change in the form of the thiamine we are giving Anna has caused a different result.

We may be able to narrow down the possibilites through further testing. Anna is scheduled for her next blood test in a couple of weeks. No matter what the cause, we know that increased lactic acid levels are not desirable. We do not know much more than that. It is not clear whether increased lactic acid levels signal any particular progression of the disease. It is not even clear that the increased levels have caused Anna any discomfort. She certainly does not appear or act any differently than she has in the past weeks when her lactic acid levels were normal.

Knowing only that this is not good and knowing little else is not particularly comforting. The circumstance definitely underscores the importance of our trip to San Diego. We spoke at length with the neurologist regarding the test results and she assures us that there is no reason to panic. In lieu of panic, we decided to shop.

There is a new mall in the metro Grand Rapids area. It opened yesterday. We decided waiting one day was enough. The trip ended up being quite therapeutic. They have a huge food court with a carousel. Anna was captivated with the lights and sounds so Kathleen took her for her first carousel ride. The first time around Anna was so excited her legs and arms just would not stop moving. By the end of the ride she had it all figured out and was happily sucking on her bottle. When she finally disembarked she was heard to remark "ooooohhh."

Tomorrow will be another day. Keep us in your prayers.

Anna's Dad

Once again, bad news about Anna's condition prompted us to seek normalcy. Just spending time at the mall watching the crowd helped us step out of that feeling of dislocation that always followed bad news.

For a couple of weeks after Halloween Anna went pretty much everywhere in her daffodil outfit.

Saturday, November 6, 1999, 10:25 p.m.
From: Anna's Mom
Subject: Saturday-anniversary eve

We were married on November 7, 1992

As John changes Miss Anna before her final bottle of the day, I can hear her coughing from her bedroom on the other side of the house. Yes, our little daffodil has managed to come down with a cold. We were told that children with Leigh's Syndrome react poorly to colds and similar illnesses, i.e., they refuse to eat and are unable to get their medications which are typically mixed in their formula. Anna has once again proven that she is tougher than nails and that the sniffles will not get her down. She has powered through the usual number of bottles today and shows no signs of slowing down! We are learning that she is a resilient little girl who is not going to fit the mold.

Also, we have no idea whether Anna's elevated lactic acid levels on Thursday were early indicators of this cold, which reared its ugly head on Friday. We would like to think so, but only time and more blood tests will tell.

On the tooth front, Anna has a matching pair of teeth showing on the bottom! They are not sticking out very far, but we can definitely feel them, as can she. She is not big on those chewable things that are supposed to soothe teething babies, but she is willing to take an offered finger or an upside down Nuk for rubbing on her gums.

Tomorrow is our seventh anniversary and our first one with Anna. Although our plans to go to Chicago for the day were delayed when Anna developed the sniffles, we are planning on a nice dinner for three.

Take care and sweet dreams to one and all from baby Anna.

Always,

Anna's Mom

Tuesday, November 9, 1999, 11:47 p.m.
From: Anna's Mom
Subject: Tuesday-a cold

Sorry we have been out of touch for a while. Anna is still in the throes of her first cold and it has kept us busy. Actually, I also have the same cold, so we are not getting much done these days except for eating and sleeping. Not a bad way to go!

John has been getting things done around the house in the beautiful weather we have been having, so at least we are accomplishing something during the day. Not much to report save for Anna's cold, which is now shifting to her throat and chest. It really bothers both of us to hear her "gurgle" in her chest. We both find ourselves coughing and clearing OUR throats in a vain attempt to convince Anna to do the same and get that darn gurgle out of there. This only appears to mildly amuse her. I never knew it could hurt so much to hear someone else have trouble breathing.

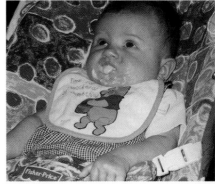

Anna in the process of recycling some medication laden cereal.

Surprisingly, however, Anna's appetite has increased during her cold. Everyone told us that metabolic kids would lose their appetites and, accordingly, would be unable to take their medications when they get colds. Not our Anna! She is bucking that trend. We are just anxious to get this one behind us and move on. She is still a challenge when it comes to taking her Phenobarbitol, as she can spit and respit and respit a microscopic piece of pureed food (mixed with Phenobarb, of course) until it becomes a huge pool of food and spit—so huge that you would need several soup ladles to catch and replace it all into her mouth. (Sorry to be so graphic.) It is a truly amazing feat.

Our little angel is asleep early tonight, so we shall also retire. The mailing to everyone will go out probably this weekend or whenever I finish revising our mailing list. So be sure to give us your address if you would like to be included. Keep those prayers and positive thoughts coming. Anna sends hugs to one and all.

Always,
Anna's Mom

Poor Anna hated the taste of her formula laced with meds or with the barium which was used to make the formula show up clearly on the flouroscopy. It was just one of the many miseries that she endured without complaint--save for a nasty look now and again. It was a little bit frustrating that Anna could muster the facial control to give you a nasty look but could no longer manage a smile.

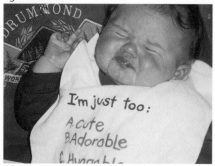

Hello again. All is quiet on the Anna front. She just finished her last bottle. All her meds are in for another day. I wish I could convey to you the sense of accomplishment we feel when we get to the end of the day and she has had all of her meds. Small triumphs I guess.

Anna is still battling her cold, but Kath and I have the sense that we are on the other side of it. She did well in occupational therapy today. Both Kath and I think we are seeing improvement in how she moves and lifts her head. We will keep up Anna's exercises with renewed vigor.

Anna had a video flouroscopy today. Once again, it showed that Anna aspirates a little bit of the fluids she ingests. The thicker the liquid, however, the more likely it all goes down the right pipe. Accordingly, we will be thickening her cocktail of formulas, cereals and medications with even more cereal.

We are nailing down flight plans for San Diego. We will actually purchase tickets tomorrow. We looked more closely into the donation of frequent flier miles. You can donate them. Virtually every airline has a program for accepting donations. The airlines also have specified charities to which they turn over the donated miles. It appears a lot of donated miles go to the Make a Wish Foundation. The Make a Wish Foundation, in turn, told us that they could not help us because they do not use their miles for obtaining medical care and because they do not help babies, only older kids.

We plan to approach the marketing department of Northwest Airlines to see if they would consider setting up an account for the benefit of Anna to accept donations of miles in her name. In the meantime, one of Anna's Friends has generously donated a frequent flier ticket to help us on the first trip. You can still donate the free tickets to a private party even if you cannot donate the miles to that party.

Finally, the long anticipated mailing remains anticipated. Hopefully this weekend. Keep the faith.

Anna's Dad

Saturday, November 13, 1999, 11:15 p.m.
From: Anna's Dad
Subject: Going to the dogs

Anna spent this morning at a dog show. Jasper was showing in the conformation ring for the second time and Anna insisted on watching him strut his stuff. Actually, Anna slept through the whole morning at the show. It did not matter because it was not really Jasper's day. He was the only dog showing in the "American bred" category, so he took a blue ribbon. At the next step, however, the judge hardly gave him a second look. We know he was the most beautiful dog there and it is apparent that Jasper certainly thinks so. Maybe next time the judge will think so too.

We are getting closer on our promises to you. Actually, we fulfilled one. We posted a couple of Anna's Halloween pictures. Just go to www.onelist.com/community/annasfriends. Once you are there, go to "Files". Two of the three pictures there are of the biggest daffodil ever. We will try to post a couple of pictures every week so you can see Anna more regularly.

We also plan to stuff envelopes tomorrow. Expect the letters to start going out tomorrow. It will take a while to get them all out. Probably by the end of next week.

It has been a trying day because Anna has been kind of whiny. We are not sure if it is a product of the cold, or teething, or something else. For a while it is kind of cute. After that, you just feel bad because you cannot seem to make her comfortable. Sometimes Anna's normal communication is a little bit whiny, so it could be that she is just being communicative. Only time will tell. In the meantime, if you moms out there have experienced excessive whinines (is that a word?) with your babies while they were teething, it would be nice to know that.

Thanks again for your thoughts and prayers.
Anna's Dad

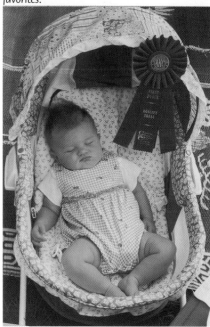

Although Anna was only eight months old, she had already attended several dog shows and dog agility trials. This photo, from a dog agility trial in Lansing during the summer of 1999, is one of our favorites.

Ruby took first place in her class that day, but Anna was the hit of the trial.

Anna and I watched a lot of football together. This night, however, Anna was too tired from working with Kathleen to watch even the first quarter.

Anna went to work with Kathleen regularly before the diagnosis. kathleen's boss, a Michigan Court of Appeals judge, permitted Kathleen to work part-time at home and part-time in the office. When Kathleen went in, Anna went with her. Anna would take long naps in the afternoon, so Kathleen could get a lot of work done. This day was the first day either of them went to work after the diagnosis.

One of Kathleen's fondest memories with Anna occurred at the office: " I was sitting in my office with my feet on my desk and Anna reclining with her bottom in my lap and her back against my thighs. Anna's head could then rest against my knees. Anna was eating from her bottle as I read the Michigan Lawyer's Weekly to her. Out of the blue, she started to laugh and smile with the bottle still in her mouth. I laughed back at her, and she returned the giggle. This went back and forth for a minute or so. It was one of the happiest moments of my life."

Monday, November 15, 1999, 11:22 p.m.
From: Anna's Dad
Subject: Monday-Anna the working girl

Anna refuses to stay up to watch the end of Monday Night Football with me. Sometimes she just is not the daughter I expect her to be. Kathleen is putting her to bed as I type.

I think Anna and Kathleen are particularly tired today. They both spent almost a full day at work for the first time in a long time. We sincerely hope that today was the first step in establishing a new routine.

On the mailing front, we have over two hundred letters in envelopes, addressed, stamped, and ready to mail. They will go out this week.

Yesterday, Kathleen had the opportunity to talk to the mom of another Leigh's patient. It is very helpful to talk to people who have experienced some of the feelings we are experiencing now. As we talk to more Leigh's parents we feel less alone.

We firmed up our travel plans to San Diego. We are leaving on December 5. Currently, we plan to return on December 15. We hope to return sooner, but the suggestion that a shorter hospital stay might suffice does not appear to be as solid as we first thought. It looks like we will be taking it day by day even out in San Diego.

The daffodil photos met with such a rousing response that we will be posting more photos soon.

Thanks again for your support.
Anna's Dad

Thursday, November 18, 1999, 9:20 p.m.
From: Anna's Dad
Subject: Thursday-Anna the workout girl

Another night is drawing to a close. Since we last reported, Anna has had speech therapy, physical therapy, another blood test, and an appointment with the neurologist.

We are amazed at the number of different therapeutic exercises for Anna. Indeed, between feeding and different exercises, we could probably consume all of Anna's waking hours. With the physical therapy, we are working mostly on Anna's neck and shoulder muscles. We think we are starting to see some improvement with Anna's head control. Maybe just wishful thinking. As part of Anna's speech therapy, we get to massage her gums and her tongue. Both Anna and I think it is loads of fun. She bit me (or half gummed, half bit me).

The blood test showed that Anna's phenobarbitol levels were okay. They also showed her lactic acid level was 3.3. This is a significant drop from her last test, but still a little high. It could be that Anna is still working on getting over her cold or it could be because we forgot Anna's thiamine that morning. At least we are moving in the right direction. Anna's next test will be just before we head out to San Diego.

We are heading out on December 5. All parents, please advise how to travel with baby. Do you bring the stroller, do you need the carseat base for cabs and buses, what do you need to bring on the plane, how do you do this? Help! Any tips would be appreciated.

Keep the faith.

Anna's Dad

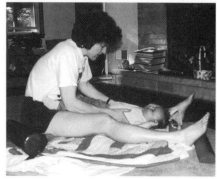

Here, Anna and Kathleen are doing physical therapy exercises. We learned the exercises from the therapists at Spectrum Health, including Lisa and Bonnie who are pictured below.

Saturday, November 20, 1999, 11:06 p.m.
From: Anna's Mom
Subject: Saturday

Anna's sharing dinner with Daddy, so I thought I would give you the update tonight. Anna has been a drool factory today, so we are guessing that she is forging new ground in the tooth department. Although all of the books talk about the fact that Ora-gel and similar products do no good because they are washed out of the baby's mouth so quickly, we may give them a try. She has been very verbal today—probably complaining about her teeth. Other than that, she has been eating well and has actually been eating faster (save for this last meal of the day). It is such a relief to have her finish a bottle in less than an hour! Yes, we live for the little pleasures.

Anna enjoyed going to the farm today and picking up the organic free-range turkey that we will be preparing for Thanksgiving dinner! We have only three words to say about turkeys: oven cooking bags. Do not spend all day cooking your turkey. Put it in an oven cooking bag and be done with it in 2 hours or so. That is Anna's Thanksgiving tip for everyone.

Thanks to all for the wonderful traveling tips. We have decided to check the car seat and we will gate check the stroller. We can transport Anna in the stroller to get around the airport and can strap carry-on luggage to the handle. We had no idea there were so many things to think about when flying with a baby. We really appreciate your help!

We have begun receiving feedback from people who received the first "wave" of our mailing. Overall, the comments are positive, so we are pleased. We will get the next wave out as soon as we can get more copies of the letter printed.

Well, Anna managed to sneak in a 45 minute nap this evening, so she will be up late again. I am fading so it is time to sign off. Go Blue and Go Green. (Anna wore outfits supporting both teams today, and it obviously made a big difference!!!)
Always,
Anna's Mom

The list was a powerful tool not only because it permitted us to broadcast, but also because it permitted us to receive. The emails we have included in this book are only a portion of the messages posted to the list. Anna's friends posted hundreds more. When we asked for tips on travelling with a baby we received dozens of responses, almost one hundred separate tips.

Well, once again, Anna refuses to drift off. So, I have time to post again. Anna had a very good day. She has been eating fairly quickly and complaining less about her teeth. Although Anna complained less about her teeth, she gave us an earful about her first long trip in the backpack instead of the stroller.

For the first time today, we loaded up Anna in her life jacket and then into the backpack. Then we took her for a long walk with the dogs. Anna kicked and threw her arms around and spoke on almost every step of the trip. We are not sure whether she liked it a lot, hated it a lot, or simply wanted to express her opinion a lot. We liked it though. Now we can walk the dogs on terrain that will not accommodate the stroller.

In our continuing effort to expose Anna to the best things in life, we let her watch "The Wizard of Oz" tonight. Although Anna is with us when we watch television, she rarely watches. For Oz, however, we pulled up a chair close to the television and she watched intently. She shrank from the Wicked Witch of the West whenever she cackled but she showed a definite affinity for the Scarecrow. As usual, Ruby preferred to follow Toto. You never realize how important Toto is to the movie until you watch with Ruby. She follows that little guy all over the screen.

The movie is a family favorite. We often sing the songs to Anna and we named Ruby based on the movie (Schatzhof Dot's Ruby Slippers). We are glad Anna was able to enjoy it.

See you later.

Anna's Dad

Anna was willing to put up with the backpack, but she preferred being carried in your arms where she could see your face. Anna's life jacket is stuffed into the backpack in this picture. When she was all strapped in she always looked like a little paratrooper.

Wednesday, November 24, 1999, 00:21 a.m.
From: Anna's Dad
Subject: The day before the turkey

Anna loved getting a massage, and we gave them to her after every bath, after her physical therapy, and whenever we were sitting together loving each other. It was wonderful to do something FOR her rather than TO her.

This is Marla Schoenborn, Anna's occupational therapist. Marla is demonstrating Anna's favorite part of occupational therapy. To provide vestibular stimulation, Marla would put Anna in a Tumbleform chair in a hammock that was suspended from the ceiling on a swivel. We would then slowly spin Anna. There was no mistaking her reaction; she loved it.

She is sleeping right now on Kathleen's lap. She is so peaceful and so beautiful. Actually, she had kind of a rough night. At 6:30 she started complaining about something, but she refused to definitively say what was bothering her. For five hours we tried everything we could think of. Then, a soothing massage from Kath and a hot bath put her to sleep. I am pretty sure that would have worked for me too. Unfortunately, Anna put Kath to sleep about the same time Kath put Anna to sleep.

Anna got rave reviews from the occupational therapist this morning. It is reassuring to hear from others that they see Anna progressing. Sometimes, I think they do that just to keep us going.

As we approach Thanksgiving we are mulling over those things for which we are thankful. There are actually more this year than we expected. We have been given so much by so many. We thank you for listening.

Keep the faith.

Anna's Dad

Saturday, Nov 27, 1999, 11:08 p.m.
From: Anna's Mom
Subject: Saturday-giving thanks

Happy post-Turkey Day to all! Anna enjoyed her first Thanksgiving very much, as she was showered with attention and kisses from her kissin' 4 1/2 year old cousins. We never knew that one baby could be the recipient of so many kisses. We felt very thankful to be all together.

We also had a bit of a scare today as Anna's breathing became very labored; she was actually gasping for air, even while sleeping. The ER docs said that her lungs were clear and all her blood work came back negative (Bonus: her lactic acid levels are no longer in the "high" range!!!), so they released us. No one, not even our pediatric neurologist, could come up with a cause for the gasping, which eventually subsided but later returned. Maybe the disease is starting to affect her pulmonary system (they warned us about this). Maybe it was just a one-time event. Maybe it will start happening more often. It is anyone's guess. We are a bit tired of guessing, however.

We are looking forward to San Diego with some trepidation. We hope that the doctors at the MMDC will be able to give us some guidance as they have seen more children with this illness than anyone else. We recognize, however, that answers are hard to come by as this disease manifests itself differently in every child and no two children progress in the same fashion. So we may not get the information that we are looking for on this trip. If not, it is unclear where we will turn as the MMDC is our first and best resource. Perhaps we are just getting ahead of ourselves—only time will tell. Go fix yourselves a turkey sandwich for us, okay?

Take care. Always,
Anna's Mom

This "attack," for lack of a better word, came on while we were driving back from our Thanksgiving celebration with Kathleen's family in Traverse City, Michigan. We were about one-third of the way into the two and one-half hour trip home when it became apparent that Anna was in some distress and that it was not going to pass. We had to choose between driving another hour and one-half to get her home or backtracking forty-five minutes to visit the hospital in Traverse City. We decided the quickest solution was the best one and we turned back.

Trying to explain Anna's unusual condition to the weekend staff at the emergency room was difficult. They treated us professionally, but they had to do some research of their own to confirm what we were telling them. We tried to stay calm but we were more than a little panicked. Previously we had been told that Anna could go at any time. We had also been told that Anna would likely succumb to respiratory distress. Was this it?

When her breathing finally returned to normal we figured it was not the end. Thereafter, we were very wary about traveling far from our already-educated health care providers in Grand Rapids. Thereafter, we always wondered whether each day might bring another attack and whether it would be her last.

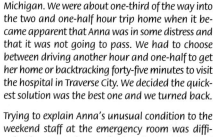

Even though the trip home was traumatic, Anna otherwise enjoyed spending Thanksgiving with her cousins.

Wednesday, December 1, 1999, 10:42 a.m.
From: Anna's Dad
Subject: One small triumph

You would expect something that costs that much would taste spectacular. It could not be further from the truth. Anna could never stand a bottle of 100% Neocate. Based on its odor, we could not blame her.

I am pleased to report that today I was able to pick up one case of Neocate, four cans, valued at approximately $170.00, and I did not have to pay for it. Children's Special Health Care Services finally got their ducks in a row. Six weeks of bureaucratic hill climbing and we finally reached the peak. It had gotten to the point that the people at the Meijer pharmacy would run when they saw me approach. But now that is over. We celebrate these small triumphs and we hope you will join us.

Anna's Dad

As the days passed after our mailing to friends and relatives, we started to get a lot of responses by mail and in person. One such response is pictured here. At the time we sent the letter, my cousin Andrew Rysdam was living in the dorms at Calvin College. His dorm, Noordewier VanderWerp, held a fundraiser and donated the proceeds to the Anna's Friends Foundation Trust. Pictured here with Anna and Kathleen are my cousin Andrew, Lisa Ponstine, and Tim Scholten. We took the picture the night they brought the check. Both Kathleen and I, remembering well our own college days, were struck by how these young people demonstrated concern and compassion for us and for Anna.

Thursday, December 2, 1999, 10:50 p.m.
From: Anna's Dad
Subject: Being a dad

Well, tonight I graduated to dadhood. Kath was getting her haircut. Anna and I were spending a quiet evening at home. I sat her in her boppy pillow on the big chair in the living room. She was happily staring at the reflections in the window, so I went into the kitchen to mix her nightly cocktail. Halfway into the recipe I heard a thump. Thumps are certainly not unusual in this house. Nearly two hundred pounds worth of dogs make this place thump central. For that reason, initially, the thump did not register as anything important. Then I realized the dogs were outside.

I rushed into the living room and found her laying on her back on the floor. She had apparently chosen my watch to perform her first serious solo rollover maneuver. In fact, as best as I can figure, she must have done a one and one half roll to make it off the chair entirely and onto the floor. I was mortified, tears filled my eyes as I checked her extremities. Nothing looked broken or bruised. Anna does not cry so she was not providing much help in figuring out how badly she might be hurt. She was only looking up trying to figure out why she couldn't see the reflections in the window any more.

I got her back in the chair after I checked every square inch of her. She just kind of cooed and babbled and kicked. Now that three hours have passed I am pretty sure she has survived the incident without harm. Now that three hours have passed my heart has stopped racing.

I know this probably happens to every parent at some time or another and I guess I am glad that I have gotten it out of the way. This certainly adds a whole new dimension to taking care of Anna. Once we got over the initial shock of the fall, we realized that all of the therapies must be doing some good if Anna is executing whole new maneuvers. What's next, walking perhaps?

Actually, even aside from tonight's dive, it has been a very busy day. For some reason, we have created a huge list of things to do before we leave Sunday morning. We are steadily working our way through it. Today, Anna had appointments with

This is Anna in the big chair. I know to most parents it would seem absurd to leave a baby just sitting in a chair on her own. But, Anna really could not move much. So long as her head did not flop forward, she would stay where you left her. I know that is not much of an excuse. When we finally acquired a reclining high chair for Anna it was the perfect solution. She could sit comfortably and you did not have to worry that her head would flop forward and take her body with it.

her pediatrician and the neurologist. Everything looks good. Her lactic acid levels are at a six week low. She seems very active (although this may be wishful parental thinking). Anna also had an appointment with the photographer today. We are anxious to share the results with you. We will, after we return. Right now the list of things to do is weighing heavily.

Wish us luck.

Anna's Dad

Chapter 4
The Trip

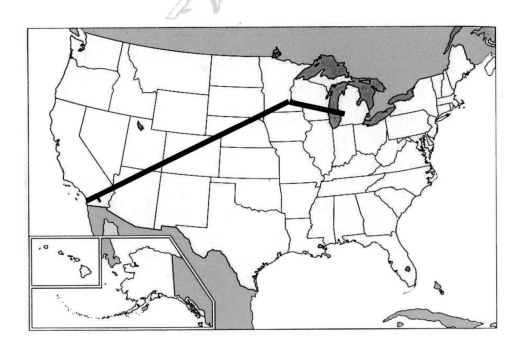

When your child is sick you want to make sure you are doing everything you can to help her. The trip to the Mitochondrial and Metabolic Disease Center at the University of California, San Diego was a big part of "everything we could do" for Anna.

Although there were experts scattered throughout the country, we knew the ones at the MMDC had experience with NARP kids. They had seen Scott, our friend from Chicago. Most importantly, the MMDC was conducting a trial of an experimental drug, dichloroacetate. Dichloroacetate (DCA) had helped Scott achieve many developmental milestones. We wanted that for Anna. We went to San Diego looking for hope and looking for answers.

This drawing of Anna with the ubiquitous rose was
done by Ryan Kimball, another of Anna's friends.

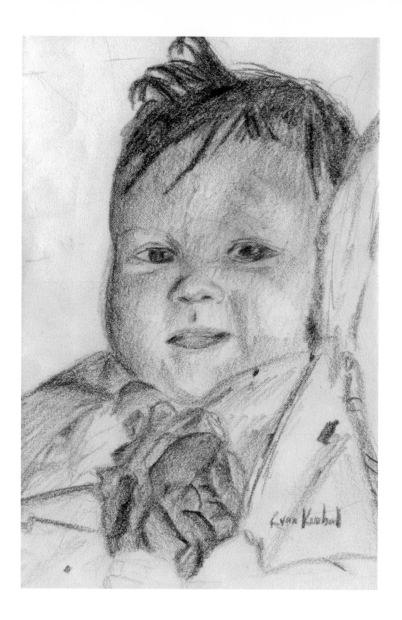

Greetings earthlings, we come to you from another planet today: Southern California. We apologize for the delay in reporting; the Bannister house (where we are now residing) has a computer with internet access, but it is down and it does not look like it is coming back up soon. Thus, I am sitting at a design station computer at Kinko's. This monitor must be a 25 incher because I have to sit back just to take it all in.

The last couple of days before we left were a blur. Nonetheless, on Sunday morning we made it to the airport in plenty of time. Anna's first flight was uneventful as far as she was concerned. She just had a hard time figuring out how she could fall asleep in the eastern time zone and wake up in the central time zone.

When she did wake up she had her first taste of moving walkways and airport bustle. While we waited for the next leg of our journey, Kathleen's cousin Rob kept us company. A special thank you to Rob for making a strange place seem familiar. Rob quickly put Anna at ease and she was sleeping again before we boarded.

We were the last ones on the plane, much to the chagrin of the lady in seat C. When she saw me squeeze by her she looked annoyed, but when Anna and Kathleen followed she looked downright scared. The flight attendant quickly found another seat for her.

Anna was awake for most of the flight. She really enjoyed looking out the window at all of the sunlight. We were on the wrong side of the plane for the Grand Canyon, but we figured she didn't know any better so we told her some other canyon was the Grand Canyon just so she could check it off of her national parks checklist.

We sat in the first coach row on the airplane. We thought we were pretty inconspicuous, but as we exited the plane, at least twenty passengers stopped to tell us what a good baby Anna was. I guess not crying has its advantages. A special thank you to all who contributed travel tips. We combined all of the tips to make a completely hassle-free trip.

The University of California, San Diego Medical Center was very different than DeVos Children's Hospital. You could almost instantly feel the difference between a public and private facility. For example, at UCSD the rooms were very spartan. The care we received at both facilities, however, was excellent.

Dr. Naviaux is in the center holding Anna.

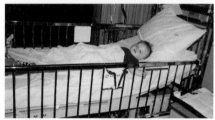

To evaluate Anna's metabolism, the MMDC carefully studied everything that went into Anna and everything that came out. To make sure nothing was missed, they weighed every piece of Anna's bedding, every piece of Anna's clothing, Anna's diapers (before and after), and, of course, Anna. They put a little piece of tape on everything that showed how much it weighed.

Anna was admitted at UCSD Medical Center on Monday morning at 8:00 a.m. They immediately started her on a glucose test and it has been constant testing ever since. She has already had an echocardiogram today and she may have a lumbar puncture, an EMG, a nerve conduction study, an EEG, a brainstem auditory evoked response test, and a fructose response test. How many of these tests she has will depend on how well she and we are holding up.

Yesterday we spoke at length with Dr. Robert Naviaux [pronounced nah-vee-oh]. He is the author of the article "The Spectrum of Mitochondrial Disease" that we found so helpful when we were first in the hospital with Anna. In him we have certainly found the depth of knowledge we were looking for. Both Kathleen and I were pleased to receive answers to questions that fit into other answers we had already received. Even if we accomplish nothing else on this journey, our first conversation with Dr. Naviaux probably would justify the trip. We look forward to additional conversations.

The tests yesterday and today (and maybe tomorrow if we run out of steam today) will determine whether Anna can participate in the DCA study. It looks like she will. Thank you for thinking of us, keep us in your prayers. I hope we will be able to post again soon.

Anna's Dad

December 6-8, 1999
Conversations with Doctor Robert Naviaux

We went to San Diego looking for answers that we could not get anywhere else. To make sure we did not miss anything, we took a tape recorder. That way we could concentrate more on trying to understand what we heard and less on remembering every word.

The first time we sat down with Dr. Naviaux it was almost a competition between Kathleen and I to see who could get their questions out first. He knew as much as there was to know about Anna's illness and how it affected her. Sometimes it was difficult for him to put it in terms we could understand. Each answer led to more questions. Fortunately, Dr. Naviaux was very patient. He answered every question. He would speak calmly and deliberately, choosing his words carefully so we would fully grasp each explanation.

We have hours and hours of tapes, pages and pages of transcript. Everything Dr. Naviaux told us about Anna was right on point. Even if we did not understand the explanations fully then, we came to understand them as we watched the entire progression of the disease in Anna. Because Dr. Naviaux's explanations were so accurate and so complete, we were sorely tempted to include every word of our conversations with Dr. Naviaux in these pages. But learning it all through the excruciating process of our inartfully worded questions is probably not the best way. Moreover, understanding Anna's disease is not the most important part of Anna's story. Please know, however, that understanding the disease was critically important to us at that time. Dr. Naviaux was nothing short of an answer to our prayers. Knowledge was power. The more we knew, the better we were able to cope, at least on an intellectual level.

We learned from Dr. Naviaux that people use different biochemical pathways to produce energy. Sustained energy is produced aerobically through the mitochondria in our cells through a process known as oxidase phosphorylation. Short term energy can be produced anaerobically outside of the mitochondria through a process known as glycolysis.

If you are interested in learning more about mitochondrial disease or Leigh's Syndrome, we recommend that you read an article authored by Dr. Naviaux titled "The Spectrum of Mitochondrial Disease." The article appeared in a 1997 Special Supplement to Exceptional Parent Magaizine titled "Mitochondrial and Metabolic Disorders-a primary care physician's guide." The entire supplement is available online at biochemgen.ucsd.edu/mmdc/ ep-toc.htm. If you have a child who has special needs, we also strongly recommend reading Exceptional Parent magazine. It is an incredible resource.

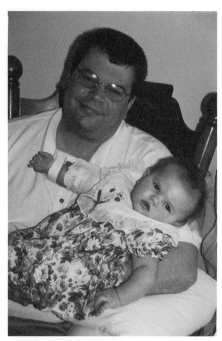

To keep Anna from thrashing her way out of the "hep-lock" that served as the portal for drawing her blood, the nurses strapped her arm to a board. Anna did not appreciate the board at all.

A significant percentage (and maybe most if not all) of the mitochondria in Anna's cells had a genetic defect that prevented them from producing energy through oxidase phosphorylation. If only a smaller percentage of the mitochondria had the defect, Anna may have had a normal life. When the percentage of mutation goes beyond a certain threshold, however, you start to have problems. Dr. Naviaux told us that when the percentage of mutated mitochondria reaches about 80%, you start to see NARP and Leigh's Syndrome.

Anna's inability to rely on oxidase phosphorylation to satisfy her energy needs meant that she did not have the energy necessary to grow and develop normally. We did not notice this problem right away because it does not take a lot of energy to be a newborn or even a three-month-old. If a normal person runs on 100 watts of energy, Anna ran on only about 10 watts. That was enough in the beginning, but it could not support her continued growth and development.

Anna's energy deficits did not mean that she had no energy. She probably produced most of her energy through glycolysis. That biochemical pathway is not appropriate, however, for primary energy production. Indeed, the parts of the body that rely most heavily on sustained energy, i.e., the brain stem, the eyes, the heart, etc., would be the first to suffer. That is what showed up on the MRI. The lesions in Anna's brainstem were areas where the mitochondria were "sick." That abnormality eventually extended to the surface of Anna's brain, manifesting as seizures. The energy deficits caused Anna to have little muscle tone and control. The deficits also impaired her eyesight and her gastrointestinal functions.

Dr. Naviaux informed us that one of the byproducts of glycolysis was lactic acid. That is why Anna's lactic acid levels were elevated. It naturally followed from her almost complete reliance on the wrong biochemical pathway. Dr. Naviaux explained that elevated lactic acid in Anna was like a "metabolic fever." Like a fever, it was a marker that something was wrong. Also like a fever, the elevated lactic acid level was a necessary byproduct of Anna's body compensating for the "infection." Also like a fever, if it got too high, it could be very dangerous. That is the problem DCA was supposed to address.

We learned a lot about Anna from Dr. Naviaux. But, that was only part of the reason we went to the MMDC. We also went to see if Anna would qualify for the

DCA drug trial run by the MMDC. She qualified. Once we knew Anna could participate, we had to decide whether she should. We have included below excerpts of our conversation with Dr. Naviaux regarding Anna's participation. We hope the transcript of our conversation will illuminate our decision to go forward.

Wednesday December 8, 1999
Conversation with Dr. Robert K. Naviaux

DR. NAVIAUX: Basically you qualified for the DCA trial.

JOHN: Just by virtue of the lactate levels.

DR. NAVIAUX: Right, right. And your diagnosis. I can tell you a little bit about how the trial runs and you can ask questions. It is a study that asks the question if low dose or high dose DCA is better for mitochondrial disease. That's the question we try to answer. The way that it is designed there are four six-month cycles. You will be on low dose for six months, high dose for six months, low dose for six months, high dose for six months but you won't know. We won't know either although technically there are ways to break the code if we need to do it. If there are any problems, we can find out quite readily. You probably want to know about some of the results to date. We have studied 50 patients over the last four years. Out of 300, more than 300 that we have evaluated, 50 qualified. About 20 to 25% of the patients show a clear benefit. About 10 to 15% of the patients actually die in the first six weeks of treatment. Another 15% of the patients go off the drug in the first six weeks because of side effects. About 20% benefit, about 20% are harmed, and you are left with about 60% of the patients that we are not really sure, they can benefit in some systems but not other systems, so it is a mixed picture.

JOHN: Of the people who have died within six weeks, is there any link between the drug and their death?

DR. NAVIAUX: It is something that we are trying to sort out. It is very difficult because DCA produces precisely the same side effects that the disease produces. Precisely. It seems to accelerate the disease in some children.

Please forgive us for starting you right in the middle of a conversation. Several of the transcripts start that way for the simple reason that we forgot to turn the tape recorder on at the outset.

I wish you could hear the tapes rather than just read the transcripts. Hearing the exchanges reveals some of the stress and tension and emotion of the moment. In addition, hearing the tapes means hearing Anna. Although Anna's voice is not reflected in the transcript, our conversations with Dr. Naviaux were peppered with comments from Anna. Anna's whines, squeaks, coos, grunts, and "oooohhhs" make you realize what the conversations were all about.

Although Dr. Naviaux was very eloquent during our conversations, Kathleen and I were not. To make the transcription more readable we have removed the "er"s and "um"s and broken sentences. Other than that, what you will read is what was said while we were at the MMDC.

JOHN: Have you been able to determine any characteristics that make it likely that the disease is accelerated by the DCA?

DR. NAVIAUX: No. What we found after a lot of time really poring over the data and testing were a lot of good leads that ended up being dead ends. One of the things we do is called indirect calorimetry. We put this little bubble on the bed and we measure the amount of oxygen they consume and the amount of carbon dioxide they produce. We measure the amount of calories they burn and the ratio of those things, oxygen and carbon dioxide, gives us also some indications of what their metabolism is doing. At first we thought we might be able to use that as a predictor of responders and nonresponders to the DCA. With 10 patients we thought we were doing well and then we did 20. There was just more variation and we could not predict.

KATHLEEN: Are the results linked to the type of mitochondrial disease? Did all of your patients have Leigh's Syndrome?

DR. NAVIAUX: They have all different kinds of mitochondrial disease. The only common denominator is that their lactates are elevated.

KATHLEEN: What percent of the 50 are Leigh's?

DR. NAVIAUX: About 15, so 35 were non-Leigh's.

KATHLEEN: Is there any correlation between whether it is somebody who had Leigh's who is receiving DCA and dying?

DR. NAVIAUX: The short answer is no. We have just as many people with other diagnoses that die or have trouble as with Leigh's Syndrome.

KATHLEEN: What about with NARP?

DR. NAVIAUX: We have patients with NARP, some that have died and some who have done well. So we can choose one, if we just focus on the T8993G mutation, we had a two year old who did well for three years. We had a nine year old who did poorly, went off drugs the first six weeks. We have a baby who died.

KATHLEEN: From the first six weeks?

"T8993G" is the NARP mutation. The number identifies the location of the mutation within the mitochondrial DNA strand and the letters identify the nature of the mutation.

DR. NAVIAUX: Yes. The first six weeks after DCA is started are a time that a lot of the metabolic adjustments go on. So a lot of things are happening. That's really the time when things sort of settle out and you can predict almost how well they will do for the next six months based on the first six weeks.

JOHN: How about other side effects?

DR. NAVIAUX: Side effects can include worsening of peripheral neuropathy, worsening of a cardiomyopathy, worsening of seizures, hearing loss, visual loss, those kind of things.

JOHN: And those again are the things that track the disease process?

KATHLEEN: How do you tell on a little baby?

DR. NAVIAUX: That's why we do all these tests. Because it is very hard to tell so we do the EEG and the echocardiogram, nerve conduction, EMG, all these things give us some foundation that allows us to tell which direction the drug has moved us.

JOHN: Next I have a whole series of follow-up questions. Six weeks being the key point, I am assuming after next week we are going to be gone, how can we determine whether or not these things are happening with her through six weeks?

DR. NAVIAUX: Because the things that really matter are not silent things. The things that really matter are, how much trouble is she having to breathe away the acid let's say, how much küssmal breathing she's doing. Whether she starts having more trouble with pooling of her feedings in the back of her throat and she is not able to swallow, whether she becomes abtunded or unarousable. Those are all things that are immediately apparent to you that are red flags that she needs medical attention.

The "küssmal" breathing was characterized by Anna pursing her lips and exhaling forcibly and rapidly to eliminate the acidic byproducts of her metabolism. When Anna was küssmal breathing we would say she was making "rosebud lips."

JOHN: One of our goals for her is to make sure she is as pain-free as possible. Are we helping her that way with the DCA or are we not?

DR. NAVIAUX: From the pain end of things, DCA has not lead to any pain in any children. Sometimes the adults will have a little neuropathy, that sense of tingling in the hands, but that has not really been a problem for any of the children. They haven't really had complaints of hands and feet bothering them even though we can show that there has been diminution of nerve conduction. Children's metabolism is different so in that sense DCA is not associated with any kind of pain. The only pain is going to be the pokes for blood draws.

JOHN: With the ones that are taking the DCA how can you tell whether the side effects are caused by the DCA and not by the natural disease progression?

DR. NAVIAUX: At the moment it is clinical experience; the statistics will eventually bear us out. I was on a soapbox very early as to the double-edged sword nature of DCA. Basically by the time we had seen 10 patients there were some red flags that some patients seemed to have an accelerated course. Very good people working in our group have disagreed with that, but now after doing 50 patients and having studied carefully certain individual cases where we lower the lactate and they get worse, then the lactate rises and they get better. This shows that there are some biologic variables. There are going to be children who get worse with lowering their lactates. We've actually tried to do statistical analyses to look at the effect. What we can say, there is another unequivocal statement that is borne out by a statistic with very high statistical power, and that is that outcome is not predicted by lactates.

JOHN: No kidding.

DR. NAVIAUX: We can say that 90% of the patients' lactates are reduced by DCA. But that reduction is not correlated with clinical outcome. It is not an inverse correlation. We can say this: if you take all of the patients, some patients will die with normal lactates, others with high lactates, others with moderate lactates. When you look at responders and nonresponders, you have exactly the same pattern of lactates. So there is zero correlation with lactates. Still there is something in addition that DCA does for some patients that seems to help.

JOHN: We are certainly interested in those benefits, anecdotal though they might be. At the same time I don't know if we would be willing to risk causing her pain, we wouldn't want to risk a high probability that it would cause her additional pain. It sounds to me that there is really no way you can say going into it.

The DCA acts like the disease process, but the worse thing that happens is the DCA accelerates it. It is still the disease isn't it, it is not the DCA?

DR. NAVIAUX: Yes.

JOHN: Okay, never mind, I won't ask that question.

DR. NAVIAUX: It is sort of hard, if a person has heart disease and you have them go out and do 50 yard sprints until they drop, which killed them?

JOHN: The heart disease killed them but they could have avoided it if they had not run the sprints.

DR. NAVIAUX: Yes. Okay. That's sort of the way that we are. So I will just leave it at that.

JOHN: So how does it work from here. We start on the DCA, do we start her today, do we start tomorrow?

DR. NAVIAUX: That's where we run into a little bit of a hitch. We have at the moment a drug supply problem with DCA. We will have drug available by Tuesday.

JOHN: That sucks.

DR. NAVIAUX: The drug is available Tuesday. What we would do is . . . what I want to do is to see what she does on the bicarbs, because I think she might need a little increase in the dose on the bicarb. See what her uric acids are because we might be able to cut that down a little bit on the allopurinol. We can have all those things done basically by tomorrow morning. We will let you go tomorrow morning. Enjoy San Diego and I will be in contact with you after the weekend. The earliest it really could arrive would be Monday which means that I would probably arrange to have you come back Tuesday.

JOHN: Now, once we come back and she starts taking the drug, then what?

DR. NAVIAUX: What we do is we give her a small dose and watch, we will do indirect calorimetry, the little bubble test, before and after.

One of the tests conducted on Anna revealed another unexplained acid in her system. To counter that acid, Dr. Naviaux prescribed sodium bicarbonate, baking soda. From that day forward, Anna's medication regimen included a little bit of sodium bicarb.

JOHN: What is it like? Is it a pill or liquid?

DR. NAVIAUX: It is just a liquid. We flavor it different ways.

JOHN: Make it taste like the Propulsid, that seems to be her favorite. So we give her the DCA and then we want to evaluate her for period of time after that.

DR. NAVIAUX: So we evaluate her.

JOHN: For how long?

DR. NAVIAUX: Well, the way that the protocol is written, we give it to you for a week, while you are still local, and then come back at the end of the week to repeat blood tests.

JOHN: Okay, so if we started on Tuesday and we would be here until the following Tuesday.

DR. NAVIAUX: If you started Tuesday, that would be the 14th, then unless we make adjustments to the protocol, if we just do it as it is written, then you would be back on the 21st, a week from the 14th.

JOHN: Okay so you just give it.

DR. NAVIAUX: We give it to you and you give it twice a day so it is given twice a day usually between 8:00 in the morning, 8:00 at night, or 9:00 in the morning or 9:00 at night. You just fall into a schedule that is convenient for you to give it every 12 hours and then you do that for a week and then we look at blood levels. Again, lactates again after one week. If everything is good, then you go home the next day, even if we make adjustments

JOHN: If we want to participate in this, we are looking at staying here until at least the 22nd as things stand on the protocol as written. And then you are suggesting the possibility that we may be able to finesse the protocol a little.

DR. NAVIAUX: Right. There is a possibility of adjusting it, compressing the one period of time. Children usually excrete DCA pretty quickly with a half-life something on the order of two hours. With chronic dosing the half-life goes to

12 and 18 hours and so that's why we give it a week to see how they do after their body adjusts. It just gives us a truer picture of how the next six weeks and the next six months are going to be.

JOHN: Okay, that's what I was going to ask you. If the six weeks is a pretty good indicator of six months, then how is the one week as an indicator of six weeks.

DR. NAVIAUX: You're maybe 20% there. It is a not a perfect picture but as far as the drug goes and the handling goes it is a very good picture, but there is a lot more to the effects of the drug than just measuring the concentration of DCA and lactate.

JOHN: Because the one thing that I wouldn't want to do is end up cutting short that period of evaluation if that gives us a sense of the six week picture. But it sounds like what you are are looking for at the end of one week is really a totally different thing.

DR. NAVIAUX: It really is a totally different thing. Honestly, it really is. There have been very few patients, a very small fraction of the patients, who have had trouble in the first week and the only thing that we really look at is specifically DCA drug levels and lactate levels. Those two things. But neither of those things are correlated with what happens in the first six weeks.

KATHLEEN: Did you guys know about the lack of DCA before we came out?

DR. NAVIAUX: No. I mean I just found out, I just found out last week.

KATHLEEN: It sounds really stupid, but this may be our only Christmas with Anna and I really do not want to spend it away from home.

DR. NAVIAUX: Even with the longest period of evaluation, you would still be able to go back on the 22nd.

JOHN: We will make it back on time.

DR. NAVIAUX: You can talk and get comfortable with it.

KATHLEEN: Would you put your child on it?

DR. NAVIAUX: It is a hope that I have no other way of giving. The DCA is a wild card, but it has a chance to help.

JOHN: And we would know within six weeks whether it's good or bad. When people go off the study, does that throw things off?

DR. NAVIAUX: Statistically yes, but medically no. I automatically put those people into the nonresponder group. Those people have declared their response to DCA and they are nonresponders that have had side effects.

JOHN: Is there any other kind of follow-up other than following what the drug does? Okay, you start this and then a week later you check those levels again, what happens from there? I assume that if there is a change in six months, that's when we come back and evaluate

DR. NAVIAUX: Actually, the way that we like to have it is you come back every six months. We will repeat all the tests to see how her heart is doing, how her nerves are going, how her brain is doing. Okay. We didn't do an MRI this time because you had a recent one done but we would do an MRI the next time. All these things would be repeated. There are some tests that will get done by your regular physician. We will get a trough DCA level to follow lactates, we will make sure there is no other problem with blood or urine. There will be blood and urine tests that the regular doctor will do. The next big evaluation for her overall progress will be in six months.

JOHN: How often will the evaluations be, how often will she need blood drawn?

DR. NAVIAUX: For that I can just show you the protocol.

JOHN: Is it weekly?

DR. NAVIAUX: No it's not weekly. It is basically one in three months.

JOHN: Okay. Although I think we will probably be pursuing that anyway to check her Phenobarb levels.

KATHLEEN: So basically what does DCA do for life span?

JOHN: It sounds like you already have your answer to that question. We do not know whether it is a good thing or not.

DR. NAVIAUX: Yes, right. That is exactly right. It lowers lactate very well. I mean there are 10% of the patients for whom it doesn't do that, but for 90% it lowers lactate very well. Some of those patients do better, others do worse.

KATHLEEN: And you don't know whether it is merely the lowered lactate or the natural disease progression, because some of the patients wouldn't be like her where she is capable of only glycolysis.

DR. NAVIAUX: All people have that, she just relies on it more.

KATHLEEN: Okay.

DR. NAVIAUX: So all people have glycolysis and use it. She just relies on it more because the other half isn't there.

KATHLEEN: Okay. Do you know what effect DCA has on glycolysis?

DR. NAVIAUX: None.

KATHLEEN: So that won't change. She will continue to be able to produce energy that way.

DR. NAVIAUX: Well, actually, I will modify that statement. Biochemically it does not affect any enzymes in glycolysis, but it is my opinion that one of the reasons that some children do worse is because cells need to get rid of lactate in order to keep doing glycolysis. So a cell that makes ATP by glycolysis and makes lactate, has to get rid of that lactate to regenerate what's called a co-factor, it is called NAD+. That NAD+ is then used again to cycle glucose and make energy. If the lactate is not removed, then you have an excess of NADH. And under those circumstances, glycolysis is inhibited. So it is a very indirect and kind of biochemically sophisticated reason but in fact that's why it is controversial. I mean it is really sort of my theory and there aren't a lot of people that have completely accepted that yet, but all the elements of the biochemical arguments are well established. It is just putting them all together that other people have balked at. So on the one hand, DCA only works on the enzyme called PDH. But because of its indirect effects on reduction of lactate, it can have inhibitory effects on glycolysis.

KATHLEEN: I thought you said that by reducing the lactate it allowed more for the NAD+.

DR. NAVIAUX: I did, but not in this. The lactate has to be pumped out of the cell. It is sort of like jettisoning. Normally when the glucose goes down to one of the end points called pyruvate, there is an NADH that has to be converted to NAD and the way that the cell does that is it shifts pyruvate to lactate and the lactate goes out. I called it an electron disposal mechanism where lactate, because it has an extra electron associated with it, . . . I don't like to get into this argument.

JOHN: No, that's okay.

DR. NAVIAUX: Because lactate has an extra electron, because it is the reduced form of pyruvate, that is the way that the cell uses to dispose of it.

JOHN: Sort of like a handle that it carries it out with.

DR. NAVIAUX: Yes. It scoops electrons out of the cell and by doing that refreshes glycolysis.

JOHN: So if the lactate isn't there to start with.

DR. NAVIAUX: Yes. If the lactate is not there, well, see what happens with DCA is that you are actually letting lactates slide back through pyruvate into mitochondria. I can draw you a picture of all this.

JOHN: That's okay.

DR. NAVIAUX: That should be a good way of just seeing. Because remember when we talked about, I still need to go over some of the brain anatomy things, too, as well as the chemical things. A drawing will also help you, give you a schematic of what's going on.

[Dr. Naviaux proceeded to sketch the biochemical paths he was talking about.]

DR. NAVIAUX: That is the argument, that is the chemical argument I use for the nonresponders.

JOHN: On the double-edged sword, that's the other edge?

DR. NAVIAUX: That's the other edge.

JOHN: And it may not happen? If it doesn't happen, that means we should expect positive effects and if it does happen that will be the cause of the negative.

DR. NAVIAUX: Right, right.

KATHLEEN: What are the positive effects you would anticipate?

DR. NAVIAUX: You would expect a child to catch up on development. Nutrition is not such a big issue in her right now because you've identified a formula that works for her. But the other issues are strength, resistance to infection, resistance to aspiration. . .

KATHLEEN: How so?

DR. NAVIAUX: Because those, remember that those white patches in the brain are not dead cells; they are just sick. So they have a chance of recovering although the lower they are, the lower the recovery potential. Nonetheless, there is a chance for some recovery.

KATHLEEN: So you need to see the EEG to figure out if she is at the low end or if she is at the middle end?

DR. NAVIAUX: I know from the MRI that she has low lesions but she has also got some upper lesions. We know that those Leigh's Syndrome lesions have a chance to come and go. So you could say with patients on DCA, lesions come and go; with patients off DCA, lesions come and go. That's the biology of mitochondrial disease. So those are the things. Strength, ideally we would like to have her rolling over. We would like to get her developmental curve going from flat to actually gaining some things. And that's what we really look for. We plan to give the child as much of a chance as they could have. So that's the positive end of things. I have spent most of the morning talking about the negative end of things but it is important to know both ends.

KATHLEEN: Again, if this were your daughter would you put her on it?

Knowing everything that you know about it?

DR. NAVIAUX: Yes. Knowing everything that I know, and knowing that if the negative things start to happen you can take her off.

KATHLEEN: Once we get her off will she basically go back to where she is now?

DR. NAVIAUX: Yes.

KATHLEEN: So it is not like we are going through a critical point within six weeks from which there's a point of no return.

DR. NAVIAUX: No. I don't think that there is a point of no return.

KATHLEEN: Are we going to put her in a biochemically or some other altered state from which taking her off it will not let her . . .

DR. NAVIAUX: . . . recover her previous baseline?

KATHLEEN: Yes.

DR. NAVIAUX: Most of the toxicity we have identified has been reversible. By taking the children off the drug or reducing the drug, there has been recovery of previous function.

KATHLEEN: If she does go on it, because you have a diminished amount of DCA available, will she go on the full dose or on a partial dose?

DR. NAVIAUX: Well there won't be a diminished amount when it comes in on Tuesday or Monday. It is just a diminished amount right now, which is zero, basically. We will get another supply next week.

KATHLEEN: Okay. I understand. Okay. Will you send us home with this stuff? Will we have to buy it?

DR. NAVIAUX: Oh no, no, no. We will give it to you.

KATHLEEN: Okay. Do you have materials or stuff that we can read about the study?

We did not discover until this day that the MMDC was out of DCA. They had none to give us. Apparently, DCA was manufactured by one drug company in Canada and, at that time, there was a supply problem. The problem was resolved the next week and we never had any difficulty getting the DCA after that. But, the lack of immediate availability on this trip probably helped us make our decision to postpone the DCA until after her surgery.

DR. NAVIAUX: A lot of it is unpublished.

KATHLEEN: No, actually about the protocol and the like.

DR. NAVIAUX: Oh yes. I will have the nurses bring it in.

KATHLEEN: That sounds fine.

JOHN: Great. Thanks a lot.

[Dr. Naviaux left and we were able to review the study protocol materials. Later he returned.]

JOHN: It is very interesting reading. What's her clinical severity score?

DR. NAVIAUX: We have several rating scales.

JOHN: But there is one referenced in the protocol.

DR. NAVIAUX: Let me see which one they use. Can you show me where it is in here? Because I developed a scale called the mitochondrial clinical assessment scale, the MCAS, that is a head to toe clinical severity scale that is introduced as a way of standardizing the clinical assessments.

JOHN: Where does she stand on that one?

DR. NAVIAUX: She is, well let's put it this way, the average number of, if we break it down by organ system, the number of defects that we find, in the average mitochondrial disease patients will have eight to ten. She is on the 15 side.

JOHN: No kidding. That is amazing. And it is amazing because we've always viewed her as being not so severely impacted. She still functions pretty well. Have you found that there is a close relationship between clinical severity and longevity?

DR. NAVIAUX: The correlation is the age of onset of the features. It turns out that mitochondrial disease can blossom fully formed at age 30, 40, 50 okay. So you can have all the same problems, heart, lung, kidneys, liver, brain, muscle, nerve, lactates, everything; it can be fully developed, but it was not present at birth. Then the clinical course can be longer than for the infants. A lot of it has to do with just the physiologic reserves. Children are more fragile.

KATHLEEN: So it is just a matter of timing, the numbers don't change as far as the mortality rate. Like for Scott, the onset came on later, the diagnosis came later at a year and half, his mortality rates are different than hers merely because she is younger.

DR. NAVIAUX: Right. Although we quote, the numbers that I always quote are the same regardless of the age of onset. Although, if you really break it down, I can tell you from clinical experience that the earlier onset, the greater the mortality, and the later the onset the lesser the mortality.

JOHN: So the 50% mortality in the first year after diagnosis that we previously talked about doesn't do justice for Anna. Does the fact that she is so clinically severe suggest that she will get less benefit from the DCA study?

DR. NAVIAUX: It is a hard question for me to answer, because on the surface my first instinct is to answer in the affirmative. But I have been surprised. Okay. I've been surprised that some patients do better than I would have predicted. So I've just learned to be humble when it comes to making that kind of prediction.

JOHN: One of things we are running up against now is bizarre travel issues, but we've got other things. What's the impact of putting her on this drug now and then putting her under the knife in January?

DR. NAVIAUX: Let me say this, one thing we know is that she needs the G tube and the fundoplication. Okay. The optional thing is the DCA. So we know if she doesn't get the G tube and fundoplication then you will have a whole other host of problems dealing with the aspiration issues. The temporizing measure that could be done to avoid the G tube would be an NG tube, but in her circumstances it is not really a good way to go.

KATHLEEN: No. No. We don't want to do that. She had one of those once and hated it. So I would rather go with the G tube.

DR. NAVIAUX: It will probably take her a month to recover from surgery and before you are thinking about starting DCA. But what we can offer, if she has problems during surgery with acidosis, is to give her acute unblinded DCA, just for the interval, the week that she is in the hospital.

KATHLEEN: Oh, okay.

JOHN: I am still not understanding completely. My question still goes to is it a problem to start her on this and then put her into surgery?

KATHLEEN: Or should we go forward and have the surgery and come back?

DR. NAVIAUX: This is what I can say with confidence: short term DCA during periods where there is significant acidosis is almost always helpful.

KATHLEEN: Okay.

DR. NAVIAUX: The thing that I can't predict is how she will do if we put her on chronic DCA before the surgery. Okay. It could be that she would be better, but it could be she is worse.

KATHLEEN: But we don't want to jeopardize her ability to be an excellent surgical candidate. I mean she is as good as she is going to be.

DR. NAVIAUX: Right. At this point, she is as good as she is going to be, she is still a high risk patient just because of her disease, but . . .

KATHLEEN: Her lungs are fairly clear, her heart is strong.

DR. NAVIAUX: Yes. That's just it. Yes, all those other things are good.

JOHN: So in your mind, I want to make sure, that it is not a bad notion to take care of the surgery first and then start her on the DCA.

DR. NAVIAUX: Right. Keeping the ace in the hole that we could provide DCA during the surgery if she needs it.

JOHN: So you actually think that that would be a good way to go. You see, I am just trying to figure out what you are saying.

DR. NAVIAUX: [to Kathleen] He is trying to read me.

The DCA trial was "blinded." You would either receive high dose or low dose, but you did not know which. Dr. Naviaux was offering us high dose DCA for the surgery if we needed it. Because we would know the dose, it was "unblinded."

KATHLEEN: He is a lawyer. You are on the jury. And he is trying to figure out which way you are going to vote.

DR. NAVIAUX: That scenario is the one where we have the highest probability of success, because it doesn't factor in the unknown of chronic treatment before surgery.

JOHN: If we don't do DCA now, in favor of doing surgery before we take on whatever the risks of chronic treatment, then in January we are getting the surgery done.

DR. NAVIAUX: It will take until February for recovery.

JOHN: Then in February, that's when we come out again.

DR. NAVIAUX: If we did it by the book, then she would come out four to six weeks after surgery, after her recovery is complete.

JOHN: I think we are both interested in going forward but there are all these complicating factors right now that we are trying to sort out. It sounds like you are not willing to go forward with this before the surgery.

KATHLEEN: Given what he said I would prefer not to go forward with it before the surgery, because every time I feed her I am in mortal fear that she is going to aspirate and then go in a downhill slide so . . .

JOHN: I agree with that but then that is presuming a high risk that she takes the chronic treatment poorly, because if she takes the chronic treatment well then there's no problem. It is only if she takes the chronic treatment poorly that this could have any negative impact on the prospects of surgery, right?

DR. NAVIAUX: Right. If we try to factor in all things and I try to take your shoes as a parent, the lowest risk scenario would be the one that I just proposed.

KATHLEEN: Okay.

JOHN: Okay. Say no more. We are into low risk.

We were fortunate that we took advantage of the opportunity to consult with Dr. Naviaux when we did. We saw Dr. Naviaux only one more time, at a United Mitochondrial Disease Foundation conference in Cleveland. After our first trip, Dr. Naviaux shifted his focus at the MMDC to research. We did not see him on our subsequent trips. We did not consult with him again face-to-face, but he was never more than an e-mail away. He followed Anna's case every step of the way. Although we would not trade Dr. Squires for any other doctor as a primary caregiver for Anna, we cannot ignore the incredible comfort Dr. Naviaux provided to us. Certainly, we were able to care for Anna much more effectively because of his assistance.

Wednesday, December 8, 1999, 6:14 p.m.
From: Anna's Dad
Subject: Wednesday

Hello again. We muddled our way through all of the tests on Tuesday. It was a very difficult day for Anna and for us. I do not even know if I can remember all of the tests she had. Three were particularly annoying for her: the lumbar puncture, the EMG, and the nerve conduction study. We wanted to know exactly what she was experiencing each time, so we had them do these tests to us as well (except the lumbar puncture which they would not do).

The EMG involves inserting a teflon coated needle into the leg muscle and then moving it around (first the needle and then the leg) to evaluate the nerve signals. We can say from experience that it hurts. The nerve conduction study is performed on the leg and the arm. They run a shock through the extremity at one point and then another to evaluate how well the nerve conducts the shock. The shock does not really hurt, but it is annoying. Anna was certainly annoyed and we promised her we would not send a Christmas card to the doctor who performed the procedures. He told us he does not get many cards from patients.

We have learned a lot already. Some from test results and some from just talking to the physicians. The nature of Anna's disease is becoming more clear to us. We have discovered how her body is supposed to work and how it is trying to compensate because of the disease. I know they are speaking in broad generalities when they explain it to us, but so many things make sense now, particularly the digestive problems we were having early on and the success we had in overcoming the problems for a while.

The doctors here have discovered a couple of distinct problems that we have already begun to address with new meds. We are told that we may see some fairly quick improvements in her condition because she will not be working so hard to fight these problems.

When we came out here, we expected the doctors would be able to tell us where Anna stands. They have. Because Anna seemed to be generally well to us, we also expected that they would tell us that Anna is doing better than average.

It was important to us to know what Anna had to endure by way of those tests. We had already figured out a couple of things. First, we did not trust what someone who did not love her might say about how it would "feel" to her and, second, if we could not bear it, we were certainly not going to put her through it. We were willing to run the risk of missing out on the DCA if it came to that, rather than putting her through an unbearable procedure.

Even though we were a long way from home, Anna received many visitors while she was in the hospital including a group of Santa Claus girls and a golden retriever. Anna even met a penguin at the hospital--up close and personal.

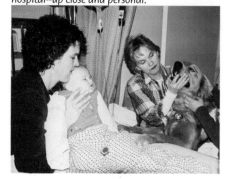

No mattter where we were hospitalized, we hung photos in Anna's room of her smiling.

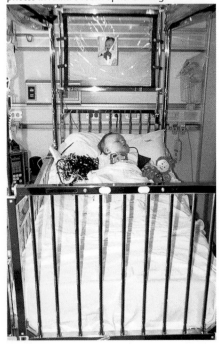

That is not the case. To our surprise, Anna's condition is considered to be very severe. Do not fret too much, nothing has changed in her condition. The prognosis they have offered is really no different than what we heard the day she was diagnosed. I think that we were surprised because we were quietly hoping for something different.

We learned today that Anna qualified for the DCA study. We first thought we would be starting on the drug immediately, but we also learned that the drug would not be available to her until sometime next week. We were told that she would have to stay a week after she started the drug. That was a week longer than we planned to stay and would require changing our Christmas plans with our families and would require making new and additional arrangements for the dogs. I would also have to fly home on the 24th or purchase a new ticket because my frequent flyer would not permit me to fly earlier than that, and Kathleen would have to pay to change her ticket. This was not welcome news.

Fortunately, after further conferences with Anna's doctor regarding the study, we decided we would be better off waiting to begin the study until after Anna has her Nissen and g-tube surgery in January (hopefully). Accordingly, we will be coming out to San Diego again four to six weeks after the surgery to begin the DCA trial.

Although the logistics of staying longer were a part of the decision to postpone the DCA, there are important reasons to wait until after the surgery that we want you to understand. When we came out here, we thought DCA was a drug that helped some and did not help others. Although that is true, there is another group that the DCA has actually harmed. If it turns out that Anna falls into that group, we can stop the treatment.

At this time, however, we do not want to jeopardize her status as a fairly good surgical candidate as it is becoming increasingly apparent that the Nissen and g-tube surgeries may be more important to her continued well-being than the DCA. If it turns out that Anna does well on the DCA, we will have waited for no reason. If she does not, we will have avoided risking postponing her surgery because the drug may have caused her to be a less desirable surgical candidate.

I hope the stuff I wrote in the last two paragraphs makes some sense. None of these decisions has come easily. We are exhausted emotionally and physically by the testing and conferences. We have agonized over the decision to not go forward with the DCA and to place the surgery first. Please keep us in your thoughts and prayers as I am sure we will face many additional revelations and decisions in the coming days.

Although we are not going to start the DCA on this trip, we will still be staying the entire time as we initially planned. They will be monitoring Anna's progress on the new drugs and we still have an opthalmological examination on Friday. It looks like we will be outpatient starting tomorrow through the weekend. After that, I am not sure if we will be inpatient or outpatient. We learn more every day.

Although this trip has been trying, we have no question it is operating for Anna's benefit and ours. Thanks for listening.

Anna's Dad

After Anna was diagnosed in September we took the monthly anniversaries of her birth very seriously. We spent Anna's nine month birthday at the UCSD Medical Center. We had cake and ice cream and we decorated her room with balloons and roses. All of the staff sang "Happy Birthday" for Anna.

Anna and Don hit it off right away.

Monday, December 13, 1999, 3:26 p.m.
From: Anna's Dad
Subject: Monday -out and about

I know for you it is Monday night, but we just got going today. We had the distinct pleasure this morning of meeting Donald Maine, another Grand Rapidian visiting the UCSD Medical Center. The weekend was certainly eventful. You may recall that it was our goal in coming to California to get answers to our many questions. We achieved that goal during last week. Our bigger goal for Anna, however, is to have her enjoy as many sights, sounds, smells and sensations as she can. This past weekend, we were able to pursue the bigger goal. Over the past three days, Anna has visited the Scripps Aquarium at UCSD, Sea World, and the San Diego Zoo. So far, it appears that Anna has a definite preference for sharks, hippos, and gorillas. Her mother has a preference for dolphins and she had the opportunity to get up close and personal with one during the dolphin interaction program at Sea World. Wait until you see the pictures.

The last few days have been a very welcome "family building" time. Last night, we dined at a fine seafood establishment on the harbor in San Diego. While we dined, San Diegans participated in their annual holiday boat parade. Upwards of 150 boats of all shapes and sizes decorated in beautiful Christmas lights and full of carolers paraded by the restaurant windows as we dined. It was as if they designed the whole thing for Anna, who fell asleep after the first twenty boats. We enjoyed it even though Anna was sleeping.

After a few days on the sodium bicarbonate (yes, we know it is just baking soda) Anna seems to have more energy. She has not taken a long nap (she usually takes a four to five hour nap during the afternoon) since she started taking the bicarb. Dr. Naviaux could explain the biochemistry of this; we only know she seems perkier.

We are off to the beach now. Tomorrow, if the drug has become available, Anna will get her first doses. If not, we may come home early. Thanks for your support.

Anna's Dad

Anna enjoyed the Scripp's Aquarium because we could hold her right up to the tanks and she could see the fish move. At Sea World, she liked the sharks best because they swam right over the top of you. She was also thrilled to see her mother in the water with the dolphins.

Although Anna liked the wildlife from the sea, she liked the wildlife from the land better. She really did react to the animals, especially the baby animals. We spent a good amount of time watching the baby hippo, the baby gorilla, and the baby giraffes. Anna also enjoyed quite a show from Ken Allen, the orangutan. He died the week after Anna did.

We went out to the Hotel Del Coronado one day, just to see what it was like. We only planned to spend a few minutes there, but we were there all afternoon. We had high tea in the dining room, roamed the halls, sat by the pool, and then walked out to the beach. There was something about holding little Anna near the vastness of the Pacific Ocean that was very soothing after a long week of difficult tests and decisions.

Thursday, December 16, 1999, 9:35 a.m.
From: Anna's Dad
Subject: Thursday-home sweet home

We are home. The last two days have been exhausting but just being home makes it worthwhile.

We decided we would wait until after the surgery to start daily doses of the DCA and the week long monitoring in San Diego that follows the initial daily doses. Nonetheless, we wanted to have the drug available to Anna during her surgery in January in case her lactic acid levels went up during surgery. To accomplish that, it was important that she receive at least one dose of the medicine before we left. She received that dose on Tuesday night shortly after 5:00 p.m. and finished an eight hour monitoring period on Wednesday morning after 1:00 a.m.

At 8:00 a.m. on Wednesday, we had our last conference with Dr. Naviaux. Once again, we spent over an hour with him. We have many hours of taped conversations with him and we are anxious to get them transcribed so we can pull it all together. After that last conference, we packed up and took off. We touched down in Grand Rapids at about 11:00 p.m.

We have lots of Christmas stuff to do in the next few days. We have scheduled Anna's surgery for January the 12th. If all goes well, we will return to San Diego near the end of February to start the DCA on a daily basis.

Thank you all again for your support. When we were first in the hospital with Anna in September, we were surrounded by family and friends. That made things much easier. In San Diego, that was not the case. Somehow, just communicating with you all through the list helped. Thanks for listening.

Anna's Dad

Chapter 5
The Surgery

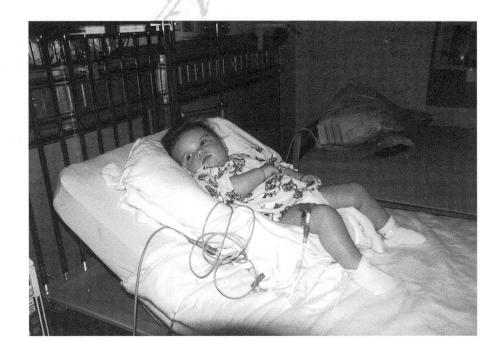

We returned from San Diego knowing a lot more about Anna's condition, but we were starting to realize that more medical information did not answer our questions as to how to live with Anna. Moreover, the trip did not confirm our hope that DCA would offer Anna significant benefits. We had mixed feelings when we got home.

We made a quick transition from the stress and exhilaration of our visit to the MMDC to the stress and exhilaration of the holidays. Do not misunderstand us; we were able to enjoy the holidays. It was particularly easy to focus on the reason for the season. But, we were also focused a little further down the road on Anna's upcoming surgery. Even with all our forethought, however, things did not proceed as planned.

About every three months we took Anna to the photographer. We were routinely pleased with the results. This shot, from December of 1999, is one of our favorites.

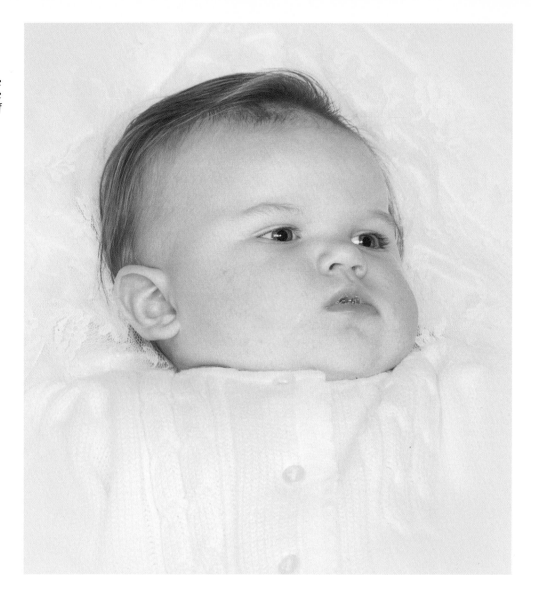

Sunday, December 19, 1999, 10:55 p.m.
From: Anna's Dad
Subject: Sunday-Happy Holidays

Well, we have now had a few days to get our feet back under us. We have made it through our first Christmas parties and with the help of family we have managed to get a lot of stuff done around the house. After feeling very burdened when we first came home, we have started to feel as if we might be able to enjoy the holidays.

After spending a long time on the road concentrating on only Anna, it was a little difficult to permit our minds to be spread across Anna, the dogs, family, home and work. Ultimately, we have decided that all of these obligations may be a little too much right now. Kathleen is going to take a leave of absence to cut down on the number of directions in which we are being pulled. We expect this will be a tough adjustment but we are confident that it is a necessary move and that it will be best for Anna.

Anna is adjusting to her new medication regimen, but she cannot seem to adjust back to Eastern daylight savings time. The dogs are adjusting to having us in charge and to being at home. I think they both preferred their "vacation" residences and they certainly preferred their "vacation" hosts. Thank you again to the gracious hosts. This may sound silly, but we are anxious to be through the holidays and to establish a new routine. Thanks for your support.

Anna's Dad

Our first Christmas party of the season was the Mika, Meyers, Beckett & Jones "kids" Christmas party. For the twelfth year in a row, I was Santa. Let's just say the suit fit me pretty well. In that role I watched dozens of kids grow from infants to toddlers to elementary school students to unbelievers.

Each year the firm adopted families in need and the kids attending the party would bring presents for those families. Unbeknownst to us, the firm adopted us that year. In lieu of Christmas presents, they presented a very generous check to Anna's foundation. After the party, I was stopped by the twelve year old son of one of the legal secretaries. I had seen him at the party every year, but he had long since passed into the category of unbeliever. He grabbed my arm and said he was really sorry about Anna. Then, he gave me fourteen dollars for her foundation. Although we gratefully received many gifts for Anna, that was the most generous gift we ever got.

Saturday, December 25, 1999, 11:15 p.m.
From: Anna's Mom and Anna's Dad
Subject: Merry Christmas Everyone!

(From Anna's Mom:) It is Christmas evening and we are relaxing with Anna. It has been quite a first Christmas for our beautiful baby, starting with our early Christmas celebration with the Feeneys last weekend and culminating with the Stuive Christmas today.

She has been the belle of the ball wherever she goes, and she has turned many a head sporting the new red velvet and white fur hat and swing coat! She was quite pleased with the fact that she could run her fingers through the fur cuffs on her jacket and hat. For you movie buffs, she looked somewhat like (but cuter than) Natalie Wood in "Miracle on 34th Street." We took lots of photos and will post them soon.

We had a bit of an exciting event this past week. During physical therapy on Wednesday, Anna picked her head up while laying on her stomach and looked at me (I was laying on the floor in front of her)! She looked at me for about 4 seconds and then put her head back down on the mat! Needless to say, it was a thrill to see her use her extensors in her neck and back in a way that she has never done before—even the therapist was impressed! [Anna never even came close to doing this again. We have come to consider it her Christmas gift to us.]

Anna continues to surprise us with what she is capable of doing physically. She is still extremely floppy in her neck and trunk, but she is starting to do many things that she did not do before, such as moving her feet more, moving her trunk when you hold her (almost like she is trying to get out of your arms), trying to sit up a lot, etc. It is hard to describe how much these little things mean to us. We see them as progress and progress of any type is very good at this point.

We thank everyone for the wonderful Christmas cards and notes that you have sent to us. We also had some of our friends' family members send cards to us and donations to the foundation in lieu of exchanging Christmas presents. The whole situation really brought home the meaning of sharing and caring during this Christmas season. Again, thanks.

We have traveled through this holiday season with some trepidation and with mixed emotions. It is hard to put our feelings into words but there is a sense of exhiliration mixed with emptiness, and we pray that God will fill that space with whatever it is that we need.

Thank you again for all your prayers and love. Happy Holidays!
Anna's Mom

(From Anna's Dad:) This has certainly been an unusual Christmas. In one respect, it has been incredibly easy to stay focused. Of course, this is Anna's Christmas. In another respect, it has been very hard. This may be the only one we get, so how do we make it the most memorable possible celebration? Trying to make it the definitive Christmas creates a lot of pressure.

Ultimately, we have enjoyed ourselves and Anna the most when we just forget about everything but the moment. In fact, some of our best times this holiday were just running around doing errands on Christmas eve day. The time we have spent with family has also been time when we knew we were celebrating the right way.

Normally on Christmas we spend a lot of time trying to get into the Christmas spirit. Not so this year. The last few months we have received so many kind thoughts, gestures, and gifts that we seem to always be in the grateful mode. We thank you all for your kindness. It makes a difference. I can see how the difficult parts of this experience might leave one embittered but I do not worry about that for a minute. This experience has done more to restore my faith in mankind than the giddy spirit of a dozen Christmases ever could.

Although I would not wish the bad parts of this on my worst enemy, I wish you could all experience the good parts.

I have tried to describe this to people in a lot of ways but I still think it is easiest to understand by putting it in the terms of a movie that I am sure everyone has seen this or some other holiday season. At the end of the movie "It's a Wonderful Life," when George (Jimmy Stewart) returns from his "if I had never been born" view of the world, he is greeted in his living room by everyone he has touched over his lifetime. They are all there to give to George in his time of need. I am always moved by that. Now I get to experience it. What a great feeling.

Anna has been exceptionally good company the last few nights. She is more than willing to carry on a long conversation or to just cuddle if you do not feel like talking. Because of you and because of her we feel very blessed.

Merry Christmas.

Anna's Dad

Friday, December 31, 1999, 4:41 p.m.
From: Anna's Mom
Subject: Happy New Year!

Here we sit on New Year's Eve watching the world ring in the year 2000 with kleenex by our sides and masks on our faces. Yes, John has a cold, I am trying not to get it, and Anna is wondering whether we have become doctors! We are trying everything to ensure that Anna does not catch this bug, which we have named "the millenium bug." A cold for her at this juncture would be very undesirable. It would not only delay the long-awaited Nissen and gastric tube surgery but also delay her participation in the DCA study. The longer we delay, the more we fight with high lactic acid levels. And Anna's aspiration problems are not improving as time goes on. So, as you can see, we need to keep this baby healthy until January 12th and hopefully during her recovery.

We will probably enter the hospital on Monday the 10th to get a PICC line established (they will use it to provide Anna with nutrients because she will not be able to eat for a few days and to get her blood levels where they should be—she operates at a deficit in several important areas due to her illness). We will be in the hospital for the week and weekend. Let us hope it is not longer than that.

Last night, we transferred our 8mm video tapes onto VHS tapes and watched our little girl grow up before our eyes. We had almost forgotten how small and precious she was when she was born, the sound of her cry, and her contagious laughter. We are so glad for these memories, but we yearn to see her face light up again with a big smile and giggle. We can only pray that God and the DCA will give us her smile back again.

We have so much to be thankful for, including all of you. We wish you good health and much love in the new year. Please know that we give thanks to God every day for your friendship and concern.

Take care. Anna sends her love.

Happy New Year!

Anna's Mom

Anna and I did not let the masks interfere with the most important part of the New Year: football.

No one ever explained why Anna could not smile after September 23, 1999--the day of her diagnosis. She could make faces that expressed her extreme displeasure, but she would never cry, laugh or smile for us. It was an unspeakable loss. Upon reflection, however, we agreed that we would go without her laugh if it meant she would not cry all the time, which is not unusual with children who suffer neurological illnesses.

Tuesday, January 4, 2000, 11:41 p.m.
From: Anna's Dad
Subject: New challenges

Anna is back in the hospital. While we were at the pulmonologist's office today for her regular checkup, he expressed concern about some recent problems we had experienced while Anna was eating. In a nutshell, Anna had started to slow down and tire while she was eating. As she got near the end of a bottle, she would start to sound "gurgly". Her throat would rattle as if her chest were congested and she would spend some minutes trying to cough up whatever formula she had aspirated while she ate.

We had already been struggling to get four bottles of about five ounces into her each day. With this new problem, we were lucky to get four bottles in and sometimes they would only be three ounces. Anna's aspiration of formula, her inability to eat in a reasonable time, and her fatigue near the end of each bottle suggested that she was having some problems with her suck and swallow skill. When the pulmonologist heard some unusual breath sounds in Anna's chest, he concluded it would be better to start a different feeding method now until Anna is ready for the surgery next week which should correct this problem in the longer term.

Accordingly, we admitted Anna tonight and she is now feeding through a tube down her nose. This will give us an opportunity to make sure Anna is fat and sassy with good blood levels before she goes in for surgery. Although we had expected to go in a couple of days before surgery to achieve this result, we are now in a week before. We were not quite ready for that, so we are scrambing to get our ducks in a row. We are certainly blessed to have friends who have been willing to take in many pounds worth of mildly annoying dogs on short notice.

Anna does not like the tube down her nose at all. She gave me very stern looks tonight. We had planned to watch football in the big chair together tonight but now she is stuck in another hospital bed which we cannot both fit in, at least not comfortably. I hope I can make it up to her when she gets out.

Anna's pulmonologist, Dr. John Schuen, and his nurse, Marion Schafer. Marion was also part of our hospice team.

118   *Anna's Friends*

Overall, admitting her today is certainly one of those "discretion is the better part of valor", "an ounce of prevention is worth a pound of cure", or "a stitch in time saves nine" sorts of things. Nonetheless, just going through the admission process and familiarizing a whole new bunch of medical professionals with Anna's idiosyncracies is draining and starts an adrenaline rush that makes it feel like an emergency situation. As far as we can tell, it is not.

Within the next day, we will fall into the hospital routine again and it will be better. In the meantime, keep us in your thoughts and prayers.

Anna's Dad.

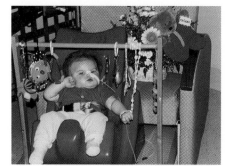

Here, Anna is showing off her nasal gastric ("ng") tube. The small ng tube became clogged not once but twice. The first time we tried to feed her through the tube we pushed the formula too fast. That made her aspirate the formula. We entered a new realm of helplessness as we watched Anna gurgle, cough, and try to clear the formula out of her lungs. We wasted five minutes setting up one and then another suction machine before we found one that worked. Eventually we were able to suction out her throat, but we thought we would go crazy watching her nearly suffocate on the formula.

Between the ng tube, the aspiration incident and the RSV test she had to undergo (where a large sharp toothpick-like swab was jabbed into her free nostril to determine if she had a severe viral respiratory infection), we are surprised that she would even look at us. Thankfully, she never held a grudge for long.

Anna never liked the hospital much. You can see her intense desire to go home--just look at her eyes.

The very first night we stayed in the hospital with Anna in September of 1999, we tried to sleep on the hospital's version of a cot. Thereafter, we brought in our own air mattress. Every night we would blow it up and make the bed. Every morning we would deflate it and pack away the bedding. We could not help but notice the residents eying our comfortable bed with envy.

Meds for Anna Evaleen Stuive as of 10/1/2000			
DCA	2.7ml bid	Vigabatrin	250 mg bid
Sodium Bicarb	17.5ml qid 1mEq	Tegretol	5.0 ml qid 20 mg/ml
Carnitor	2.7ml bid 100mg/ml	Vitamin C	1.0 ml tid 100 mg/ml
Super B-50	1 cap bid	Vitamin E	2.0 ml tid 50 IU/ml
50 mg B-1, 50 mg B-2, 50 mg B-6, 50 mcg B-12 50 mg Niacinimide, 400 mcg Folic Acid, 50 mg Pantothenic Acid, 50 mcg Biotin, 50 mg p-Amino-benzoic Acid, 50 mg CholineBitartrate, 50 mg Inositol		Coenzyme Q	1.0 30 mg cap bid
Topomax	37.5 mb bid		

This is what the labels looked like. They were especially useful in the hospital because you might get ten different people each day asking for the same information. Whenever they asked, we would just peel off another label.

Greetings to all from Anna's tired mom. I just thought I would give everyone the update before I hit the pillows. Dad is staying with Anna tonight—we hope that by changing shifts, at least one of us will get sleep. We will see if that plan works.

The good news of the day is that Anna does NOT have RSV, a rather nasty viral infection that drastically affects infants. She is also negative for several other viral infections. We did a little dance of joy in her room when we received that news! (After hearing her gurgle now and again and having a resident and a nurse say that the gurgling plus the temperature she had this morning of 101.1 degrees were clear indicators of RSV, we've learned not to believe anyone but the pediatric pulmonology docs. Sorry to all our friends who are becoming doctors or are nurses!)

Anna's x-rays did, however, show that she may have a bacterial infection in her lungs. She may have aspirated something or she may have picked it up like any other bacterial infection, but the treatment is the same. So tonight, she is starting a new antibiotic. Add it to the ever-growing list of her medications.

All of the doctors and nurses have been amazed at the "medications labels" that John put together. He took some nice Avery address labels and printed on them a listing (color-coded by form of medication) of Anna's med regimen. You should see their eyes light up when we peel off a label and hand it to them when they are poised to write out some 15 different meds! It is fun to tackle adversity with organization.

Anyway, Anna spent most of the day sleeping off her fever and getting used to her second "ng" tube (nasal gastric). The first one became blocked on two different occasions and we used (hold onto your hats) Coke and meat tenderizer diluted in warm water to clear the gunk from the little plastic tube going from her nose into her stomach. It will be the ONLY soda she will ever get, so I told her to enjoy it. Due to the blockage, we pulled that ng tube and put another in its place. She squirmed a bit and fell asleep again as soon as #2 was put in. It was surprising given how much she hated the first ng tube. She regularly tried to pull it out. Because Anna primarily breathes through her nose, the tube always got in the way and made her breathing very labored. What a trouper!

She was very talkative tonight and is enjoying the photos that Dad scanned in and printed off on photo-quality paper, then hung on her hospital room walls. It makes the room feel more like home. Speaking of photos, we have a unique request. PLEASE SEND US A PHOTO OF YOURSELVES! We would love to see all of Anna's Friends hanging around Anna's hospital room.

We will probably be in the hospital through next weekend, so if you mail them now, we'll get them in plenty of time. Many thanks! Also, for our healthy friends, please feel free to visit us. We are at Spectrum Downtown Hospital (the old Butterworth). Our current room is much larger than the tiny room we had last time, so we promise we will have room for you.

We still need to keep Anna healthy, so we have surgical masks for those who wish to take no chances. For our friends with sick children or who are sick themselves, feel free to call us and chat.

Finally, rather than individually thanking all of you who have sent us well-wishes today, I will thank everyone collectively for the continued prayers and positive thoughts. Without them, we would not have the strength to keep going.

We love you all and will give Anna many kisses and hugs from all of you.
Sweet dreams.
Anna's Mom

Although Anna did not like being in the hospital or having the ng tube, she did very much like having company. Having visitors was important for us too. When people were visiting Anna, Kathleen and I could slip away and eat dinner together or just go for a walk. It was harder to do that than you might imagine. It seemed every time we walked out the door we would miss an important conference with a doctor. After a little while, our family members became very effective surrogates for us and it became easier to leave for a little while.

It is Friday. It is almost noon. I actually got a full night's sleep last night. I am a new person. Certainly not a better person, but a new person nonetheless.

I just talked to Kathleen at the hospital. For Kathleen, Anna manages to go to sleep at midnight and sleep until 8:00 a.m. For me on the other hand Anna likes to stay up until after 2:00 a.m. and then, though she gets to sleep through the morning, I have to get up at 6:00 a.m.

Tonight, I am going to trick Anna. I will leave and then get Kathleen to stay until midnight so Anna falls asleep. Then I will come back and Kathleen can sleep at home. I will let you know if that works.

This stay in the hospital is certainly different than the last two. At least until the surgery, there is not much tension or uncertainty. Although it is nice to not have tension or uncertainty, we are actually getting a little bored. I think that is in part because we have lost the biggest concern that has animated our day to day existence for months: the need to get Anna to eat enough and thereby get her meds. Now, the tube does all of that. The hours we would spend either feeding Anna, preparing to feed Anna, or worrying about whether Anna was eating are now available for other things. Unfortunately, the hospital does not offer a lot to fill those hours.

Please do not take my comments as complaints. The tube represents such a radical shift that I simply must comment. For months we have hung on by our fingernails with regard to feeding Anna. Now that primary focus is irrelevant. It should continue to be irrelevant when Anna gets her g-tube. I am just realizing now how different our days will be.

Please send sleep thoughts to Anna at about midnight.

Anna's Dad

We did suffer some anxiety those first few days in the hospital. For one thing, Anna had to recover from her aspiration pneumonia before she could endure the surgery. We also had to get Anna's blood bicarb level over 20 before surgery per Dr. Naviaux's explicit instruction.

When you are parenting a terminally ill baby you start to focus a lot on numbers. Your child cannot tell you subjectively how she feels, so you turn to the objective numbers generated by all the tests. When Anna was first diagnosed we gauged how she was doing by her lactate numbers. When we were preparing for surgery, we focused on her bicarb numbers. You do not have a choice, it is all you have. Although we relied heavily on all the numbers, we never really knew exactly what those numbers meant for Anna.

Kathleen let me come home for a while to pay bills and do laundry. She also told me to post to the list, so here I am.

It appears Anna's respiratory infection is not particularly troubling with regard to the surgery. It is troubling her a little in that she has a hard time coughing up the junk inside her, especially with the tube down her throat. Periodically, respiratory therapists visit and suction her out.

It was my turn to not sleep last night. Anna was willing to compromise a little. She settled down at 1:00 a.m. Give or take a few minutes, however, one or another monitor went off about every hour and a half. Thus, deep sleep was simply not an option.

Amazingly, although I usually sleep through any noise or interruption, I cannot sleep through a medical device beeping. Fortunately, Anna can. I think she likes to make the monitors go off because she kind of smiles in her sleep when I dash to the bedside to figure out what is going on. Please do not be alarmed, the monitors rarely indicate anything dramatically wrong even when they are beeping. Typically, Anna either kicks a cord or slips an electrode. She is certainly talented at defeating technology.

Kathleen and I were able to go to dinner together last night for the first time all week. Although trading off is a team effort, it does not promote togetherness. In fact, between our holiday illnesses (which we desperately tried to avoid sharing) and the tag team hospital responsibilities, we have not slept in the same room for almost two weeks.

Things are going well. There is no new medical news to report. It appears our lives will be pretty uneventful at least until Tuesday. On Tuesday morning, Anna's case will be presented at grand rounds. That afternoon, I think, she will have a central line installed to permit her to receive nourishment even when she is out for surgery. Wednesday is the surgery. She will spend some recovery time in peds ICU, although we are not sure how long that will be. Then hopefully as soon as Thurs-

The respiratory therapists would suction Anna and then they would give her an albuterol treatment with a nebulizer. After a while, Anna became accustomed to the mist of the albuterol being nebulized in her face. She even appeared to taste it from time to time, especially when she was nebulized while sleeping.

Eventually we learned that Anna did not necessarily intend to set off the alarms, she was doing it quite by accident. You see, they would hook up the pulse/ox monitor to Anna's toes. Right where they hook it up there is a little red light. There was a clear plastic cover over every hospital bed she ever slept in. When she kicked her feet, the red light on her toes would reflect in the plastic over her head, giving her a little light show. Whenever she got bored she would start her light show, it would tug at the connections, and the alarms would sound.

Everyone who visited on January 9 got to eat birthday cake. Anna celebrated her ten month birthday in the hospital. That was two in a row. Here, Anna is relaxing in her Aunt Lauran's arms before blowing out the candles.

day she will return to a normal hospital bed.

It takes some time before her stomach will be ready to take food through her new tube. Once she is able to regularly take food that way without incident, I anticipate they will let us go home. Right now, that looks like at least a few days after surgery if all goes well.

Please feel free to visit (if you are healthy) or to call. We are at De Vos Children's Hospital which is part of Spectrum Health's downtown campus (Butterworth Hospital for you old-timers).

Keep the faith and thanks for your thoughts and prayers.

Anna's Dad.

Monday, January 10, 2000, 8:23 a.m.
From: Anna's Dad
Subject: Monday

The waiting for this week is over. The quiet weekend yields to active preparation for procedures, presentations, and surgery.

Anna is breathing more freely and seems to have beaten back the respiratory infection for the most part. This is welcome news as the antibiotic used to overcome the infection has a very annoying side effect: horrible diarrhea. I am sorry, I am sure you did not want to know that.

We certainly look forward to the replacement of the ng tube with a g-tube. Although feeding will still take some time, it will not be the Herculean effort it has been for the past months.

Moreover, the last few days have been the first extended period where we have known Anna is getting all of her meds. Blood tests yesterday demonstrated that fact. Her levels were as good as they have been since she was diagnosed.

Today is still the calm before the storm, but we are already noticing a higher tension level. Please keep us in your prayers.

Anna's Dad.

Anna's first procedure in anticipation of the surgery involved the installation of a central line in her femoral vein. The line would permit Anna to receive nutrition and medication before and during her surgery. Due to Anna's inability to handle sedatives, they had to insert the central line without anesthetics. We felt it critical to be with her to comfort her during the procedure in the PICU (pediatric intensive care unit).

When we brought Anna to the PICU for the procedure we did not realize we would be staying there until the surgery. The floor administrator, however, was very aware of that fact. While we were in the middle of the central line procedure, she decided to order all of our belongings in our regular hospital room to be collected and removed. No one told us that this would occur, and we had over a week's worth of stuff collected in that room.

John had to leave the procedure room to deal with the chaos that the floor administrator had created. This event threw us both out of sync for days and stole the precious little energy we had reserved to deal with the upcoming surgery. It was essential for the two of us to be on the same wavelength, especially when we were in the hospital. We found it impossible to get that peace and oneness back after this act of administrative shortsightedness.

Fear was a huge problem for me before and during the surgery. When we handed Anna to Dr. Visser, the anesthesiologist, on Wednesday morning, I was sure that was the last time I would ever see her alive. As we waited in the surgical waiting room, I could barely contain myself. Kathleen's reaction was very different. She was troubled until she put Anna in Dr. Visser's hands. Then, she was fine.

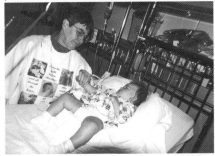

These pictures of Anna in the PICU show a lot of interesting things. First, in the picture on the right you can see Anna's central line. Anna was noticeably pleased to be rid of her ng tube. Moreover, the TPN (total parentaral nutrition) she received through the central line did wonders for her. She had a tough night right after the surgery, but other than that her time on the TPN was one of her best times ever. She was bright as a penny and very talkative.

Another interesting thing is evident in both the picture on the right and the picture of Anna with her Oma. As you can see from both photos, Anna always slept in a little U-shaped nest made of rolled cotton blankets with pillows behind and under her to keep her at a 45-degree angle. We started building Anna's nests after she was diagnosed; it reduced the possibility of reflux and gave her a more natural sleeping posture. Even after her surgery, when reflux was no longer a threat, Anna continued to sleep like this. We hoped it would make her feel cradled, even in her sleep.

Wednesday, January 12, 2000, 1:55 p.m.
From: Anna's Dad
Subject: Anna's surgery

I am pleased to report that by 12:30 this afternoon, Anna made her way from surgery to recovery. Our greatest fear, that she would not be able to come off the vent proved groundless. Her critical blood levels remained at excellent points throughout the surgery. She is now resting in PICU.

The surgery appears to have been an overwhelming success. Anna will feed by IV for the rest of the day. Either tonight or tomorrow, they will begin shifting her from IV to tube feeding. Although we have many challenges in the days ahead, we are overjoyed and thankful for the results so far. Thank you for your support.

The last couple of days have been exhausting and I will provide more detailed reports over the next couple of days, but I am also pleased to report in brief that Anna was the star of pediatric grand rounds yesterday and that the installation of her central line yesterday was also a rousing success.

Prayers are answered.

Anna's Dad

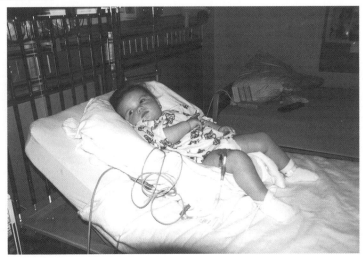

Friday, January 14, 2000, 11:08 a.m.
From: Anna's Dad
Subject: Friday-recovery

I am at home for a couple of hours and I thought I would update you. As I mentioned before, the surgery went better than we ever hoped. Anna had a couple of difficult periods of pain over the ensuing 36 hours, but she is one tough cookie.

She is feeding in part through the g-tube and it is going very well. They are slowly weaning her off of the IV feeds onto her formula again. We expect the transition will be complete by the middle of the day on Saturday. She has been remarkably talkative (in her way) and other than giving her new tube a couple of very firm yanks, it does not seem to bother her at all.

We hope to be out of PICU by the end of Friday. We anticipate at least a couple of more days in the hospital. Her lactic acid and bicarb levels (the objective measures we use to gauge her status with respect to her disease) are the best they have ever been. No one can offer a truly compelling explanation for this, but we believe it is nothing short of a miracle.

Kathleen got her first full night's sleep in weeks last night. Anna did too. Thank you again for your support.

Anna's Dad

Even though Anna did not cry, you could tell when she was in a great deal of pain. She would whine and thrash her arms and legs, and nothing could settle her. There was only so much that the medications could do after surgery. We gutted out the rest. I never want to relive the pain she felt that evening and morning after.

Although we still believe that Anna's recovery from surgery was miraculous, we have since learned that Anna was doing so well because of the IV feeding with TPN (total parentaral nutrition). Probably for the first time Anna's body was receiving exactly what it needed in a form it could easily handle. You could tell instantly from looking at Anna that the TPN was good for her. She was incredibly chatty. We asked all the medical professionals why we could not feed Anna TPN all the time. They noted that ultimately Anna's liver would fail if she was fed only TPN. Given Anna's life expectancy, that did not frighten us too much. In the end we learned that specially formulating the TPN for an individual each day was remarkably expensive. That was probably the real reason no one would recommend it as a long term therapy.

This is the core of the team that got us through those days in PICU and the surgery. From left to right, Dr. Dan Visser, Anna's anesthesiologist, Lynn Fagerman and Dr. Neil Uitvlugt, Anna's surgical nurse and her surgeon, and Joanne Decker, the PICU sedation specialist.

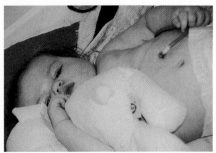

Anna's nimble fingers always gravitated towards that tube. It worked best to coil it up and hide it under the velcro tab of her Pampers. Even then, every once in a while she would get to it and give it a yank that would make you wince.

Eventually, Anna's tube was replaced by a button that she could not grab. The button (illustrated below) was fairly simple. Anna had a hole in her stomach. With the balloon (C) deflated, you pushed the tube into the hole. Then, you used water to inflate the balloon through valve A. That held it all in place. To feed Anna, you would put the end of the feeding tube (b) into the main valve of the button (B), Then you take the cap off the feeding tube (a) and place a two ounce syringe in it, fill it with formula and let gravity take it in little by little. Occasionally, we forgot to put the plug in the med port (c) and the formula would go into the feeding tube (a) and shoot out the med port (c).

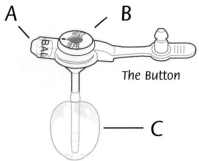

A   B

The Button

C

Saturday, January 15, 2000, 7:37 p.m.
From: Anna's Mom
Subject: Saturday-tubes and buttons

I am home only for a short while but thought I would post for a change.

Anna is handling her feedings through the gastric tube better than anyone could have imagined (once again, our little one is exceeding all expectations!), and she is feeling ready to come home. Our pediatrician is anxious to get us out of the hospital, which is crawling with children who have viral pneumonia (better known as RSV). Better to keep her healthy!

Her bicarb and lactic acid levels are fluctuating unpredictably, however, and we have yet to determine a reason. So we just sit and speculate while the doctors consult with each other. Still, we pray that they will discharge us some time Sunday. By the way, we are now in a new room (the smallest of our 3 hospital rooms). Please feel free to check up on us.

There is so much I want to tell all of you but I must return to my baby, so I will close with the oft-quoted phrase that best sums up the past twelve days: "What a long, strange trip it's been." May God bless us all and give us strength and accept our prayers of thanksgiving for Anna's successful surgery!

With all our love,
Anna's Mom

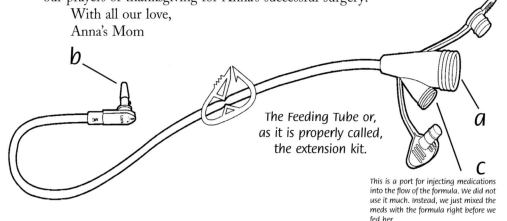

b

The Feeding Tube or, as it is properly called, the extension kit.

a

c

This is a port for injecting medications into the flow of the formula. We did not use it much. Instead, we just mixed the meds with the formula right before we fed her.

Tuesday, January 18, 2000, 10:31 p.m.
From: Anna's Mom
Subject: Tuesday–a welcome change

Greetings from Anna, who just finished her 5th bottle of the day at 10:00 p.m.! She is adjusting well to her new eating regimen and we are starting to get the hang of feeding her through the g-tube. Had someone told me three months ago that I would be enjoying the g-tube, I would have called that person a liar. Three months ago, we viewed the g-tube as something—some monster—that carried with it all kinds of consequences and meanings...all of them bad. It represented the beginning of the end, a drastic change of life, and a giving in to the disease.

Now, we are three months smarter. Now, we see the g-tube for what it is: a means to an end that we embrace and accept for exactly that but nothing more. We have now replaced 5-6 hours of frustration and struggling each day during Anna's feedings with 5 sessions of 15-30 minutes where she can sit and play while we feed her. Our lives, once again, have changed...for the better.

Anna is showing off her new g-tube while getting a sponge bath. Anna liked to keep her hands near her head. Her fingers were almost always playing with her hair or ears. It made it easy to tickle her. She would not laugh, but she would squiggle and try to push your hands away. We have a lot of video tape of us tickling her. Perhaps we did it so often because it was one of the few things we could do to elicit a reaction from her.

We are still reeling from our hospital stay and the mess in our house is proof of the chaos we feel. Anna is trying to get into a more regular sleeping pattern now that no one is coming in at all hours of the morning to take her temp, blood pressure, or to "nebulize" her with albuterol for her lung infection. We could all use about 2 weeks of solid sleep, but we will take one night at a time.

Anna is going to continue her physical therapy on Wednesday (no rest for the weary), and she returns to the surgeon's office next Tuesday for them to look at her sutures and at the g-tube.

The dogs were beside themselves when we picked them up on Sunday and Monday! Poor Ruby had a horrible time once Jasper returned. He constantly pestered her, obviously making up for missed time. We finally put him outside at 4:30 a.m. to get him to stop whining. What a silly pup!

Time to get Baby Anna ready for bed. She sends kisses and thanks for all the prayers. Ditto from her dad and me!

Take care,
Anna's Mom

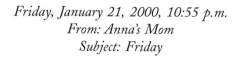

Friday, January 21, 2000, 10:55 p.m.
From: Anna's Mom
Subject: Friday

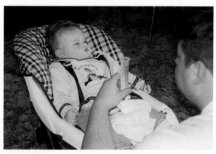

Anna ended up with several reclining high chairs. The one pictured above was at Opa and Oma's house. We had one at home and we kept one in San Diego at the Bannister House. It is probably still there.

Anna is relaxing after a busy day and a fun night out with friends. It has been a long time since her Dad and I have been out on a Friday night—obviously, she is making sure that we enjoy the night life and not just that time between 12:00 a.m. and 2:00 a.m. when she wants to have a party in her crib! Anna does great in restaurants and was wonderful today as well. It must be her good upbringing.

Fortunately, there is little news to report. Anna is doing beautifully with her feedings. We are also getting better about feeding her in public without drawing a large crowd. We are anxious to have her weighed next Tuesday during her doctor's appointment to see if she has crossed the 24 or 25 pound thresholds.

We also acquired a new "feeding chair." They now make reclining high chairs for kids that work great during her feedings. It is still somewhat cumbersome for one person to hold her and feed her, although we do it for at least two feedings a day. Thus, the chair has been a new and interesting addition to the household. Anna is also adjusting beautifully to her new car seat. With seven different adjustments for reclining the seat, Anna rides comfortably and without the possibility for her head to flop forward (as it often did in her old car seat). She is still puzzled at why she cannot just stay in her new seat rather than being lifted into and out of it, particularly in the cold weather. I think she just adds it to the list of odd things that we do to her.

We are still trying to get our lives together but it has been less than a week since we were discharged from the hospital. We have a long way to go.

We are also waiting for word from San Diego regarding when we can return. That date will then determine when Anna will receive the DCA, which will be during the week prior to our trip. That way, when we go back, they will be able to see how she is doing on the drug. So that is our next hurdle of sorts.

Wishing all of you a good and quiet weekend. Thanks for all the prayers.
Anna's Mom

Sunday, January 23, 2000, 6:36 p.m.
From: Anna's Mom
Subject: Sunday-football

Anna is having a great day watching football, snoozing, and helping us make chocolate chip cookies. She is truly living large.

Today after church, as I bundled her back into her car seat, I swear that she exercised some facial muscles that she has not used since September. It sure looked like she was working on an open mouth grin, and I was thrilled! Dad, who was driving the car, was able to see her do this not once but twice as he looked in the rear view mirror. What a great way to start a snowy Sunday!

Anna had a wonderful visit with her 5 year old cousins yesterday. They were fairly inquisitive about the gastric tube and, due to some good preparation by their parents, were not surprised or "grossed out" at all. Hooray for them! All the company must have tired her out as she fell asleep in Dad's arms around 11:00 p.m. and slept until almost 10:00 a.m. Hooray for us!

Although it has been almost two weeks since pediatric "grand rounds," we thought we would give you some idea of what that experience was like. "Grand rounds" are held at the hospital as a means of educating the interns, residents, doctors, and area physicians, who are all invited to attend. They typically choose unique cases to present during these teaching experiences.

The doctor in charge of grand rounds was excited about Anna's case and the prospect of having her as the first "live" pediatric patient to be presented at grand rounds. This same doctor, however, was concerned about having the patient's parents present. He believed our presence would inhibit the free flow of information among the attendees (i.e., the doctors would feel uncomfortable talking about her case in front of us). Our doctor prevailed, nonetheless, and we reached a compromise: we would be there with Anna, answer questions, and then leave during the last ten minutes of the hour-long presentation.

When the long-awaited morning for grand rounds arrived, we had been in the hospital for a week, Anna had a nasal-gastric tube in place (which we used to

Anna almost always had a balloon in her hand or within reach. If you look closely, you will see that she is sleeping and clutching the ribbons attached to two of her favorite balloon pals. Also, as you can see, Anna was a great snuggler who could make almost anyone fall asleep holding her.

Here, Kathleen is posting to the mailing list. We purchased this computer so Kathleen could work at home after Anna was born. We used this computer, a printer donated by Kathleen's parents, and a scanner donated by John's parents, to generate all of our prayer cards, brochures, letters, magnets, and even this book.

The revelations during grand rounds made it clear that we need to give doctors, nurses, and medical students a safe place to ask often difficult questions regarding how parents deal with medical information, terminal diagnoses, and difficult decision-making processes. Upon reflection, we believe that grand rounds was one of the defining moments in our life with Anna. We had something of value to share with people who could make all the difference in the lives of families with terminally ill children. That discovery was exhilirating. One would assume that all doctors and nurses received training on how to deal with dying children. In reality, they receive very little training in palliative care involving adults or children. This is one area where we believe we can, and will, make a difference in the future.

feed her prior to surgery), and we were a bit nervous about the whole thing. The senior resident presented Anna's condition when we entered the hospital in September.

Next, the radiologist spent a fairly long time reviewing her MRI films to show the docs what to look for. It was actually difficult for me to watch that part of the presentation because the neurologist held up those same MRI films when she first explained to me that Anna had Leigh's Syndrome.

We got through that part, however, and then the neurologist gave her presentation. When she finished, she asked us to take Anna and sit on the stage of the auditorium. It was then that we realized that the auditorium was packed with interns, residents, our pediatric surgeon, our pediatrician, our pediatric gastro doc, the anesthesiologist, John's pediatrician, Anna's physical, speech and occupational therapists, and a host of others. All told, there were probably over 120 people there, which was a huge crowd according to our neurologist.

The neurologist showed the group Anna's capabilities and then handed her to us. She sat on my lap looking adorable (despite the ng tube hanging from her nose) and yawned at the crowd. John and I answered questions posed by the neurologist and by members of the audience.

We actually wish we could have had about 50 minutes more to talk because the questions were becoming increasingly less about the disease and more about dealing with a terminal illness. I personally thought that the doctors would not be interested in how the parents of a very ill child deal with that illness, but I was wrong. Apparently, they have few chances to ask the tough questions of parents in our situation who are their own patients, so this was a unique opportunity for them to ask us.

Our neurologist concluded the event 65 minutes after it began. Only two people had left before it ended, which was amazing according to knowledgeable sources. Several doctors and residents who saw us around the hospital expressed their thanks to us for coming and bringing Anna. It was the first time that a pediatric patient attended grand rounds, and we are sure that it will not be the last. The doctor who was concerned about our attending asked us questions during the event and was one of the first to thank us for coming.

We have also considered appearing with some Hospice folks to present a related clinic for doctors dealing with terminally ill patients. The idea is exciting to us and we hope to be able to share more with others. Perhaps this is one of the greater goods that Anna and her family may realize. We will keep you posted.

Sorry this post is so long. I promise shorter messages in the future. Take care and thanks for the continued prayers.

Anna's Mom

Anna and Jasper spent a lot of time together. Jasper just assumed that all babies laid on their backs on the floor so they could talk to him. Jasper also thought that all babies tasted as good as Anna did. One can only hope.

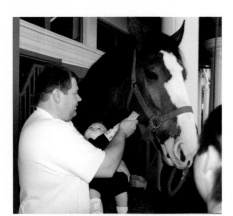

Anna and Jake the Clydesdale met at Sea World. You might notice in this photo John is clean shaven. In many other photos in this book he has a beard. He tells me that he grows a beard when he is tired of shaving and then shaves when he is tired of trimming his beard. He goes back and forth quite a bit.

Anna has been enjoying the first half of the Big Game and is currently cheering for the Rams. We think she is REALLY enjoying the commercials, however, particularly the ones with animals. She was really, REALLY excited to see the Budweiser Clydesdales; she met Jake, a beautiful Clydesdale, when we were in San Diego and enjoyed petting that beautiful beast! She recognized Jake right away on the commercial, and now she is trying to convince her Dad that she needs a horse. Good luck!

Anna has had a great, relaxing weekend. It is the first weekend since Thanksgiving that we have not been busy or in the hospital, so we are thrilled about our open schedule. This past week was really hectic and poor Anna spent a little more time in her high chair than usual, but sitting at that height did permit her to watch us as we worked on the computer completing several urgent projects. Based upon the look on her face now as she sits with Dad in the big recliner, I think she has forgiven us.

The occupational therapists were really excited at how much progress Anna has made in the past month or so. She is using her body much more and you can see much more expression in her face. She even seems to be exercising her lips—maybe a few words will be on the horizon.

Also, the surgeon was thrilled at the condition of Anna's incisions. Contrary to other predictions, she has not been "crabby" due to the surgery. Talk about prayers answered! Our little rose keeps surprising all of us.

We just confirmed with the docs at the MMDC in San Diego that Anna will be able to start the DCA within the next week and we DO NOT need to go back out to San Diego to get her started. Although this is good news, as we do not have to make the long trip, we are somewhat reticent to take this big step without the protective arms of the MMDC around us. We are in the capable hands of our pediatric neurologist, however, so we are confident that everything will go well, and we will keep all of you informed.

Finally, we want to thank all of you who have been sending us cards and e-mails full of encouragement and words of wisdom. You are all God coming to us again and again to remind us that we are not alone. He is sending you to us, and we are grateful for the gift of you.

We also send our prayers to many of our friends who have lost loved ones recently, especially our friends in Chicago whose five-year-old son, Scott, died a week before Christmas. Although we never met Scott, we feel connected to him and his family. Scott, like Anna, had NARP causing Leigh's Syndrome. His family continues to be in our thoughts and prayers.

Take care, and thank you for your continued prayers.

Much love,

Anna's Mom

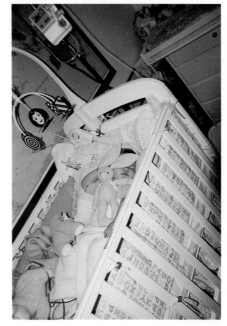

One of Anna's best friends was her floppy green bunny. As you can see, Anna would often count on her friends to shield her eyes from the morning sun. You can also see the kangaroo pump hanging on the pole behind her crib; we used that for a few weeks after Anna's surgery to feed her at night. Once she started gaining weight, we increased her daily feedings and stopped using the pump. We were glad to stop. It seemed odd to feed her during the night. It was also dangerous. On more than one occasion Anna managed to pull the pump connection off her g-tube, filling her crib with formula.

For the first time in her life, Anna was getting 8 ounces of formula plus medications and free water at each feeding. Plus, she no longer threw up her meals. Thus, we were able to greatly increase the volume of food that Anna could enjoy.

Anna and Dad are enjoying Anna's last meal of her waking day, and Dad is trying to get her to say "cheese." She seems amused by the whole thing. We have been working on "Anna," "momma," and "daddy;" we often get "aahhs" in response, so we take that as a good sign.

On the doctor appointment front, the gastroenterologist thought that Anna is gaining weight at a respectable pace, so we are adjusting her caloric intake downward a bit and increasing her fluid intake a bit. Let's hope it gives her little body what she needs to be "regular."

Tommorrow, we have a blood draw, physical therapy, and a video fluoroscopy. The video will help us see whether Anna can still manage food well enough to eat by mouth again. Her stomach and esophagus should not be swollen any more and she should be able to handle pureed food and thickened formula, but if she still aspirates, we will not take the risk. Needless to say, we are anxious to get the results.

Anna is very talkative this evening and a lot of fun to have around; she says to say hello to everyone and sends kisses across the world wide web to all of you.

Take care and thanks for the prayers!

Anna's Mom

I truly regret that I do not have a picture of that memorable moment, but I was surprised to find we had many pictures of Anna and me sneaking a nap. Here are a few of them.

Things are going well. Really not anything to tell you about, so I will tell you about nothing.

Last night, I came home from work with a nasty headache. I thought I would crash on the bed for a while and snooze the headache away. Eventually, Kath brought Anna in to help. I was laying in bed and Anna was less than two feet from my face. She drifted off but I could not.

I just watched her sleep. After about twenty minutes, Anna woke up. As she woke up she just looked me in the eye. Actually, we stared at each other. Totally at peace. It probably did not last more than a minute, but if I could live in that minute forever, I think I would.

Anna's Dad

Before we left for San Diego the second time, Anna received a very special gift from a very special group of people. The ladies in the Clerk's Office at the federal court made Anna her heart quilt. The quilt came with a poem penned by Melanie Vugteveen.

Anna's Quilt

This quilt was made by many hands. It was amazing to see people making the time in spite of life's demands

Some of us are quilting experts; however, many of us are not. It was a challenge we were willing to take on no matter how hard it got.

Certainly not the same as the challenges that you are all going through. But we felt it was at least "something" we could do in hopes of it being a bright spot for all of you.

This quilt was created with love for an incredibly special girl who, from the very first visit, gave our heartstrings a twirl.

Maybe it was because you were so adorable and wonderful to hold. Or maybe it was the obvious love and pride we could see and hear in your parents, even with words untold.

You have a very special place in all our hearts. The hearts on the quilt represent just a small part. . .

Of those who are praying and holding thought of "all" of you high, in faith, that all our prayers of healing and thanksgiving reach the Lord, who is <u>always</u> nearby.

May this quilt bring you comfort and keep you warm. Enjoy the bright colors, and drool and chew on it, it all adds to its charm.

This quilt represents the love and many prayers from all of your dear friends. It has many pieces and threads stitched together by the love that it lends.

The quilters: (back row) Diane Kettner, Kathy Devlin, Gloria Frayer, Diane Hopkins, Sheila Blasingame, (front row) Kelly Van Dyke, Leigh Ann Certa, Mary Jo Schumacher, Lois Ripma and Melanie Vugteveen.

Chapter 6
The Second Trip

With Anna's surgery and her recovery complete, it was time to travel to San Diego again and start the DCA trial. As we began to plan that second trip, we found ourselves less excited about going back. If DCA could help Anna develop without hurting her, we had to at least try it. We still wanted to do everything we could to help Anna live her life to the fullest extent she could. But, we were starting to realize that there was a cost: disruption of day-to-day routines, invasive tests, and just the hassle of living on "hospital time." In hindsight, it is apparent that we were starting to value the quality of our time with Anna more than the quantity. We do not regret going back. We are confident the DCA helped Anna, but you can start to see a shift in our attitudes on this trip. We were no longer counting on the medical profession to show us how we should live with Anna.

Monday, February 7, 2000, 10:32 p.m.
From: Anna's Dad
Subject: New stuff

In the category of "things change," today we found out that we will travel to San Diego to start Anna on the DCA and for her initial tests after the first week on the drug. If that sounds like a different course of action than the one we had discussed recently, it is.

There had been some miscommunications between doctors in the pacific time zone and doctors in the eastern time zone. The result, if we waited another month, maybe we could do the tests here. Anna thought a month was an awfully long time to wait. Accordingly, eight hours after we found out that we could not start the drug here, we have travel plans for San Diego. We will leave on the morning of February 16 and return the evening of February 25.

This swapping of horses midstream has been draining, but there are some definite benefits including some additional evaluations Anna will undergo while she is out there. We will enjoy the expertise of the MMDC as we start the drug, and we will see a little bit of warm weather.

Undoubtedly, this turn of events is the way things are supposed to be; we just need to get used to it. Other than the new plan, all is well. Anna tipped the scales at over 26 pounds today and she stands (or lies) 30 inches tall just two days shy of her eleven month birthday. She comes from hearty stock so her husky build is of no surprise. As the PICU doc at Spectrum Health so politely put it, "she has a lot of tissue."

Also, we are pleased to announce that Anna pooped today without the assistance of medication or suppositories. She did not want us to tell you that, but we are pretty excited about it as this has not happened in months.

Keep the faith.
Anna's Dad.

It is strange how experience can change the way you look at the same event. Back in December, we had a much different view of our first trip to UCSD. It was not that we thought they would tell us something miraculous; maybe it was the hope of knowledge that we would possibly acquire. This time, it all feels different. Not bad, just different.

We are fairly tired and maybe that is clouding our view. Maybe we are just unsure of where this road will lead us. Given the severity of Anna's condition, we came to the conclusion that we had little to lose. Others have made us wonder whether we also have little to gain. But, we are eternal optimists and the glass is more than half full. So we move forward, blazing a new trail that we hope will lead us to better days, at least better than we would face without the DCA.

Rest assured, we are not willing to pursue this path if Anna begins to stumble while on the DCA. We can stop our participation in the study as quickly as we start it.

On a lighter note, Anna is getting her g-tube out tomorrow—actually, she's getting it replaced with a "button." The button resembles a beach ball valve. The button sits close to the skin and there's less of a chance that Anna's nimble fingers will be able to pull on it (she has given her current tubing several hearty yanks in the past weeks—yikes).

With the button, we just open the valve, snap on the long tube that we use to pour the formula in, and go. It should be less of a hassle to access. Anna is hoping for a bright purple or maybe a hot pink button. We told her she may not have a choice.

She still seems excited about this next stage in the process. We will be in touch while we are in San Diego. Thanks for keeping us in your prayers!

Always,
Anna's Mom

In hindsight, we realize that the second trip to San Diego "felt different" because we were beginning to realize that the medical disciplines were not going to answer our question as to how we should help Anna live her life.

Dear Family and Friends:

We are writing to update you on Anna's condition since our last correspondence because so much has happened in the last three months.

UCSD

On December 5, 1999, we left Grand Rapids to visit the Mitochondrial and Metabolic Disease Center (the MMDC) at the University of California, San Diego. Perhaps the most amazing thing about the trip to San Diego was that it was uneventful. We had received so many helpful tips about traveling with babies through the Anna's Friends mailing list that we must have appeared to be seasoned pros at flying with babies. Anna paid little attention to this new mode of transportation. By the end of every flight, however, all of the passengers complimented Anna, saying what a good baby she was. Rather than telling them she does not cry, we simply took it as a credit to our parenting skills.

When we arrived at the MMDC, it was a little different than we expected. The MMDC is simply part of the UCSD Medical Center's Clinical Research Center. It consists of eight of the many rooms on the top floor of the hospital. I think we expected that it would be bigger.

Although we might have been a little disappointed by the size, it did not take long for us to realize we were in the right place. The first day we enjoyed one of several long conversations with Dr. Robert Naviaux, one of the researchers responsible for establishing the Center. Dr. Naviaux was able to give us a new perspective on Leigh's disease and the NARP mutation causing the disease in Anna

Before we left for San Diego, we put together our second mailing. You will find this second letter restates much of the information we provided in our posts over the previous two months. The principal purpose of the first mailing was to inform; the principal purpose of the second mailing was to say thanks. We had received over $40,000 in contributions to the Anna's Friends Foundation.

It was not an easy thing to ask for help, particularly financial help. When Anna was diagnosed both Kathleen and I had good jobs and insurance. Nonetheless, there was a lot of uncertainty. Would we be able to keep working? Would insurance cover the significant and unusual costs of caring for an infant with a mitochondrial disease? The funds from the foundation represented a comforting security blanket when we did not know the answers to those questions. The funds proved a necessity when we found out the answer to both questions was "no."

We anticipated the foundation money would last a long time. We were wrong. The expenses for Anna's care increased exponentially as she reached the end of her life. By the time everyone was paid the foundation had $83.69 left, we had drained our savings, and tapped our retirement account. Without the foundation, we never would have made it.

Along with the letter we sent thank you cards to the foundation's donors and a special gift: refrigerator magnets featuring pictures of Anna. We have reproduced all of these items in the following pages.

Thank you for your generous donation to the Anna's Friends Foundation

John, Kathleen & Anna

We now understand that Anna cannot produce energy the way we do. The energy source she relies on is incapable of producing the same amount of energy and, accordingly, as Anna grows and develops, the energy deficiency becomes more pronounced. This has led to the lesions in her brain which in turn affect her abilities to do many things.

Anna sends her thanks and love

The doctors at the MMDC were particularly struck by two things: first, on their objective scale of clinical severity, Anna is the most severely affected infant they have seen; and second, Anna is surprisingly very well-nourished considering her clinical severity. With regard to Anna's clinical severity, please be aware that this is really no different than what we were told when Anna was first diagnosed. We were quietly hoping that the severity of the diagnosis might have been wrong. It was not.

The fact that she is so well-nourished (particularly given the early problems we had with nourishment) might be considered a mere fortuity, but we prefer to think of it as miraculous or at least divine providence.

Anna sends her thanks and love

Early on, when Anna was having feeding problems, one of the components of her "cocktail" was Karo syrup. The syrup is almost straight glucose and was exactly what she needed to produce energy her way. It was only when we traded breast milk and Karo syrup for Maltsupex that Anna started having the problems that led to the initial diagnosis and hospitalization. I am sure Dr. Naviaux would shudder at these oversimplifications, but we believe that explanation is consistent with the science of her disease.

Anna was subjected to an intensive battery of tests during the first two days at the MMDC. That was not pleasant for her or for us. By the end of the second day, Anna was very agitated and it was apparent she was at the end of her rope. Fortunately, she was also at the end of the tests. Anna had qualified for the drug study.

Anna sends her thanks and love

The MMDC is studying the effects of dichloroacetate (or DCA) on patients with mitochondrial and metabolic diseases. Actually, they know the principal effect: it lowers lactic acid levels. We were surprised to learn that lowering lactic acid levels does not appear to help everyone.

For those the drug helped significantly, the effect was dramatic. Some children who had never walked or talked gained those skills after a short period on the DCA. For those the drug did not help, the effect was equally dramatic. For some, the drug appeared to accelerate the disease process. It was difficult to tell if the acceleration was the result of the drug or the disease as the drug effects may mimic the disease process. For most people, the drug did not

significantly help or hurt them.

Ultimately, after agonizing discussions and a lot of prayer, we decided to proceed with the drug trial. We had been in contact with a mother whose son also has Leigh's caused by the NARP mutation. She had witnessed the dramatic benefits of DCA in her son. As these benefits are consistent with our goal that Anna live the fullest life possible, and because the possible detriments appeared to be exactly what the disease offered anyway, we decided to go ahead. We could end the drug trial at any time if things did not go well.

Although choosing to go forward, we did not want to risk Anna's status as a good surgical candidate for her Nissen and g-tube surgery by starting the drug before that surgery. Thus, while we were in San Diego, Anna only had an initial dose of the drug to study its effect so she could have it available if needed during surgery in Grand Rapids. That first dose immediately lowered Anna's lactic acid levels and had no apparent detrimental effects.

Although Anna was an in-patient for much of the stay in San Diego, she did get to see the sights. We showed her the Pacific Ocean, Sea World, and the San Diego Zoo. She was particularly fond of the baby animals, especially the hippo and gorilla. Anna's mom got to swim with the dolphins at Sea World. This "vacation" allowed us to feel like a family.

BACK HOME

After ten days in San Diego, we returned home and, as much as we were able, readied ourselves and our home for the holidays. Anna enjoyed her first Christmas but paid little attention to her first New Year's Eve.

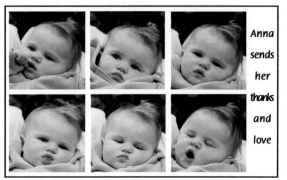

Anna sends her thanks and love

Thanks from all of us

We arrived home with a new formula for Anna. The goal was to increase the calories over the minimal volume we were able to get her to take through the bottle. Despite the reduction in volume, Anna started to slow in her feedings and particularly struggled with the last ounce or so. She would cough and a couple of times she even sneezed the formula out her nose. We anxiously awaited the Nissen and g-tube surgery scheduled for January 12.

On January 4, we visited Anna's pulmonologist for a regular appointment. He was concerned by the sound of her lungs and believed that she was aspirating her formula. He immediately admitted us to the hospital a week earlier than we had expected. To prevent any further aspirations and the risk of pneumonia, Anna began feeding through a tube that went down her nose and into her stomach. After a few days of respiratory therapy, "ng" tube feeding, and antibiotics, Anna was ready for surgery.

To ensure that Anna would get sufficient nutrition before, during, and immediately after surgery, the doctors recommended the installation of a central line in her femoral vein. With the line, Anna could take intravenous nutrition for an extended period. Without the line, Anna would probably have to fast for a long time (fasting increased Anna's lactic acid level).

The nutrition Anna received through her central line proved to be very beneficial. Because the IV nutrition could go straight into her system, her liver never got the chance to produce excessive lactic acid. The days immediately before and after the surgery were perhaps Anna's healthiest days. This was apparent in her lactic acid and sodium bicarb levels and in her demeanor. Unfortunately, it is not healthy to stay on IV nutrition for too long. We are hopeful that Anna is as bright and bouncy on the DCA as she was on the IV nutrition.

The doctors had prepared us for the worst with regard to Anna's surgery. We were warned that she might have problems with the anesthesia, that she might not be able to come off the ventilator after surgery, that she might become exceedingly bad tempered, or that she just might not be the same person after the surgery. The warnings were appropriate because there are so many unknowns when you are dealing with a child whose system simply does not work the way it should. So, we prepared for the worst, tried to get Anna in the best shape possible, and prayed. By the time we handed Anna off to Dr. Visser, the anesthesiologist, we knew she was in good hands, on all levels.

We are thankful that the surgery was a complete success. Anna came off the ventilator without incident before she even returned to ICU. She had no problems with the anesthesia and she has been a good-tempered angel since. Anna has been feeding through her new g-

Anna sends her thanks and love

Anna sends her thanks and love

Anna sends her thanks and love

Anna sends her thanks and love

tube since the second day after surgery. The tube, initially one of our greatest fears, has become a welcome addition to our daily routine. Anna is able to handle almost two and one-half times the volume of food in a fraction of the time it took before the surgery. It has greatly freed up our day and reduced the worry that we will not be able to get Anna to take the medications she needs.

Anna was discharged four days after the surgery. After waiting two weeks for the internal swelling to go down, we repeated Anna's video fluoroscopy to determine whether we could feed Anna by mouth and use the tube as a backup. The test revealed that Anna was unable to handle even thickened formula by mouth. Because she permits the formula to slide too far down her throat before swallowing, the formula can slide right into her airway and her lungs.

Even though we can no longer feed Anna formula by mouth, we will be able to feed her some pureed foods. She is able to handle pureed foods because they are not so "slippery" and she swallows more often while eating them. We still have to get past Anna's suspicions that everything we put into her mouth contains nasty tasting medicine; her negative reactions to the first few bites of food may take some time to overcome.

We are happy to report that Anna has gained five pounds in the last month. Since her surgery, Anna has been more communicative with her hands and voice and seems to be moving her body much more than before. All of her therapists have observed these changes. We hope that they continue.

She is now becoming proficient at the game of "where's Daddy" or "where's Mommy" as she turns her head and eyes to find the designated person or dog in the room. She is also less tolerant of having her head falling forward leaving her chin resting on her chest. Using her

Anna sends her thanks and love

Anna sends her thanks and love

Anna sends her thanks and love

arms, legs, and body, she works very hard to get her head back up. Anna is quite a fighter.

Now, we await the commencement of the DCA regimen. Although we are not anxious to add a new drug to the already formidable array of drugs and vitamins Anna takes each day, we are anxious to see the benefits of lower lactic acid and higher bicarb levels.

We are returning to San Diego to start Anna on the DCA. We will arrive on February 16 and return home on February 25. Six months after we start the DCA, we will return to San Diego to redo the entire battery of tests Anna endured in December. That is the price we pay for participating in the study. We will keep you posted.

The Foundation

As we mentioned in our November letter, we formed a non-profit trust/foundation (the Anna's Friends Foundation) to raise funds to help cover the extraordinary expenses associated with caring for Anna. The response has been overwhelming! To date, we have raised almost $40,000.

We started the Foundation amidst an atmosphere of uncertainty. At that time, we did not know which of Anna's care expenses insurance would cover, how much we would have to travel, or if we would be able to continue working. The Foundation offered us significant peace of mind in the face of these uncertainties.

Some of the uncertainties have now been resolved. We will probably not need to travel more than twice a year for Anna's care. Kathleen has taken a leave of absence from work while John has been the beneficiary of hundreds of hours of vacation time donated by his colleagues.

To date, our insurance, as supplemented by Children's Special Health Care Services, has covered most of Anna's direct medical expenses. We can only hope that will continue.

We are thankful for the many donations--the peace of mind they have provided as well as the expenses they have covered. We anticipate that we have raised sufficient funds to cover the unusual expenses associated with Anna's care for at least the next few months. It is not clear whether we even need to worry beyond that point.

We cannot know how much we will need for Anna's care, but any funds left over after Anna is gone will go to research regarding mitochondrial and metabolic disease or to organizations that provide hospice services. In that regard, we are currently working towards the establishment of a satellite clinic for the MMDC in Grand Rapids.

Anna sends her thanks and love

Anna sends her thanks and love

Anna sends her thanks and love

Anna sends her thanks and love

Ironically, while we were in San Diego in December, Dr. Haas of the MMDC was here evaluating Spectrum Health's DeVos Women and Children's Hospital as a possible site for a Midwest extension of the MMDC. The funds necessary to accomplish this goal far exceed anything we could raise alone (in the seven figure range), but we are doing everything we can to make this happen.

Although Anna's disease is rare, we have been amazed by how many children have similar diseases in the Midwest. It is extremely difficult for many to travel to the west coast to get the care and information they desperately need. Kathleen is certain that our efforts to bring the MMDC to Grand Rapids is part of the greater good that will come of this experience.

Again, we continue to thank God for all of our family, friends, and colleagues who have come to our rescue. Thank you for your support and prayers. We are frequently moved by the expressions of love for Anna and for us. Rest assured that we are doing well. Your generosity has afforded us the greatest gift possible: more time with Anna. She is very good company. Your support has permitted us to achieve many of the goals we have for Anna. You have shown us that we are not alone. You have given us peace.

May God bless all of us with His love and mercy.

Much love,

Anna's family—John, Kathleen, Anna, Ruby and Jasper

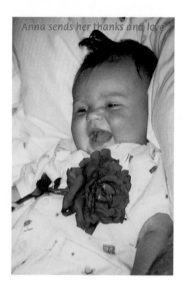

Anna sends her thanks and love

Thanks

Anna sends her thanks and love

Thursday, February 17, 2000, 10:21 p.m.
From: Anna's Dad
Subject: Thursday-fortuities

Good evening all. Well, I guess for most of you it is good night. It is a quiet evening here and a good chance for us to catch our collective breath (or is it breaths).

The last few days have been exhausting and we have been pushed to our absolute limits. But, now we are here and things have been going very well. We flew out of Grand Rapids at 5:10 a.m. on Wednesday. That followed an absolute whirlwind effort to wind up our affairs at home (including the recent mailing). So, for the four days leading up to our very early flights, we were operating on little sleep and it was apparent. We were pretty much at each others' throats, except for Anna.

The flights out were very pleasant (a special thank you to our Anna's friend benefactor who helped us with the tickets). We came to San Diego with no plans for lodging (that's how busy we were the last few days before we left). The Bannister House where we stayed last time was full with a waiting list. We also came without resolving our transportation needs. When we arrived, however, everything fell into place. The rent-a-car place had exactly the vehicle we needed for Anna and her ever growing pile of equipment (a Ford Expedition), and miraculously a room opened up at the Bannister House. I am typing on the House computer now. We thank God for smiling on us despite our lack of preparedness for this trip.

We met a new MMDC doc, Dr. Barshop. He spoke with us this morning regarding our itinerary for the week. Anna started the DCA yesterday. So far, so good. Today she had a neuro-psychological evaluation. Tomorrow is a neuro-opthalmology evaluation. Then we are free until Wednesday when she will undergo the pharmokinetic evaluation for the DCA, indirect calorimetry, and some other stuff which will take a whole day. It appears we will have a lot of rain during our stay, so you may be hearing from us often. Thank you for your support. Feel free to post messages for us to the list; that is the only way we are getting e-mail for the next ten days.

Anna's Dad.

John's Aunt Trudy helped out with the tickets to San Diego. Actually, it was John's Uncle Ron. Uncle Ron passed away before Anna was born, but he had accumulated a lot of frequent flier miles and Aunt Trudy donated them to the cause.

Anna thought the Expedition was a definite step up from her normal ride, a minivan.

We arrived at the Bannister House on Wednesday over the noon hour. Every Wednesday, the Bannister volunteers make lunch for the "guests." We walked in, they all greeted us with a hug and several plates of food, and gave us a room. We were home, even though we were thousands of miles away.

Thursday, February 17, 2000, 4:44 p.m.
From: Melanie Vugteveen
Subject: Poem

Hi John, Kathleen, and Anna:

Hope all is going well on your trip! We've been praying for many blessings and answers to your prayers. I've been working on a poem and I would like to share it with you. (I'll warn you...it's not a short one.)

John and Kathleen, I just want to let you know that you two are phenomenal people and Anna is so very lucky to have you as her guide. Your faith, thoughts and actions are earthly examples of how God wants people to abide. God bless...

Melanie :)

FINDING COMFORT...
By Melanie Vugteveen February 14, 2000

It's known that we are all on loan to earth for a set number of days. God has plans for all of us....He works in mysterious ways.

Each life is a gift from God, that is more precious than gold. No matter the package, a parent's love goes to depths untold.

Parents should feel extremely proud that God trusted them with such a beloved gift. That thought can give our inner strength and spirit such a lift.

Circumstances in life prove that God didn't promise to give us easy roads to travel. Everyone, sometime, hits something that causes their life to unravel.

We don't always know why we are dealt the hands we got. Sometimes we even question Him, when we're trying to make sense out of the whole lot.

I don't think God expects us to always deal with the cards with a smile on our face. To many of us, some cards hold experiences that are too painful to erase.

The Bible says that God doesn't give us more than we can stand. That brings some comfort when dealing with trials and challenges at hand.

But even more comfort lies in knowing (and believing) that God had faith in us even before dealing a particular card. Knowing full well that somehow we would persevere....no matter how hard.

It's during those times that God has a way of bringing certain people into our life, special people who give support and heartfelt prayer during our times of strife.

There is great peace and comfort in the thoughts above. There is also great peace and comfort when seeking and finding God's love.

However, I'm learning there is another thought that will help when peace and comfort are what you seek, in those times when the future may seem a bit hazy and bleak.

It's not only important to rely on your faith in God to help you get through. But don't forget to also rely and draw on the faith that God has in you.

Hi all. We have been busy recreating the last couple of days. As this is Presidents Day, we will be goofing off today as well. Before we head out, however, we thought we would let you know how things are going.

Anna's appointments with the pediatric neuro-psychologist and the pediatric opthalmologist went well. We were a little disappointed with what we heard regarding Anna's eyes. The opthalmologist noted that Anna's right eye was diverging. We had noticed this too, but did not think much of it. He noted that this could be corrected surgically, but that we might want to wait and see how things go with the DCA first. He also noted that Anna tracked (followed with her eyes) but that her responses were quite slow.

Although he did not tell us anything we did not know, hearing it all again was depressing. It brought up again the questions we have regarding Anna's ability to see and recognize us. No one can measure that ability and we proceed as if she can based on her reactions. There is no way to know for sure. But doubt loomed large on Friday.

Once we were done with the opthalmologist, we were looking forward to a few days without doctors or hospitals. In the first few hours of that free time, I realized why we stay so busy sometimes. When your time is free, your mind can wander. And when a seed of doubt has been planted, it is not good to let your mind wander. The balance of Friday was a tough day for both Kathleen and me. But the best cure was readily available: a good dose of Anna. When we spend time with her the doubts are erased. She is good company and reacts in ways that evidence her ability to see and recognize us. The fact that no science can confirm this is of little significance.

On Saturday, we ventured to the San Diego Wild Animal Park. On Sunday, it was the San Diego Zoo. Today looks like maybe Sea World, maybe downtown. We are free until Wednesday when they will do the pharmokinetic testing for the DCA. That will take all day.

These shots of Anna with Mission Valley and the ocean in the background were taken from our balcony at the Bannister House.

Anna's eye diverged for quite a while. It must have made it difficult for her to focus and probably resulted in double vision. To try to help her, we would keep our faces or other objects close to her face when we played. Her poor eyesight led us to focus on aural stimulation. We played music, read books, and sang to her constantly. There is no evidence that Anna's hearing was detrimentally affected by the disease.

So far, Anna does not appear to be responding particularly well or poorly to the DCA. We are watching her very closely. Anything out of the ordinary gets analyzed exhaustively.

Kathleen is coming down with a cold. Obviously, she cannot handle warm weather and sunshine. We are very happy to get your messages. Although the Bannister House is a familiar surrounding, only friends and family can make it a home.

Please keep in touch.

Anna's Dad.

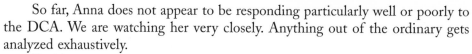

The fun stuff is over, today the tests begin again. There is nothing particularly difficult about today's tests. They consist primarily of periodic blood draws to evaluate how the DCA is affecting Anna's lactic acid levels. We anticipate the results will be the same as they were in December: the levels will be down.

We have continued to watch Anna with some trepidation, because we do not want her to get Kathleen's cold and because we are ever vigilant for undesirable side effects of the DCA. That is the down side of an experimental drug.

We should be done with the tests by about 6:00 p.m. We spent Monday bumming around downtown and the harbor. We saw our first sea lion in the wild. Anna was not impressed. Tuesday, we hit Sea World again. Anna slept through most of it, including the sharks. Last time, she really liked the sharks because they swim right over the top of you. Today the killer whales were her favorites.

We are about San Diego'd out right now. We tried to switch to an earlier flight home, but nothing was available. We are in the process of scheduling our trip back in August, God willing. Hopefully, we can schedule the trip for a time when all of the specialists Anna has seen over our two trips will be available. Well, it is my turn to spell Kathleen on the Anna watch.

Keep the faith.
Anna's Dad

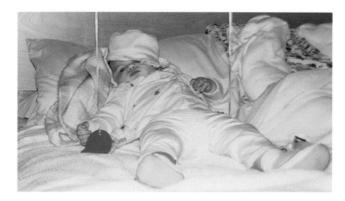

Anna at the Bannister House after a long day of entertaining Kathleen and me.

Jasper again stayed with Kirsten and Frank Marshall. Ruby stayed with Dawn Wichmann, her kids Lisa (pictured above) and Steve (pictured below) and Baylee, their Bernese Mountain Dog. Baylee loved Ruby, but Ruby always played hard to get.

It's Saturday night, the house is a mess, Jasper is annoying me, and Ruby is watching television. Yes, we are home again.

A special thank you to the friends of Anna who watched her dogs for the last ten days. When we do not have time to even think about them, we are confident we do not need to because we know they are in such good hands.

Now that our schedule looks unencumbered by hospital visits for a few months, we hope to reassure Ruby and Jasper that they hold very valued places in our house. Since they have spent one month of the last three in other houses, it may take some convincing.

We have a lot to do around here, but I am sure our "to do" list is no longer than yours. So far so good on the DCA. We have perceived neither dramatic improvements nor setbacks. We are anxious to fall into a routine again. Medical travel should not be necessary for another six months.

Anna's first birthday open house will be 3/11/00 from 2:00 to 5:00 p.m. at Clay Art Studio, where Plainfield meets the Beltline, next to Mr. Burger. Cake, munchies, and soda will be served. Anna thinks she has enough stuff already, so no presents. She just wants your company.

I put the February and the November mailings on the files section of the site as well as some more pictures. If we missed you with the mailing and you want to get that stuff, send your snail mail address to me at jcberner@iserv.net and I will add it to the database.

Thanks.

Anna's Dad

Tuesday, February 29, 2000, 2:06 p.m
From: Anna's Mom
Subject: Tuesday

Greetings from Anna's Mom. Our little almost-one-year-old darling is sitting in her chair and falling asleep as she hangs onto the trinkets that are sewn into her new "tactile" bib. Our therapist who does home visits every week brought it for Anna. This extra long bib has nubby balls, little plastic coils, stretchy hair tie backs, plastic netting, beads, fuzzy balls, and plastic rings sewn onto it for Anna to touch and pull on. It is intended to encourage her to bring her hands to the center of her body and encourage reaching and stretching. Right now, it is only encouraging sleep, which she always deserves after a morning of therapy and her bath.

We are enjoying day two of our return to routine. Given our hospital visits in December, January, and this latest trip in February, we are all out of sorts. We relish the mundane and the ability to have dull (or at least predictable) days. Who am I kidding—our days are far from dull with little Anna around!

Although we have yet to notice any dramatic changes in Anna since she started her daily DCA treatments, I think that she is feeling better now that her lactic acid levels are not elevated all the time. In the past, we have been able to predict with a fair amount of accuracy when her levels were high because she acted lethargic. Lately, she has been moving her arms and legs a lot and seems to be exercising her voice more. These changes are not great but they are something. In any event, she has not exhibited any of the reported negative side effects of the DCA, although it is difficult to know whether she is experiencing the tingling in her hands and feet that many DCA patients report.

We will keep you posted. I will give Anna hugs and kisses from all of Anna's Friends as soon as she wakes up. As always, thank you for your continued prayers!
   Love,
   Anna's Mom

This is Anna with Linda Dodge, her home visit occupational therapist from Ken-O-Sha. Linda came every week to see Anna. She would give Anna quite a workout. Anna always knew when Linda was there because she would pretend to be asleep in the hope that she would not have to do her exercises. Linda had a very keen insight into the things that would most stimulate Anna. Many of Anna's favorite toys were on loan from Linda.

Thursday, March 2, 2000, 4:54 p.m.
From: Anna's Mom
Subject: Thursday-working out

We fought long and hard to get Anna's physical therapy paid by the insurance company. The PT strengthened her muscles and joints. It also made it easier for her to breathe and protect her airway. Insurance did not want to pay because the PT was not "curing" her condition. But without the PT, we are sure she would have lived a shorter, less full and less enjoyable life.

Because we saw Anna's therapists so often, they became our close friends. They started working with Anna only a day or two after her diagnosis and they kept working with her until October of 2000 when we stayed at home with her around the clock. Then, they came to our home to spend time with Anna. This meant the world to us.

Just a quick note to let you know that Anna really impressed her physical therapist on Wednesday. We had her on all fours (her knees and elbows), and Anna was rocking her body back and forth like we have never seen her do in the past! Bonnie, the therapist, said that Anna was really giving HER a workout, as it is difficult to keep Anna in the correct position while she is squirming and moving so much. Anna still chose to leave her head down while she was doing all of this, but it was exciting to see her using all those muscles.

Anna has also started to use her arms to support her trunk when she is sitting with our help. By using her arms, legs and torso, she is getting better at pushing her body up by placing her hands on her thighs when she is placed in a "slumped forward" position. It is hard to describe, but basically, she does not appear to enjoy sitting slumped forward and tries really hard to straighten and lift her back and shoulders. Again, her head remains tipped forward, but we have to strengthen the torso and shoulder girdle before we can see strength in the neck. I thought we would pass that little ray of sunshine on to all of Anna's friends!

Keep us in your thoughts please, particularly this next week and a half, as we are reliving many of the exciting events that occurred this week a year ago. It's going to be an emotional time.

Hugs from Anna.

Anna's Mom

Chapter 7
The Spring

When we returned from our second trip to San Diego we knew we had done everything we could for Anna medically. As the season shifted from winter to spring, we were a little bit at loose ends. Up to now we had always been looking ahead to one upcoming medical event or another. Now the calendar was clear.

We were adjusting to that transition in our day-to-day lives as Anna's birthday approached. We agonized over how we should celebrate Anna's birthday. When a life is going to be short, it is sometimes very hard to celebrate the passage of time. Nonetheless, we decided to throw a big party and invite everyone. We were not disappointed with the result.

This work of art, a prayer quilt, was created for Anna by an elementary school class at Holy Spirit School. They heard about Anna by way of one of our prayer cards. This was their response.

158   *Anna's Friends*

Sunday, March 5, 2000, 11:37 p.m.
From: Anna's Dad
Subject: Sunday-anticipation of celebration

Hello all, it has been a busy weekend and an emotional one. It is hard to predict how far out the pendulum of emotions will swing. This weekend it went a long way out.

We do not know why some days are harder than others but we have theories. Part of it is Anna's upcoming birthday. A birthday is a time to look backward and forward. Both directions make us wince a little.

Looking back, we can both recall those heady days right before Anna was born. We had just put the finishing touches on Anna's room. Every night we would come home from work and just sit in that room and imagine how bright and magical it would be when it was truly finished and filled up with a baby. I remember well my total fear the first time I held Anna. Over the course of that first day fear turned to wonder. I can recall holding her as she slept and telling her all about how wonderful her life would be. These are the things that filled our minds a year ago. Although I am sure a time will come when we will consider these memories to be precious; right now, they are just painful.

Looking forward is also tough. Will this be Anna's only birthday? What will the next few months hold? Will the DCA significantly improve Anna's quality of life? Will she ever walk or talk?

In September, making it to Anna's first birthday was a major goal. Now that we have reached it, we only want more. Although we want more, there is nothing more we can do for her. She has had the surgeries. She is already taking the experimental drug. We can only wait.

We will never rule out miracles, but sometimes hope runs thin. As these thoughts run through our minds, it is easy to find ourselves staring into the distance, our eyes filling with tears for no reason. It is unusual when we both fall into that kind of malaise at the same time, but that is what has happened this weekend.

This weekend has also offered some almost forgotten pleasures. On Saturday, thanks to Opa and Oma [that is Dutch for Grandpa and Grandma] for babysitting

Anna's room was a very special place. During Kathleen's pregnancy we asked to be kept in the dark regarding the baby's sex. That left us without guidance as to how we should decorate the baby's room.

We ultimately decided that we wanted to give our baby the whole world. So, we acquired a 4 foot by 8 foot colorful world map, framed it, and hung it over the crib. We used that multi-hued map as the pallette for decorating the rest of the room. Using the map's colors we stenciled the alphabet and the digits all the way around the room. We made curtains from world map fabric and bedding from fabric with the alphabet. We hung framed prints that featured the alphabet and the digits. Between the maps and the alphabet and numbers, we figured the baby would be able to go anywhere and do anything.

To give you a sense for it, we have included some pictures on the next page. Below and above you can see the stenciling in progress.

The gift certificate we enjoyed so much was one of many wonderful things in a gift basket Anna received from the staff at the Clerk's Office of the United States District Court. Anna was a little intimidated by the basket because it was bigger than her.

Here is Anna's room with the stenciling completed.

and the angels at work for a gift certificate we could not ignore, we went to our first movie together since Anna was diagnosed. On Sunday we also managed to enjoy a meal out.

The bulk of the weekend, however, was spent compiling information in response to a questionnaire from the Governor's office relating to Kathleen's continued pursuit of a judicial appointment. She has her next interview on Tuesday. Perhaps the flurry of activity, uncertainties, and potential dramatic changes attendant to that appointment have contributed to the swing of the pendulum this weekend.

Finally, yes I am aware that Michigan State beat up on Michigan on Saturday. Fortunately for me and Anna, we both decided that we are going to give up college basketball for Lent and we got an early start this weekend. Come talk to us again when football starts.

Despite the tone of this note, rest assured we are doing well. Anna is still the best medicine.

Anna's Dad.

Wednesday, March 8, 2000, 11:10 p.m.
From: Anna's Mom
Subject: One year ago today . . .

One year ago today at 10:45 p.m., John and I were relaxing in the Birthing Unit at Spectrum Hospital. I was lying on a table that was about 6 inches too short for me and left my ankles hanging in mid-air, my arm was being squeezed every few minutes by the tightest blood pressure cuff in the world, and I was feeling no pain due to the miracle of the epidural.

Truly, we were about as relaxed as we could get. I had enjoyed a leisurely jacuzzi before demanding my epidural at 9:00 p.m. and was feeling pretty good, considering the fact that I had only been in active labor since 6:30 p.m.

One year ago at this time, I could barely feel the contractions and John was lounging in the lazy boy chair next to my bed. The baby was responding beautifully to the contractions; the resident was amazed that the baby's heartrate would increase with every contraction and then settle back into the 120-130 beats per minute range. I told them it was all the exercising the baby and I did at Tae Bo class—the baby was obviously in good shape!

One year ago today, John and I watched a rerun of Law and Order from 11:00 p.m. to 12:00 a.m., and then they said I was ready to push. I did not feel ready to push, but being the obedient pregnant one, I pushed. One hour and sixteen minutes later, the doctor pulled the baby to freedom. John laughed and said "Hello, Anna!" I was so surprised that our "Orville" (the baby's in-utero name) was a girl and not a boy.

The first thing I remember thinking (after the shock of learning that our baby was a girl) was "my gosh—she has really long feet!" Given the enormous shoe sizes in our family, it is no wonder. Her long fingers were the next thing I noticed. She was so long and had so much hair—it all seemed too amazing. Our gift from God had arrived in beautiful form without a mark on her perfect, round, cherubesque face! I will not bore you with the gory details that occurred after that point one year ago today.

I will tell you that the first song we ever sang to her was the song Farmer Hoggit sang to Babe the gallant pig: "If I had words to make a day for you, I'd sing

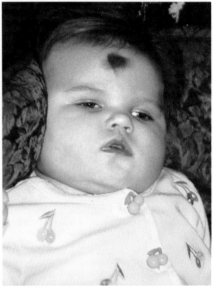

Wednesday, March 8 was also Anna's first Ash Wednesday service.

a morning golden and new. I would make this day last for all time, and give you a night deep in moonshine." Both Anna and Babe really enjoyed it!

John also made up a song telling her all about life and the things she would do. For some reason, we cannot remember the tune. Maybe it is better that way.

A lot has happened since one year ago today. It has been a busy day...for a reason. I thought it would be good to stay busy, and I am glad we did. I did inform Anna regarding all the highlights of what happened one year ago today. I think she enjoyed hearing her story told in real time! We will do the same tomorrow. It is amazing how quickly time goes by when a new life comes into your heart. I can only hope that each day will last a lifetime for all of us.

Happy almost Birthday to our wonderful, beautiful baby girl, Anna Evaleen! We love you more than words can say!

Anna's Mom

Although we saved the big party for the weekend after Anna's birthday, we did celebrate a little on the actual anniversary of Anna's birth, March 9. We met Opa and Oma and Uncle Oscar and Aunt Lauran at a local restaurant where Lauran and Oscar were playing that night (they are musicians, among other things). Anna had a wonderful time, but as you can see, we kept her up past her bedtime.

> You are invited to Anna's First Birthday Open House
> Saturday, March 11, 2000 from 2:00 p.m. to 5:00 p.m.
> at Clay Art Studio, 5157 Northland Drive NE, Grand Rapids
> Where Plainfield meets the Beltline, next to Mister Burger
> (call for directions if you need them 616-447-2529)
> Cake, soda, and munchies will be served.
> Anna believes she already has plenty of stuff so
> PLEASE NO GIFTS.
> Anna has worked a deal with the wonderful ladies at Clay Art Studio. You
> will have the opportunity to paint a clay birthday tile for her if you like.
> Please come visit, paint, and have fun.

We sent invitations to the Anna's Friends mailing list, everyone on Anna's address list, and then we handed out a few dozen more. The "wonderful ladies" referenced in the invitation were Melissa and Shellie, the proprietors of Clay Art Studio.

We prepared instruction sheets which were handed out to each guest.

Welcome to
Anna Evaleen Stuive's
First Birthday Bash

1.   *The preliminaries.* First, we thank you for celebrating this milestone with us. Please sign the guest register and then fill out a nametag (Anna has a hard time remembering names).

2.   *The necessaries.* Next, say "hi" to Anna, enjoy the cake, munchies, and soda, and mingle. When you start to feel creative, we have a couple of outlets for you.

3.   *The balloons.* You might notice the significant number of balloons floating about. They are not just for decoration. Balloons are Anna's favorite toys. Grab a permanent marker and a balloon and personalize a balloon for Anna. A favorite saying or verse, a picture, a song, anything you think she will like is perfect. Be sure to sign it. We have a helium tank at home and the balloons can be refilled so they will last for months.

4. *The tiles.* Each of you may paint a 6x6 tile for Anna free of charge. Please be aware, we are paying for the time you are in process. That does not mean you have to hurry; it just means that it is best to prepare before you get your tile. Some instructions and hints are on the back of this paper. We are paying for the first tile. If you want to paint more than one tile for Anna, any additional tiles are $4 each. Alternatively, feel free to paint some pottery for yourself (on your own nickel). The charges for each type of "raw" piece are right on the sample pieces in the back of the shop. The cost for the time is $4 per hour. You will be amazed at your own talent.

5. *The thank yous.* Thank you to Clay Art Studio for their gracious hospitality. Thank you to the Mahones (a.k.a. Uncle Oscar and Aunt Lauran) for sharing their musical talent. Thank you to the many tireless workers (too many to name, but you know who you are) who helped set this up and will help clean it up. Finally, thank you for all of your support and for sharing this special day with Anna.

Hints and Instructions for Painting the Tiles

1. Get a plan. Plan what you are going to paint before you start. You may even want to first draw it on a piece of paper (the paper on the tables works great). If you need some decorating ideas, check out the idea books or copy one of the samples you see in the studio. Feel free to use any of the sponges, stencils, or stamps.

2. Get your paints. Choose your paint colors from the chart on the paint rack, not the color in the bottle. The chart shows how they will look after firing. Keep in mind that one coat gives a translucent look, three coats give an opaque finish. Use as many colors as you need and remember that a little paint goes a long way. Pull together what you need and set up a spot to work.

3. Get your tile. When you are all set, go see the wonderful ladies at the counter. They will give you your tile and sign you in. (They also are very talented and can help you with design and color ideas.)

4. Get going. The first step is to wash your hands. Then use a damp sponge to remove any dust and dirt on the tile. Make sure you wipe it off well. If you want, you can draw your design right on the tile with a pencil. The pencil marks will burn off when the tile is fired.

5. *Get painting.* Go ahead, start painting. When using sponges, stencils and stamps, a small amount of paint achieves the best result. When layering colors, paint the lighter colors on the bottom, darker colors on the top. When stamping, apply two thin coats of paint to the stamp and then press down. When sponging background colors, do a couple of coats. It will lighten up significantly when it is fired. When you are done, return the tile to those wonderful ladies. Be sure to sign your tile on the back with the "special pencil." It will not burn off. They will sign you out.

6. *Get tidy.* Just put the brushes, sponges, stamps, etc. in the bins on the counter. The wonderful ladies will clean them later. Put the paints back on the rack.

7. *Get patient.* It will take a week before the tile is fired and finished. We will leave them at the studio for two weeks after that for your viewing pleasure. Then, we will be using them in a project for Anna.

Anna gave us many special days. Her birthday party was certainly near the top of the list. We had no idea how many people to expect or what the mood would be. Nearly everyone Anna knew showed up and the mood was nothing short of joyous. Anna only got one birthday party, but it was the best birthday party we ever attended. The tiles and the balloons always bring us back to that day.

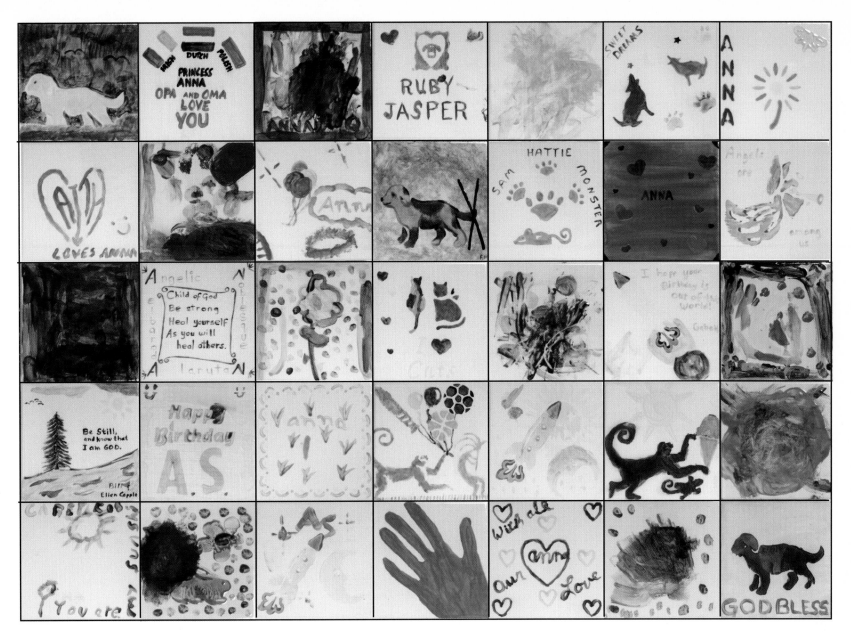

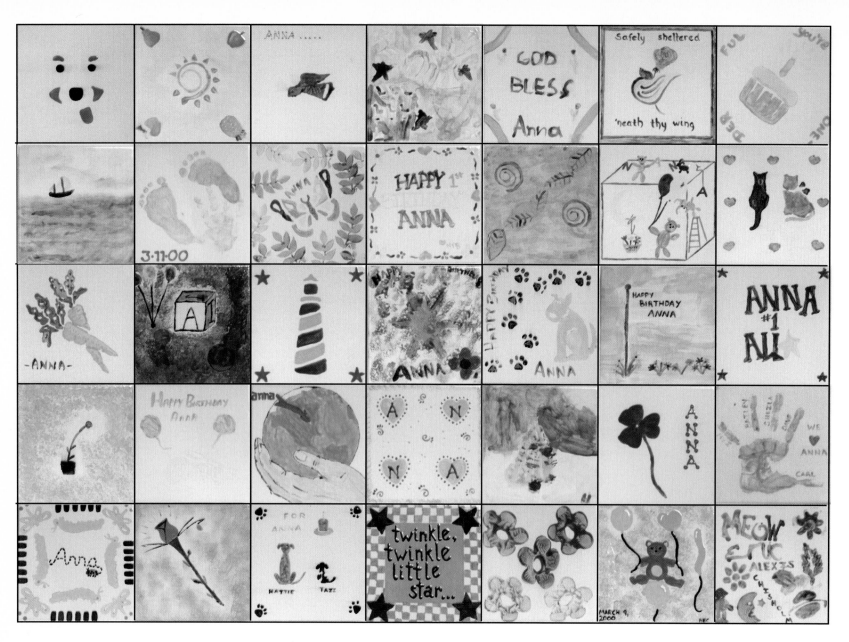

We have been celebrating Anna's birthday for a few days now. I think we might still sing Happy Birthday and eat some more cake tomorrow, but it is pretty much all over. The party was a big success. At about 3:30 p.m., there were so many people there you could barely breathe. I think everyone had a good time and Anna certainly ended up with a lot of tiles.

We know there were a lot of other people who wanted to make it but, for one reason or another, could not. If you fall in that category but still want to paint a tile for Anna, we have worked it out with the wonderful ladies of Clay Art Studio that you can paint a tile for Anna through the end of the month. Just go in and tell them you want to paint a tile for Anna and they will know what to do. If you want to get some sense of what happened at the party, we have put the "instruction sheet" on the files section of the Anna's Friends site. We will post pictures as soon as we have them.

We went through three big cakes and sang happy birthday to Anna each time we cut a new cake. She slept through about a third of the party but was otherwise a very gracious hostess. A special thank you to everyone who helped us celebrate, to Aunt Lauran and Uncle Oscar for playing music, and to the Clay Art Studio gang. It was more wonderful than we possibly could have expected.

When we first thought about throwing a party, I was a little leery. I was worried that it might feel wrong and that Anna's illness would hang over everything like a dark cloud. That is why we celebrated where we did. I wanted to make sure that if the mood turned somber we would have something to distract us.

Boy was I wrong. I guess by now I should know better. The party turned into exactly what it was intended to be: a celebration of Anna's life and of what a wonderful gift she has been for us (and apparently everyone else). Although deep in our hearts we always know that is true, it is very nice to have that fact validated by the scores of party-goers today.

Thank you for all of the good wishes and the cards.

Anna's Dad.

Wednesday, March 15, 2000, 6:47 p.m.
From: Anna's Dad
Subject: Anna is proud to announce...

Anna is proud to announce that her Mom may now be properly referred to as your Honor. Governor Engler has appointed her to the Kent County Circuit Court bench. She will assume her new duties on March 27, 2000. We will keep you advised as to the date and location of her investiture ceremony. Anna recommends Clay Art Studio, but we think we might try something else this time.

Anna is also proud to announce that she and her Dad are going to have a lot of fun once we get Mom out of our hair. Anna has already decided she wants to be a judge now too. Maybe for Halloween.

Anna is doing well, but is somewhat frustrated by the difficulty in pushing her teeth through her gums. Other than that, we are thankful for this new and interesting direction.

Keep the faith.

Anna and Anna's Dad

Anna and I sat together at 4:30 p.m. day in the big green chair by the picture window. The Governor's Office had just called to determine where they could contact me within the next hour. I had no idea what it meant, so Anna and I talked about both possibilities. I asked her if she approved of me becoming a judge. She looked at me, we examined each other's faces, and then she cooed a few times. I thanked her for giving me her blessing. Then she and I discussed what I would say if the Governor offered me the job and what I would say if they told me that someone else got the job. I wish I could describe the anticipation and the fear of the unknown. We should have been getting used to that.

During December of 1999, a judge on the Kent County Circuit Court announced his intention to retire. It had always been Kathleen's dream to be a judge; however, opportunities to be appointed to the Circuit Court bench are rare.

The appointment process involved several steps. It was a demanding process. It was certainly not a process that one might expect parents of a terminally ill child to pursue. In fact, if it had been solely up to Kathleen, she probably would not have taken up the challenge. But, it was not just up to Kathleen. We made the decision as a family.

Looking back, I do not know why we never really mentioned the process in the posts. Maybe we did not think Kathleen would really get appointed. Maybe it just did not seem that important compared to Anna.

Kathleen threw her hat into the ring by a letter to the Governor dated December 2, 1999, three days before we went to the MMDC for the first time. We sought the recommendations of local leaders by letters we drafted and sent when we were in the hospital with Anna before her surgery. We completed the Judicial Qualifications Questionnaire as soon as we were out of the hospital after Anna's surgery. Kathleen appeared before the Judicial Qualifications Committee right before we went to the MMDC for the second time. We completed the Governor's questionnaire after we got back from San Diego. Kathleen interviewed with the Governor's legal counsel right before Anna's birthday. We were all together at home the night the Governor called.

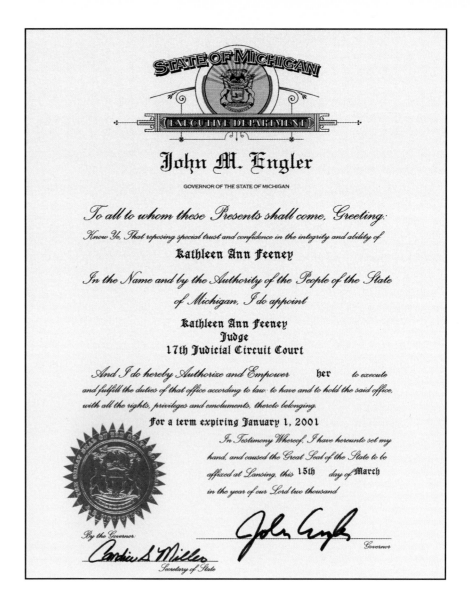

Anna is getting used to hearing people refer to her Mom as "Judge," but I fear that it will take her Mom much longer to get used to the new designation.

It has been a busy few days and my head is still spinning, but I will take this kind of head rush any day! Anna will be going to work with Dad on Friday while I sit and watch one of the other family law judges during "motion day." And so begins my new career.

I will be sworn in on March 27th and will keep my fingers crossed that no one decides to run against me in this fall's election. So, we have a lot on our plates right now, but it is a good heapin' helpin' of wonderful stuff. Anna is still having problems getting that right front tooth to drop down. It looks so painful. Our little angel is taking it all in stride, nonetheless. She sends her love to all and says that she is unsure whether her diet is doing much good (she looks bigger to us all the time!).

Take care and thanks to all of your for your good wishes and continued prayers.
Love,
Anna's Honorable Mom

Here is Anna with Anja. We participated in the interview because we wanted to do everything we could to help our neurologist. It was not an easy thing to do. Anja asked some very difficult questions that took us straight back to the day of the diagnosis and all the emotions of that day. Anja and her crew edited together clips from the interview and put in a musical background. I wish you could hear it as they played it on the radio. Not because of what we said, but because you can hear Anna cooing and chortling in the background. We have included the transcript of the edited interview, unfortunately minus the coos and chortles.

Children's
Miracle ▼ Network®
hospitals helping kids

Friday, March 17, 2000, 10:16 a.m.
From: Anna's Dad
Subject: A Worthy Cause

One of Anna's friends is working the evening and night shift on the Children's Miracle Network Radiothon now taking place on EZ105.7. If you have been listening already, it is possible you have heard parts of an interview between Anja Downe and Kath and I regarding Anna.

We decided that it was worthwhile for us to participate in this event, which raises money for DeVos Children's Hospital, because of our experience with Anna's diagnosis. As you may recall, starting last summer we struggled with some seemingly minor health problems with Anna. Last September, however, when Anna started having seizures, DeVos's chief pediatric neurologist, Dr. Liza Squires, immediately moved us up on the extensive neuro waiting list and got us in for an MRI. The very day of the MRI we got the tentative diagnosis of Leigh's syndrome which was confirmed the following week.

Of course, that is not a particularly happy story. But, from a parent's perspective, it is a far more comforting story than many others we have heard from the parents of other children with mitochondrial disease. It would make you cringe to hear how often these kids are misdiagnosed or simply not diagnosed for extended periods of time simply because these diseases are so rare.

Although knowing your child has a terminal disease is a difficult thing, I believe it is worse to know that some unknown thing is wrong with your child. I am incredibly thankful that we found ourselves in an up-to-date facility with incredibly competent physicians and staff on September 23, 1999. If we had been somewhere else, it is entirely possible that we would be still searching for answers today instead of enjoying Anna's company in the time we have left.

We thank you so much for the support you have given to us and Anna directly. We think we are all set now for a good long time into the future. If you still want to do something that will help, the Children's Miracle Network Radiothon for DeVos Children's Hospital is a worthy cause.

Your donation will help the next parents who are not sure what is wrong with their child. Indeed, some of the money raised will go directly to help kids with mitochondrial and metabolic diseases because the funds will be used to bring prominent specialists to DeVos to consult on the mitochondrial and metabolic cases. They are working right now to bring some of our friends from the Mitochondrial and Metabolic Disease Center at the University of California, San Diego to DeVos for direct patient consultations.

I can assure you that there is no greater benefit when your child is ill than to know that you are being treated by the best in the world. To be able to bring that level of expertise here is a wonderful thing.

If you are interested, contributions can be made by calling 1-877-953-KIDS. One way to give is to sign up for the EZ KIDS COME FIRST CLUB. Under this plan, contributors pledge $10.57 per month for 12 months ($10.57 will be deducted from their credit card each month for one year, totalling $126.84). 100 PERCENT of any donation goes directly to helping kids at DeVos Children's Hospital — not one penny goes to cover administrative costs.

The radiothon runs through Sunday afternoon (March 19th). A good time to call and contribute is during the evening on Thursday, Friday, or Saturday, when Anna's Friend Larry McLain will be doing a special "Dollars For Dedications" edition of EZ Love Songs, where contributors can request or dedicate a song in exchange for their donation. Also, do not forget to listen so you can hear Kathleen and I talk about Anna (they air the interviews or excerpts from them at different times). We also plan to see if we can get Anna to talk on the air.

Thanks,
Anna's Dad

We went to the hospital for an on-air interview on Saturday afternoon. Michael Sirianni spoke with us for a few minutes, but we had a hard time getting Anna to say anything. Anna was very popular, even though she was silent. The phones were ringing constantly while she was on the air. The radiothon raised over $115,000.

DeVos Children's Hospital

A Member of Spectrum Health

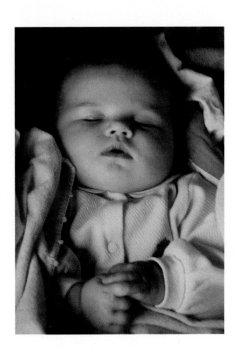

KATHLEEN: Anna is almost a year old. At nine weeks she was 9 lbs. 9 oz. and she was 8 lbs. 11oz. when she was born. She was not gaining weight or developing as she should have. We changed her diet and she started to gain weight, but she still had some developmental delays. She wasn't lifting her head up, she wasn't sitting up, she wasn't rolling over. There were just little things along the way. We had her tested for a lot of different things. They all came up negative. Eventually at around six months, she started to have really noticeable delays and she was starting to lose milestones. She began to stop smiling and laughing. At that point, they said we really need to get her in. She underwent an MRI scan and it confirmed a terminal diagnosis. She has Leigh's Syndrome. It is a rare metabolic illness. She has a rare form of a rare disease. The mitochondria in her cells, they have their own DNA, and within that DNA strand there is a mutation. It is kind of a like reading a long sentence and the noun in the middle of the sentence is misspelled so the sentence makes no sense. And because of that DNA mutation her cells can't produce the energy that they should so she is operating on maybe about 10 watts of energy while you and I are operating maybe on 100 watts. And because of that, she has malfunctions in her brain, her brain is smaller than it should be. There are lesions in her brain. Basically, it is a terminal illness. It will eventually lead to her early death.

JOHN: After the MRI, no one showed any concern so I went back to work and Kathleen stayed at the hospital with Anna. Later, Kathleen called me and gave me a hint of what it was. Miraculously my parents just showed up and they took me to the hospital. Once we got there we got more information from Dr. Squires. This was a very serious illness. We learned that Anna's life would be measured in months rather than years. We were just floored. When I first heard the news, I fell to my knees and I was just making sounds not really crying and then everything was really foggy from there.

Right then it was a lot of mourning what we weren't going to have. School functions, hearing her say "daddy." Seeing her walk, seeing her develop, seeing her have friends.

KATHLEEN: I think about how much we will miss her. How hard it is going to be to walk into her room that we spent a lot of time decorating. I think about not smelling the way she smells after I give her a bath. But I also know that there is going to be an angel who we will be able to talk to all the time and we are going to know her name and her face.

From almost the first moment that we found out, all of our friends, family and colleagues, everybody just started coming and calling and sending cards. We figured out that all these people were God coming to us again and again and saying "look, you are not in this by yourself. I am in this with you and I am sending all these people to you because I know that you need them."

JOHN: One of the nurses stayed with us for several hours that first day in the hospital. I tell you without Laura I don't think we could have gotten through it at all.

KATHLEEN: You know people always say that God doesn't give you anything that you are incapable of handling. Already we have had so much joy despite all the sorrow. Every morning that she gets up it is a great morning and it is going to be a fabulous day, and we have to give thanks for that. We have tried really, really hard not to sit and have self pity because if you only have so much energy in a day and you waste a lot of it on feeling bad, there is not enough to go around to take care of her and to make sure that she knows that we love her and to do everything we can for her.

At the beginning, I couldn't deal with the thought of her degenerating. Now, that's changing because she has been with us so much longer. Although she is unable to take food by mouth anymore, we have to feed her through a feeding tube, still it is every day that we are just relishing and living for. Right now, we are just focusing on her and loving her as much as we can and exposing her to as much as we possibly can. Then later on we will worry about us.

You may recall that Laura Wagner drafted the script that got us through the first night after the diagnosis. This is Laura with Anna and me.

In Kathleen's words here, you can see a road map for the rest of our journey with Anna.

There is a saying from one of my favorite musicals, "The Sound of Music:" when God closes a door, he opens a window. While Anna's illness may have been the closed door, the judgeship was the open window. Sometimes, while Anna was still with us, that open window seemed like a pretty significant burden and I certainly would have preferred that the door stayed open. Nonetheless, after Anna was gone, that open window helped me keep going. With Anna, I was privileged to care for one very special little girl. Now, I am privileged to care for hundreds of children in my divorce, delinquency, and abuse and neglect cases.

Anna with her Aunt Lauran.

Tuesday, March 21, 2000, 10:45 p.m.
From: Anna's Dad
Subject: Tuesday night

Well, we apologize for allowing so much time to pass since our last message. We are in the midst of preparing for a big transition. Kathleen's new job has been very demanding even though, technically, it has not started yet. Kathleen is working hard to build relationships with her colleagues on the bench, her new staff, and the bar. Right now it seems like everyone has a legitimate claim to her time. There is also a lot to learn about the new position.

At the same time, I am working at a transition for my work. It appears that I will still be working part-time for a few months, to permit a smooth transition and adequate training for my replacement. To make sure Anna is not watching too much television while I am working half-days, Anna's Aunt Lauran has agreed to keep an eye on her when I cannot. We will keep you advised as both of these transitions progress.

The next big milestone for Kathleen will be Monday, when she takes the bench for the first time. The official investiture ceremony will be at the end of April. We will let you know when the date is set.

Last Saturday we went to Clay Art Studio and looked at all of the tiles that were finished. Standing alone, the tiles are wonderful works of art. When you see them all together, they are an incredible expression of love and support. Thank you again.

On the Anna front, so far so good with the DCA. We are reluctant to report any dramatic improvements because we are always afraid it is just wishful thinking. But, over the last few days, Anna has pooped on her own several times. This is certainly different. That is an aspect of baby care that we are used to controlling. When we control it, it is an every couple of days sort of thing; whenever she looked like she was trying, we would help. For the last few days, it can happen any time. It has been happening a little more frequently and it is always a surprise.

Again I apologize to our more sensitive readers for focusing on Anna's toilet habits. Beyond this change in Anna's day-to-day activities, the changes are not so objectively apparent. We believe Anna is generally more bright and active. Others have said the same.

We are thankful for these changes even if they are not so readily quantified. We have felt the support of our friends and family over the last busy week. We will certainly need it as well over the next weeks.

Good night.
Anna's Dad

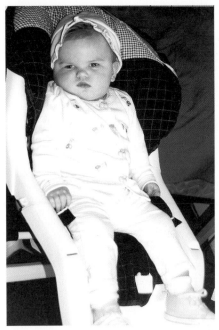

Anna being bright and active in her pink tennis shoes.

Anna added to her wardrobe everywhere she went. This is her panda sweatshirt and panda t-shirt and panda hat from the San Diego Zoo.

The swearing-in took place in one of the courtrooms in the Hall of Justice. Those courtrooms did not seat many, thus we did not invite many to attend. Nonetheless, Kathleen was surrounded by family, friends, and colleagues during the ceremony.

Friday, March 24, 2000, 10:11 p.m.
From: Anna's Mom
Subject: Friday–sworn in

Today Anna was in court for the first time in her life. She was there to see her Mom get sworn into office. Yes, at 4:30 p.m. today, I officially became a judge of the 17th Circuit Court, the youngest judge and the first woman to sit on the Kent County Circuit Court bench. The courtroom was very full and all of the Circuit Court judges (plus a few Court of Appeals judges) were there.

Please keep us in your thoughts and prayers as this has been an interesting week for us. Pray that the Good Lord will help me to make the right decisions, to base justice on love, and to help the people who come before me for guidance. And pray that we will continue to take one day at a time as we transition into our new roles. We gather so much strength from your prayers—that is why we ask for these special prayers from all of you.

For those of you who do not live in the Grand Rapids area, there have been several articles in the paper opposing my appointment based on an area judge's suggestion that I am incompetent, unqualified for office, and that my appointment is purely a political move. We know it is not true, but it is difficult to read in print.

Anna continues to do well! She is moving her arms a lot more and is getting stronger biceps. The bowel movements are getting more frequent and she had another on her own this morning. We think this indicates improved muscle tone and a good level of hydration. Both front teeth are visible but are slow to drop down. Anna's learning that she can rub her lower teeth on her upper gums to relieve the pressure, but it makes a mess of her gums. Poor baby!

We are looking forward to a relaxing weekend. We have to go and do birthday tiles for her on Saturday, and we are going shopping for all three of us (a first). Anna is now heading for the 3T and 4T sizes in almost everything. What a little munchkin!

Thanks to all of you for your cards and letters of congratulations. Please know that your kind words touch our hearts!

Much love,
Anna's Mom

On March 16, 2000, the governor's appointment was heralded in a headline on the front page of the Grand Rapids Press: "Engler's choice for judge lauded." A week later I made the front page again. This time, however, the tone was different. A local district judge had publicly criticized my appointment saying I did not have sufficient experience and suggesting I was incompetent for the job. The headline read "Judge blasts governor for judicial appointment." Other articles followed, and then a flurry of letters to the editor. Some supported me; others echoed the district judge's concerns. In the end, the Grand Rapids Press printed an editorial which set the facts straight and encouraged everyone to give me a chance. That is all I wanted.

Getting to see your name and picture in the paper is one of the interesting consequences of being a public figure. I know it ripped John apart to see me publicly criticized. It was a little easier for me. I could just look at Anna and know that the furor of the debate over my qualifications at its worst could not compare to the worst days that we had endured together. Similarly, no matter how well the debate was resolved, it could not compare to the best times that Anna and I shared. That certainly kept things in perspective. Nonetheless, for a few weeks in March and April of 2000, the Grand Rapids Press had a profound effect on our lives.

This photo appeared in the March 16 article announcing Kathleen's appointment.

Her honor: *Kathleen Feeney and her husband, John Stuive, will switch roles to care for their daughter, Anna.*

< *This photo by Press photographer Rex D. Larsen, captioned "Judicial Succession," appeared in the March 17 Grand Rapids Press. It features Kathleen standing next to her predecessor Judge Robert Benson and his wife Mary. At the far left is Judge John Letts, Judge Benson's predecessor. Next to Judge Letts is Ealry Lyons, who served as court clerk for all three judges. Anna and I were at the party, but we did not make it into the picture.*

Sunday, Mar 26, 2000, 9:37 p.m.
From: Anna's Dad
Subject: A new day

Kathleen and I were too busy to paint tiles at Anna's birthday party, so we painted tiles another day. Here, Kathleen is painting a tile while Anna and dolly watch from her stroller.

Well, it looks like the furor over Kathleen's appointment is starting to die down. Today, the Press editorial set everything straight. All of the facts we were hoping to get out got out. I know you are supposed to just let the stuff roll off, whether it be good or bad. Kath is pretty good at that. That is part of the reason she is going to be so good at what she does. I, on the other hand, am not good at it, not even a little bit. Trust me, it sounds a lot easier than it is.

Now that the great debate is over, Kath can get down to doing what she has to do. Whenever things got dicey this week, we usually got past it by focusing on Anna. She has been bright and bouncy all week. She does not read the Press. Well, ok, she reads the comics and the diaper ads, but nothing else.

She has not needed any assistance with certain bodily functions all week. We are attributing this to better muscle tone and better hydration. We think that it fits in with her improved brightness. We hope and pray it continues.

We stopped in to Clay Art Studios today. We painted our tiles and made the first attempt at photographing the finished ones. What a joy to see them all side by side. It is a moving experience. This was just our first attempt at photos. I am betting it will take a few tries before we get something usable. As soon as we do, we will proudly display them to Anna's friends first.

Again, we ask that you think of us this week as it is the first week of a new order for us. We thank God for the blessing of Anna. She has really helped us keep perspective this week.

Anna's Dad

Saturday, April 1, 2000, 5:40 p.m.
From: Anna's Mom
Subject: Saturday-away too long

Sorry that we have not been in touch lately—we know that it causes a fair amount of consternation among our faithful readers and for this we apologize.

We both survived our first week under the "new arrangement." Work for me was hectic but exciting; there was little time for lunch let alone wondering about what John and Anna were doing without me. John found the week to be equally challenging as he began assuming primary care duties for Anna while still working. It is not an easy job balancing work and Anna's therapy, doctor's appointments, feedings, bottle making, exercises, and just spending quality time together. Rest assured, he is up to the task and Anna is thrilled to have him around more!

It's been a quiet Saturday for us. Some stomach problems put me out of commission for most of the day, so Anna kept me company by playing songs for me on her piano. The piano says "let's play a song" and then sends lights running back and forth along the baby-sized keyboard. She watches and then touches one of the keys, and out comes a wonderful song. We think she is quite pleased with her musical abilities, as she will select song after song for quite a while.

John accomplished a lot today, which made up for lazy old me. It is so wonderful to spend a day at home. It does not happen often enough around here.

We are going to pick up the birthday tiles from Clay Art Studio tomorrow. We have seen most of them already and they are WONDERFUL!!!

Anna is having a sleepy kind of day, which her dad attributes to the fact that I put her hair in a top knot this morning. John is against cutting her hair ("it will rob her of all her power") and against putting stuff in her hair. So my attempts at dealing with her long tresses must be causing her to nod off. All you moms out there with kids who will not sleep, try putting their hair up.

Sorry this is not as exciting as our usual posts, but it is par for the course on this casual Saturday. Thanks again for the wonderful cards you have sent to us and for your continued prayers (as well as those letters to the editor).

God Bless- Love,
Anna's Mom

Friends began to tell us that they looked for our e-mails as soon as they turned on their computers in the morning. No news to them was not good news. We tried very hard to be sensitive to their need for information as they provided us with immeasurable support, love and prayers.

This is Anna's piano. It provided hours of entertainment for her and for us.

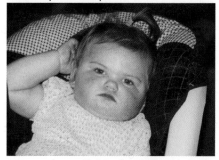

Anna was born with lots of dark brown hair. She grew a full head of sun-kissed sandy blonde hair that brushed the back of her shoulders. If we didn't pull her hair up, she just kept flipping her long tresses into her face. Her hands were always up by her ears twirling her hair. We often had to untwirl hair that was tangled around her chubby fingers.

This is Jim outside the log cabin home he is building. Jim is quite a renaissance man. He is also quite an artist. On the following pages you will see a sketch he did for Anna during an RCIA class when we were discussing the sacrament of Anointing of the Sick. You will also see Jim's painting of Kathleen, Anna and me under the protective wings of an angel. He gave the framed painting to us just a few weeks before Anna died.

Jim Wisnewski was one of the leaders in my RCIA class (I will explain more about the class in a few pages). That class met weekly beginning in September of 1999. Accordingly, Jim was aware of Anna's illness as soon as she was diagnosed.

Jim was also a teacher at Catholic Central High School. In that role, Jim had shared Anna's situation with his students. In his words:

> "When I found out about baby Anna's illness I immediately asked my students to pray for her. I passed around the card with her picture on it in my sophomore religion classes and in my art classes. We faithfully remembered her in our daily intentions and I would occasionally update the students on her progress and changes. They would ask questions, so I had the idea to make a videotape to answer some of these. Kathleen and John agreed, so one night after RCIA class we videotaped, doing it in one sitting with no editing."

We transcribed the video interview and we have included excerpts below. Because you already know the background information, we have removed it from the transcript.

JOHN: Hi. I am John Stuive and this is my wife Kathleen Feeney. First of all we would like to thank you for all the support you have given us over the past weeks. Jim has told us about that and we would also like to introduce our daughter, Anna Stuive. You already know the situation with Anna. She is very good company. That's one of the things we have come to treasure over these past few months as we have watched her develop to the extent she can. We have learned to deal with our daughter who is a little bit different than a lot of kids.

No one can tell us exactly how long Anna is going to be with us and that has really given us a different perspective on life. For the first few weeks after she was diagnosed, the one thing we searched and searched and searched for was someone who could tell us how long do we have, how will this happen, which way is she going to go? For a while that was the most important thing in the world. And then, as we got more used to the situation, that wasn't the most important thing anymore. What was the most important thing was to be able to spend time with her and to enjoy her for whatever time we have left. That has left us in a situation where we really live day by day with her. We don't spend a lot of time planning for the future or anything. We just kind of take today and then tomorrow and the next day as they come.

Right now it is kind of a game, waiting to see what happens next. No one can tell us which system in her body will fail next. As the disease usually progresses, it usually is just a cold or the flu or pneumonia or something happens and then the child starts to lose a lot of the developmental milestones that she has already gained. That is what we are looking at in terms of the future. I think that is part of the reason that we live day by day because we are just looking at her vital systems shutting down.

KATHLEEN: It is amazing, though, how much strength we have taken from everybody's prayers for Anna. We realized early on that all the people who are praying for her and coming to her all the time, coming to us and saying how much they care about her, how much they love her, how much they are praying for us, they are just God coming to us over and over again to let us know that we are not alone, that we are all in this together. We feel very blessed that Anna is part of our lives. It has been an amazing experience to see how such a small little girl who can't even talk can touch so many people's lives so deeply. It is amazing to watch God working through her to show us His grace and His mercy and I think a lot of people have been touched by her like that. So we really are blessed.

JOHN: And we are really learning a lot. Early on knowing that people were praying for us would be a little frustrating for me because I would sit there and ask what good is that doing? What's that going to change if we have a 1,000 people or 2,000 people or 2,000,000 people, what difference is that going to make? But as time has passed it really has become a

source of peace, a source of strength. There is a lot of time where all of this just exhausts us and it is at those times where knowing that you are not alone is probably the most important thing.

JIM WISNEWSKI: I have a question. How have your lives changed? You are both lawyers and, well, you are a judge Kathleen. But certainly you had hopes and dreams for this baby and I had heard you even picked out her university, but certainly a lot of that has changed. What has this done to you in your personal lives?

KATHLEEN: It has made us realize that you have to live for today. You can't worry about what is going to happen in the future. It has made us realize that when we pray about fulfilling God's purpose here on earth, He does listen and answer, maybe not in the way that we had expected. It is undeniable that she is supposed to be our daughter and we are supposed to be her parents and that's for a very specific reason--although we don't know what that is and maybe never will.

JOHN: And that's another thing we've learned is that you don't have to sit around and think "what should I be doing to fulfill God's purpose for me?" You have to be doing it right now and we are doing it just by being her parents.

KATHLEEN: Yes, and you don't realize that until something like this happens. This has given us guidance for the rest of our lives. From now on, we look at different opportunities as God opening windows or maybe He has closed doors and it is up to us to decide whether or not we are going to step through those doors or look out those windows that He has opened.

JOHN: The living day-by-day thing has meant some fundamental changes. We are both professionals and one of things you get as a professional is money. Although I hate to admit it, money was a driving force in our lives. At least it was something that we paid a lot of attention to. Now, it is something we've just stopped paying attention to. Much to both of our surprise it has not made a bit of difference. When we sit down and pay the bills the money seems to be there. It is just a change in focus that I know has made a big difference for me.

Both of us were very career oriented. Right now, my career is taking care of Anna and I am perfectly happy with that. When that career is done, I am sure that there will another career out there and I am not worried for a minute. And that is not something that I would have expected. If you would have asked me that question a year ago. "What if you lose your job?" I would have been running around worrying. It just hasn't been that way. It is just not the way things are anymore.

KATHLEEN: I think it has really opened up our eyes to the way God is working around us. You have to be aware of what is happening now and not always hoping for things to change in the future. I think it wasn't until she became ill that we realized that this was our purpose. This was our calling.

JOHN: And fulfilling that purpose was not some noble thing we were going to do in the future. I think that is the biggest change. It is something we are doing right now and that we have to do everyday.

JIM WISNEWSKI: Well thank you very much. Anna, are you going to wave to us?

KATHLEEN: Anna, you wave bye and say thank you so much for all the prayers and support.

Jim showed the tape to his classes. We asked him about their reaction.

"When I first showed the tape to the classes, the initial reaction in each hour was dead silence. Even though they knew of Anna, the video seemed to make her 'real' and they were stunned that this beautiful child was slowly dying. I saw a few tears and then came the rest of the emotions: sorrow, disbelief, anger over the unfairness of it all, and great sympathy for her dad and mom, as well as admiration of them. Their attitudes and prayer changed and 'their baby Anna' became part of their lives, touching them as she has touched us all."

Ruby with her cast. As you can see, Jasper was never far behind.

Kathleen and I had a bet. If her school went farther in the NCAA basketball tournament than mine, we would buy Anna a new Michigan State outfit. If my school went farther than hers, we would buy Anna a new Calvin College outfit. Both schools were national champions so Anna got two new outfits. Anna and I wore our Calvin College shirts together often so people would know we were together.

Today I took Ruby to the orthopedic specialist. She had been limping; we assumed arthritis. Instead, Ruby had blown her anterior cruciate ligament. She had surgery this afternoon. She is spending a night in the hospital recuperating far away from Jasper's annoying interest in everything Ruby. We sat with her at the vet for a while tonight. Ruby is very unhappy about today's events. She will now face four weeks as a couch potato and then six weeks of gradually increasing exercise. We have explained all of this to Jasper, but right now he misses Ruby. We will spend much of the next ten weeks keeping him away from her. It seemed strange today to be worrying about the medical condition of someone other than Anna.

On the Anna front, she has started to have problems a couple of times a day coping with her own saliva and secretions. She will cough and struggle for air for a second but she has been able to clear it out herself, especially if we can help her by holding her upright. We are told this is no cause for immediate alarm, but this is something to watch. It is also a difficult reminder that these past several weeks with relatively few hospital and doctor visits may be just a brief respite.

This past weekend we were able to get Anna's birthday tiles up in Kathleen's office on a ledge that is about a foot below the ceiling. I have now had the privilege of viewing these works of love/art several times in their new setting. Together they form a masterpiece which is even greater than the sum of the individual masterpieces. If you have the opportunity to stop by and visit Judge Feeney's office you will be amazed (by the tiles as well as the principal occupant of the office).

Congratulations to the Spartans and all of their fans. That was truly a team of destiny. I never doubted once that the team would win the championship. I am glad they were able to join the ranks of the Calvin College Knights as 2000 NCAA national champs.

Anna sends her best wishes. She has agreed to take care of Ruby and nurse her back to health. We are hoping they will give us a group rate at physical therapy.

Anna's Dad

Monday around here is garbage day. That means I have to take out the garbage. I will do anything to put off that task so I thought I would take this opportunity to post.

First, after a couple of doctor visits, three new meds, and three new pieces of medical equipment, it appears we are prepared to address whatever is making Anna cough and causing her congestion. As you may recall, we wrote recently that Anna had started to demonstrate some difficulty in handling her secretions. We now believe that because Anna is teething, it has increased her oral secretions. Because she typically is sitting in a reclined position, the secretions tend to pool at the back of her throat. Because she has trouble swallowing, she would end up trying to breathe through the pool and start to choke. This was happening a couple of times a day. It was usually easily corrected just by changing her position, i.e., getting her more upright. Eventually, she would get a breath in and start to drool out the saliva.

After a few days of watching this new problem, Anna also started to get congested and cough more frequently. We were concerned that Anna might have aspirated some of her secretions and that she was developing an infection in her lungs. The past two doctor visits, one to the pediatrician and one to the pulmonologist, have apparently ruled that out. Nonetheless, we were still left with the swallowing problem and the congestion, whether or not they were related.

To help Anna deal with secretions, she will soon be starting a new med that will dry her out a little. Because the drying may actually result in thicker secretions, we will also have a suction machine available to vacuum out her mouth. To make sure the problems do not get critical while she sleeps, we will also have a new pulse/ox monitor to alert us if Anna is having problems breathing at night. (Anna has routinely been on such monitors in the hospital and we already tried one at home for a little while last October, so it is not anything new.)

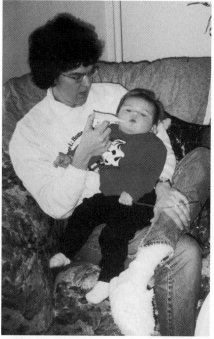
Kathleen is administering an Albuterol treatment.

Anna's new nebulizer (on the arm of the chair).

Anna with a few of her many balloons.

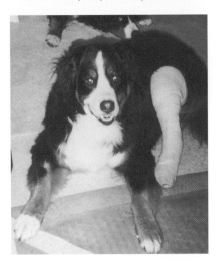

In addition, to address the congestion issues, we will be using our new nebulizer to administer Albuterol (a bronchodilator) and using a nasal decongestant spray as well. I think if we get one more piece of medical equipment or three more prescriptions, we will qualify for a free Disney World vacation from our pharmacist/medical equipment company.

Anna appears no worse for all of these problems. She is sitting next to me right now in her high chair explaining what she wants me to type. Sometimes she explains using squeaks and squeals, but primarily she communicates through balloon sign language. She grabs a handful of balloons by their ribbons and pulls them up and down in rapid succession. Presumably, the colors, directions, and speed of the balloons can be translated into English. Kath and I just have not figured it all out yet. Not surprisingly, this leaves Anna rather frustrated and she ends up pulling on the ribbons all the more furiously. It is starting to scare Jasper.

Ruby is recovering well. For the first couple of days she was not interested in moving around much. Every time someone came to visit, Ruby would limp to the door and whine to tell them what horrible things we had done to her. Now, she is just like her old self. She even puts her weight on the leg with the cast. I am sure she will be disappointed when she loses the cast because it has proven a real attention getter. Jasper is also adjusting. Even though he has been surprisingly gentle with Ruby, he has been compelled to spend more time alone. Jasper was not meant to live alone and he was certainly not meant to pass the day without having Ruby to pester at regular intervals. He has become very clingy and that is saying something for Jasper, who would rather be in your lap than anywhere else.

Kathleen's new job continues to be challenging. We are in the process of planning the formal investiture ceremony which will take place at the end of April. Shortly after that, we will travel to Wisconsin for the Bernese Mountain Dog National Specialty Show. This was to be our first specialty show with two dogs, but now it looks like we will only have one as Ruby will not be ready to travel. Oh well, she will certainly enjoy the week away from Jasper.

Anna says it is time for me to shut up. Good night.

Anna's Dad.

It is a beautiful sunny day. I am ready to go to work, but I am waiting for Lauran. The dogs have already been outside to do their business. For Ruby, that is the only time she is permitted outside. Before she can go out, we have to put a plastic bag on her cast. She can only go out on a leash, otherwise she might tear up the scar tissue that is building up in her knee to replace the ligament. It is very hard for her. Every time I take her out in the front yard, she tries to push the envelope a little further. She insists that we go farther out each time and is now very reluctant to come back inside when she is done. Although she acts this way whether it is raining, snowing, or sunny (we have experienced each in the last week), I imagine that she feels like I do: that it is a shame to waste such a beautiful day inside.

Normally, by now Anna is awake. I just went into her room and she is still sleeping. She was so peaceful I did not have the heart to wake her up. Instead, I raised the shades. Even she cannot resist the sun. I can hear her stirring.

We obtained new meds and equipment to address her recent coughing, but we have not yet used them. The problems have calmed down significantly and we are reluctant to start new meds which may have their own detrimental side effects. The med should dry up her secretions, but it may also result in thickening them. The new pulse/ox monitor is really for use if we use the new med. We are supposed to hook it up to Anna at night to make sure the thickened secretions do not cause her any problems. The alarms, however, are not particularly discerning. We have found that her typical nighttime stirring will cause an alarm even if there is no problem. Accordingly, we will wait until we use the meds to use the machine.

We are finishing preparations for Kathleen's investiture ceremony. There is nothing like planning a party for three hundred in the midst of lives in transition. We have gotten so used to strange schedules that we hardly notice.

Kathleen's schedule is still very hectic. We are both looking forward to our vacation at the beginning of May.

Thank you for your support and prayers. Anna is doing well and so are we.
Anna's Dad

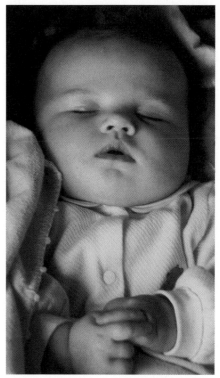

Watching Anna sleep among her stuffed animal friends was the highlight of each morning. We hated to wake her with anything but a song, so most mornings she woke to us serenading her.

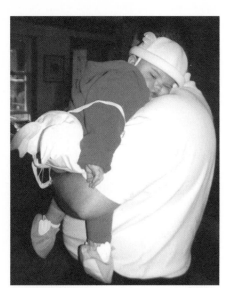

Anna had many hats and she was not afraid to wear them. This winged chapeau, which we dubbed her mercury hat, came complete with winged backpack and winged booties from one of Anna's friends in Japan.

Thursday, April 20, 2000, 8:58 a.m.
From: Anna's Dad
Subject: Thursday-a bouncy baby

Anna is sleeping soundly. Until she wakes up, I am free to do as I please. I thought I would catch up with the list.

We have decided that Anna is brighter and bouncier on a regular basis. Of course, we do not know whether that is attributable to the DCA, the natural waning of her disease symptoms, or a recent increase in her dose of Tegretol, an anti-seizure medication. We have some scientific interest in the answer, but we are pleased by the result even though we remain ignorant.

Anna is still growing. I will take her in today for a weigh-in to see if we need to adjust her food intake again. Anna is no longer suffering the symptoms of a cold or whatever was bothering her last week. She still has trouble with her secretions a couple of times a day, but we also think she is developing skills to deal with it. Accordingly, we have not used the med to dry her up, the suction machine, or the monitor.

Kathleen is starting to really enjoy the daily challenges of her new position and we are getting into a new daily rhythm. I have been officially replaced at work. I will be continuing to work half-time through the end of May, but then it will be just me and Anna. Anna has mixed feelings about it because she prefers to spend the early part of the day with Aunt Lauran.

Ruby had her cast removed yesterday. When you see her leg without all of the fur, it looks hopelessly too skinny to support her weight. The new challenge is to keep her from licking her leg too much. If we have to, we will make her wear an Elizabethan collar to prevent this. Then she can knock down things with her ever-wagging tail on one end and her satellite dish collar on the other end.

The past two months have been very busy. We have sort of looked to Kathleen's investiture on the 28th as the end to this initial craziness. After that we will have a week of sorely needed vacation in Wisconsin. Although we have had a lot of time off work in the last year, this will be our first vacation since September of 1998.

Thanks for listening.
Anna's Dad

There are a few subjects that we never posted to the list about even though they were very important to us at the time. For example, we never posted about those first few days in the hospital or about Kathleen's quest for a judicial appointment, but we filled those gaps in this book. We also never posted about my journey from being a Protestant to becoming a Roman Catholic. That was my biggest transition in a spring filled with transitions. Let me fill that gap now.

I grew up in a Protestant church, the Christian Reformed Church, while Kathleen grew up in the Roman Catholic Church. That difference was significant to us even when we first started dating. As is typical of Kathleen, we explored our religious differences head-on. We took an inter-faith marriage class over a weekend even though we had dated for only a short while.

The class did not really help us that much, although it did reveal that there were a lot of couples in the same situation and that there were a lot of different ways to address the problem of a two-church household. Eventually, we decided to continue what we had been doing prior to the class: worshipping in both churches. When we had kids, we reasoned, we would expose them to both churches.

We pursued that plan with vigor until Kathleen became pregnant with Anna. Then, some of the more difficult practical questions came up, i.e., in what church will the baby be baptized. We agonized over that one for a while, both of us presenting our arguments in a very lawyerly fashion. Neither of us convinced the other. Ultimately, we decided not to decide. Instead, we determined if the baby were one sex, it would be baptized in one church; otherwise, it would be baptized in the other church.

That left us the seemingly not difficult question of which church got which sex. Unfortunately, both of us were quite convinced that Anna was a boy, so the same partisanship that made the decision difficult in the first place carried through to this question. Accordingly, we devised an elaborate multi-step random selection method. In the end, a boy would be baptized in the Christian Reformed Church and a girl would be baptized in the Roman Catholic Church.

Anna's baptism in early June, 1999. Father Bozung baptized Anna while we and Anna's godparents, Neil and Angie Jansen, watched.

Anna with Sister Felicia at the Easter Vigil Mass.

Simply recounting our means of making that decision makes me uncomfortable all over again. That was no way to resolve an important decision. I wondered how many times we would have to set up elaborate multi-step random selection methods to decide issues relating to our children. More importantly, I wondered how a kid, especially a teenager, would react when presented with two similar but mutually exclusive churches. I knew if that kid were me, I would reject both. That was certainly an unpalatable result. I was convinced that we had to present a united front. I knew Kathleen could not change, so I decided to explore whether I could.

After Anna was born, we took a baptism class at Kathleen's church. The class was taught by Sister Felicia Bertaina. Sister Felicia had ministered all over the world, but she ended up in Belmont, Michigan of all places. She was from Italy, but she spoke in very precise English glazed with an accent that compelled you to listen to every word she said. Sister Felicia had an uncanny ability to understand every question you asked and to give you her best answer. I had gone to Christian schools all my life, I had endured countless hours of Sunday School and catechism instruction, but I never met anyone who understood questions and answered them as well as Sister Felicia. We hit it off right away. I mentioned some of my concerns to Sister Felicia and she encouraged me to take the RCIA (Rite of Christian Initiation for Adults) classes which she would lead in the fall of 1999.

We started the classes in September of 1999. I say "we" because I made Kathleen and Anna go with me. After only the first couple of classes, Anna went into the hospital. After that I knew Anna would never be a rebellious teenager. I knew she would probably never know the difference if we worshipped in one church, two churches, or a dozen. Nonetheless, Anna and I kept going to class.

The RCIA classes were challenging for me. I did not have a hard time accepting what the Roman Catholic church believed; I had a hard time leaving behind thirty-five years of a different doctrinal education in home, church and school. I also had a hard time differentiating myself from my family and friends. I can offer an analogy from another point of conflict between Kathleen and I that might help explain how I felt.

As you know, Kathleen earned her undergraduate degree from Michigan State University. I earned my law degree from the University of Michigan. She grew up a Michigan State fan; I grew up a Michigan fan. During the first few years of our marriage, we had season tickets to Michigan State basketball (hey, East Lansing is closer than Ann Arbor). When it came to watching basketball at Breslin, I became quite a Michigan State fan. I cheered as loudly as anyone else and I meant it-- except when Michigan State played Michigan. Then, even though it was the same Michigan State team on the floor and even though I tried to cheer for them, my heart would leap if Michigan did well and sink if Michigan State did well. Three decades of supporting the Maize and Blue had left an indelible imprint.

That is kind of what RCIA was like. I could understand the beliefs of the Roman Catholic Church, I could even like or prefer those beliefs. But, when they butted up against the Christian Reformed doctrine I had studied since I was a child, my upbringing tended to win out. I tried to explain all of this to Jim Wisnewski, part of the RCIA team, after class one night. I spent about five minutes describing some of the doctrinal differences and how ingrained my beliefs were. He put his hand on my shoulder, looked me in the eye, said "God is love," and walked away.

At the time I thought Jim's comment was less than helpful, but it stuck with me. As I ruminated upon it, I realized a few things. First, there was no way in the world I could blithely put behind me things I had been taught since I was a kid. Second, the fact that moving forward with RCIA was not easy did not mean that moving forward was wrong, particularly where the goal of bringing Kathleen and I together to present a united front to the world was a worthy one. Third, even if I would never be as good a Roman Catholic as I was a Protestant (because I could never go back and be brought up Roman Catholic) it did not mean I could not be a good Roman Catholic. Fourth and finally, God is love and I trusted He would judge my actions accordingly.

Much to my surprise, and Kathleen's, I continued through RCIA to completion. I was confirmed as part of the Easter vigil on Holy Saturday. I carried Anna on my shoulder as I participated in the Eucharistic celebration for the first time. I carried Anna with me every time thereafter as well. I so closely associate the celebration of the Eucharist with Anna, that even now, more than a year after she left us, I cannot make it through that part of the Mass without crying.

Kathleen, Anna and I with Jim Scales, my RCIA sponsor, and his wife Cheryl.

You are cordially invited to attend
an Investiture Ceremony
for the Honorable Kathleen Ann Feeney
Circuit Court Judge, 17th Judicial Circuit

The ceremony will take place at the
Gerald R. Ford Museum
303 Pearl N.W., Grand Rapids, Michigan,
on Friday, April 28, 2000

The doors will open at 5:00 p.m.
The ceremony will begin at 5:30 p.m.

Hors d'oeuvres and refreshments will be served
after the ceremony
The museum's exhibits will be available for your perusal
until the doors close at 8:30 p.m.

R.S.V.P. on or before April 21, 2000,
by telephone to
616-364-1068
or by e-mail to jeberner@iserv.net
Please indicate the number of people who plan to attend

We sent out hundreds of invitations.

Friday, April 28, 2000, 5:00 p.m.
The Investiture Ceremony

Close on the heels of our special celebration at Easter was our formal celebration of Kathleen's investiture. An investiture is the judicial version of an inauguration. Kathleen had already taken the oath of office in March, but it was hastily arranged to permit her to start working right away. We still needed to go through the formal ceremony with all the pomp and circumstance.

It was up to Anna and I to plan the ceremony and the reception that followed. We selected a location, arranged for a number of speakers, hired a caterer and a band, and prepared invitations and a program. We held the event at the Gerald R. Ford Presidential Museum in downtown Grand Rapids. We invited hundreds of colleagues, family, and friends. We were also honored by the presence of many elected and appointed officials.

Although Anna slept through a significant portion of the ceremony, she did wake up long enough to help me hold the Bible as Kathleen was sworn in. We will let the investiture program and the pictures tell the rest of the story.

State of Michigan
County of Kent
17th Judicial Circuit Court

Investiture Ceremony for the
Honorable Kathleen A. Feeney

April 28, 2000
Gerald R. Ford Museum
Grand Rapids, Michigan

Call to Court	. . . . **Ealry M. Lyons**
	Clerk to the Honorable
	Kathleen A. Feeney
Invocation	. . . . **Sr. Rosemary Smith**
	Principal, Assumption of the
	Blessed Virgin Mary School
Introductions	. . . . **John C. Stuive, Esq.**
Salutation	. . . . **Hon. John P. Steketee**
	Presiding Judge,
	Family Division,
	Kent County Circuit Court
Remarks	. . . . **Hon. Jane E. Markey**
	Michigan Court of Appeals
	Rep. Vernon J. Ehlers
	United States Representative
	3rd District of Michigan
	Dr. Liza A. Squires
	Director of Pediatric Neurology
	DeVos Children's Hospital

GERALD R. FORD

MUSEUM

Request for the
Oath of Office. . . . Hon. Stephen J. Markman

Michigan Supreme Court

Oath of Office . . . . Hon. Elizabeth A. Weaver

Chief Justice
Michigan Supreme Court

Presentation
of the Robe . . . . John C. Stuive, Esq. &
Anna Evaleen Stuive

Presentation
of the Gavel . . . . Lisa A. DeFerrari, Esq.

President, Women Lawyers
Ass'n of Michigan,
Western Region

Acknowledgment. . .Hon. Kathleen A. Feeney

Family Division
Kent County Circuit Court

Adjournment . . . . John C. Stuive, Esq.

Saturday, April 29, 2000, 4:12 p.m.
From: Anna's Dad
Subject: Sorry for the wait

I am sorry we have been so delinquent in our posts. The last few days have been a whirlwind of doctor's visits, therapy visits, conferences with the caterer, the musicians, and the museum personnel, preparing programs, drafting speeches, and, finally, the investiture itself. But now it is done. Last night was truly magical. We were honored by the presence of nearly three hundred guests, including state Supreme Court Justices, Court of Appeals Judges, Circuit Court judges, District Court judges, Federal judges, our United States Congessman, a couple of representatives from the state house, county officials, Anna's doctors, nurses, and therapists, as well as family, and friends. By the end of the evening Kathleen was positively glowing. Even Anna got in on the festivities; she helped present Kathleen with her robe. For the last two or three weeks, the investiture has been a huge wall that we were not able to see over. Now that it is done, we are pleased to be on vacation.

We will spend the next week in Wisconsin for the Bernese Mountain Dog National Specialty. That will be a welcome change of pace. Anna is thriving. We have achieved some level of control on her diet. She has stopped gaining weight so quickly. She continues to be as bright as she has ever been. Each day she seems to be a little more communicative and a little more active. She has really started to enjoy talking on the phone. When you put the phone to her ear she just starts cooing and squeaking as if she is reporting her day's activities to whomever is on the other end. When the listener talks back, Anna looks at the phone as if it is an enchanted device. She will now sit and play in her tumbleform chair for more than an hour at a time. Despite all of this activity, she is not taking longer naps. Her therapies are going well, she is still not very strong with her head, and she still cannot roll over, but we are becoming more hopeful.

Right now we are riding incredibly high. Anna is doing well. We just spent an evening which was packed with warm and positive feelings and emotions. You have been there for us when we were down and we want to be sure to share these good times as well. Thank you all.

Anna's Dad

Chapter 8
The Summer

All of the transitions of the Spring yielded to the steady warmth of the Summer. Usually, when I think of Summer I think of June, July, and August. Technically, of course, Summer begins with the summer solstice on June 21 and ends on the autumnal equinox on September 21. Even that is not entirely correct. In the southern hemisphere Summer starts on December 21 and ends on March 21.

The fact that definitions of "Summer" are somewhat variable works well for us. Our Summer with Anna stretched from the beginning of May to the end of September. It corresponded roughly with the warm weather, but that is not why we called it the Summer. It was our Summer because, other than a little cold at the beginning, it corresponded exactly with a period of time that was very sunny and steadily pleasant for Anna.

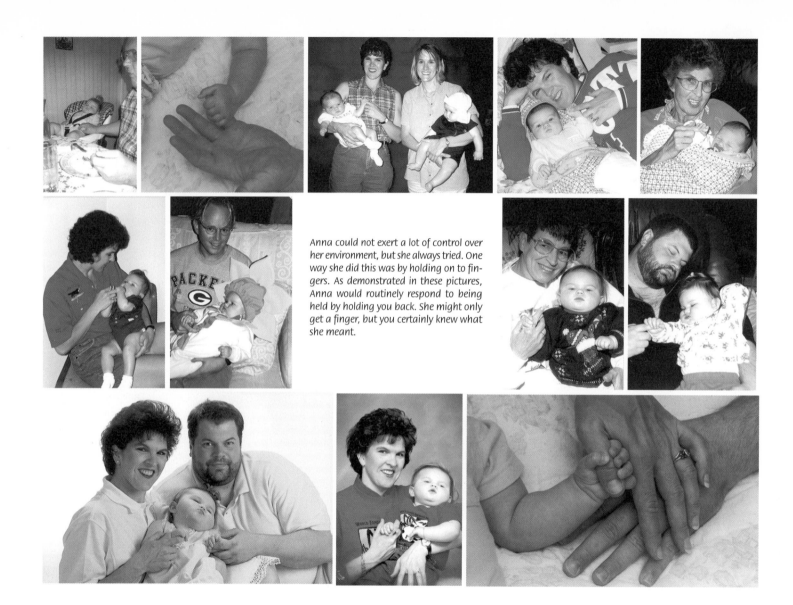

Anna could not exert a lot of control over her environment, but she always tried. One way she did this was by holding on to fingers. As demonstrated in these pictures, Anna would routinely respond to being held by holding you back. She might only get a finger, but you certainly knew what she meant.

Thursday, May 4, 2000, 11:37 p.m.
From: Anna's Dad
Subject: Thursday-dog days

Well, I should be coming to you from the wilds of Wisconsin where the 2000 Bernese Mountain Dog National Specialty Show is in full swing. Instead, I am coming to you from beautiful Belmont, Michigan.

We have returned home a few days early because things were not going all that well. The second day out, Anna began to cough and gag very miserably. We ended up taking her to the Med Center in Wisconsin. They took x-rays and listened to her chest. She was running a mild fever so they figured it was some sort of viral infection. We put her on antibiotics. That night, however, she was up almost all night with breathing problems. We decided we were better served to come home. We are going to see the pulmonologist tomorrow.

Once we decided to go home and once we started packing, Anna seemed much better. Although she still has a nasty cough, she has not gagged for some time and she is in very good spirits. I think either Anna caught her infection from me or we both caught it from the same source, because I have had some of the same symptoms. The place we were staying was beautiful, but it was an old resort. It is possible the somewhat antiquated air handling systems left something to be desired and both Anna and I suffered because of it. I am fine now, so Anna will probably be fine as well in a couple of days.

Anna was not our only patient. Yesterday, as we hurried to pull everything together to go to the Med Center, Kathleen shut her thumb in the sliding door of the van. Normally that is something I do to my thumb, but this role reversal thing is going a long ways. She fractured the tip of her thumb and they had to burn through her thumbnail to relieve the pressure. Although we thought Kathleen was otherwise in good health, she also got sick on the way home today. Under the circumstances, we are just glad to be home where at least we know the doctors.

Despite the tale of woe above, we did manage to enjoy many of the wonderful things we normally associate with the national specialty. We saw a lot of old friends,

For the second time we found ourselves in a situation where we were far from home and where no one knew anything about Anna's condition. Because Anna had such a rare disease, emergency room doctors were somewhat befuddled regarding how they should deal with us. Once they had an opportunity to check their medical databases and confirm what we told them, they were less skeptical and much more engaging.

At the specialty, Anna finally got to meet Ruth Nielsen and Max (Ruby's boyfriend) from Seattle. We have enjoyed the company of Ruth and Max at national specialty shows in Estes Park, Colorado and Warwick, Rhode Island.

Whenever Anna had problems breathing we would pursue a therapy called "percussive thumping." It involved thumping her chest, side, and back with a rubbery cup-like device. Whenever we first started this therapy Anna would look at us like we were crazy. After a couple of minutes, however, she seemed to find the rhythm of it soothing.

Anna, Jasper and I are enjoying the breed competition at ringside. Our shade was on the far end of a virtual tent city created by the shelters of fellow Bernese Mountain Dog fanciers from Michigan. These friends included the Torstensons and the Becktels who started the Anna's Friends mailing list.

a lot of berners, a lot of beautiful scenery, and ate a lot of food. Of course, we were hoping for a few more days' worth of all of these things, but right now I will settle for a couple of good night's of sleep in our own bed.

Good night.
Anna's Dad

Greetings to all of Anna's friends on this beautiful, sunny Mother's Day! We are glad to report that our absence from your e-mail this week has merely signified the hectic pace of our schedules these days.

Anna is doing well—much better than a week ago this time. She is sitting in the sunshine that streams through our picture window, entranced by the helium balloons that she masterfully controls via the ribbons in her hands. Her chest congestion, coughing and gagging spells are few and far between these days, so we suspect that she is on the mend. Thanks to all of you for your extra special prayers to help her get over this infection. Considering that this was only her second cold in 14 months, we are doing quite well.

Anna treated me to a wonderful Mother's Day gift by buying me some roses (she picked the color by kicking at the bunch she liked the most) and helping me paint a ceramic heart box at Clay Art Studio, the site of Anna's first birthday party. John, ever organizing our lives and Anna's meds via colored caps for her oral medication syringes, painted little jars with the same colors as the caps. Now we are organized and color coordinated!

Later on Saturday we took Anna to the home of our good friends, Mike, Sheri and Brianna, for a few hours so John and I could attend a fundraiser at the Amway Grand Plaza for Spectrum Health's Pastoral Program. We benefitted greatly from the talented and caring people who comprise this pastoral group, and we enjoyed the opportunity to honor them.

Additionally, we decided to treat the event as our "prom," because neither one of us ever really did the prom thing in high school. With John in his tux and me in the blue formal we purchased Friday night, we had a wonderful time. We even danced a bit before heading home. All in all, it was a wonderful start to this Mother's Day weekend.

Despite our best intentions to head North and spend today with family, we are woefully behind in our housekeeping chores and are somewhat exhausted from

While we attended our "prom," Anna stayed with Mike and Sheri Volkhardt and Brianna. Anna was certainly no stranger to the Volkhardt home. Sheri took care of Anna on Fridays during the summer of 1999 before she was diagnosed. Anna loved visiting her buddy Brianna.

the harried pace of life, so we decided to delay the trip for a week. To our Moms and all the Moms out there, we send our prayers that you will have a wonderful Mother's Day and that God's grace will be with you every day of the year.

As Anna slept in my arms this morning, I could not help but feel that my arms were wrapped around the manifestation of God's blessings upon us and I felt the warmth of His light shining in her face. What a gift!

God bless you all. Love,
Anna's Mom

Greetings from Anna's house. We have been busy caring for Anna since our last post. She recovered well from her viral infection and used up all her antibiotics. But she must have known that we were leaving home again for the weekend, so she decided that we needed another medical problem to keep us busy while we were on the road. This time the gastric tube became infected. It was quite a sight and seemed to cause our sweetie a lot of discomfort, but the doctors were not overly concerned. We have her on another round of antibiotics and things seem to be progressing beautifully. It is odd that in 14 months, she would come down with two infections in the same month. Maybe we have just been lucky until now.

Most recently, we have noticed that Anna has been very active, almost overactive during the day. The movement of her arms and legs seems to reflect uncontrolled or unchanneled energy and it is difficult to discern whether she is excited or in distress. We are taking steps to capture these "sessions" on tape so the docs can see what we are seeing. This is a very recent development, one we had hoped could be related to something else, such as the new DCA refill we just received (i.e., did they accidentally switch the form of DCA that Anna is currently taking now?). No such luck. So we are back to scratching our heads and trying to make these active times as fun and enjoyable as possible for Anna.

It is hard to convey just how much these sorts of situations can steal comfort and calm from our lives, but we gain strength from all of your continued prayers. The feeling we get when we hear that you and your children always remember us and Anna in your prayers is indescribable. Please keep up the good work!

Anna is requesting my attention, so I must close. She sends chubby cheeked kisses to all of her Friends!

Much love,
Anna's Mom

Anna gets a massage from her Opa.

Often it was difficult to know if a new behavior in Anna was a sign of improvement or a symptom of her disease. Shortly after the diagnosis Anna used to nap for long periods. At first we were happy that she could get peaceful and undisturbed sleep without "night terrors." Later, we learned that the seizures occurring in her brain would make her sleepy. Then, we perceived long naps much differently.

The new medications that followed our trips to San Diego made Anna more awake and alert, and she moved around a lot more. That made us happy. Eventually, however, that movement turned into jerky motions with her arms and legs. That again bespoke seizures. When the positive and negative are so close together it keeps you on your toes.

Saturday, May 27, 2000, 8:55 p.m.
From: Anna's Mom
Subject: Memorial Day weekend begins

Yes, it is Memorial Day Weekend and it is raining. So we went shopping. Success: we located several Gerber brand "Wrap and Snap" onesies in the extra-large size that Anna loves! We had called the manufacturer and had searched high and low for these onesies, so this was a great coup for us. (It does not take much to get us excited these days.)

We also visited the Sears Photo Center where I had my "judicial" photo taken in my robe (the photographer was very nervous) and Anna posed with me for a few shots. We will try to load these photos on the web site very soon.

Anna has been a big "tickle bug" for the last few days. When Dad tickles her chest, she almost giggles as she squirms and gives Dad big open mouth "Aaaahhhhhs." It is so fun to see her responding to this stimulus. She is still focusing on faces and voices, which is great, and her frantic movements have been fewer and farther between lately. Thanks for all the extra prayers in this direction.

In response to a recent post, I am pleased to inform you that I will be on the ballot in Kent County this November with NO opposition! This is truly a blessing and we are very excited that I am running unopposed. It was impossible to predict how things would play out and I was expecting some competition. I owe my judge, who predicted that I would have no opposition, a nice lunch. My pleasure.

Anna is snoozing in her Dad's arms right now with her right hand up next to the side of her head; this is her favorite sleeping position. She did the same thing at the store today and attracted a lot of smiles from fellow shoppers. What a cutie.

Here is hoping for sunshine by Monday so we can work in the gardens.

Love to all,

Anna's mom

Wednesday, May 31, 2000, 10:49 p.m
From: Anna's Mom
Subject: Wednesday-Ohio bound

Just a quick note to let you know that we are off to Cleveland on Thursday after I am done with court at Juvenile Hall for a seminar hosted by the Cleveland Clinic and the United Mitochondrial Disease Foundation (UMDF) regarding mitochondrial problems. Our specialists from the MMDC will be presenting and Anna's neurologist will be attending, as will 3 other families from this area.

The docs meet on Thursday and Friday and the families attend Friday and Saturday, so there is some overlap with the presentations. I am hoping that we will meet other families dealing with NARP causing Leigh's Syndrome, but I will not be disappointed if we do not. It should prove to be an interesting event.

Anna has been having some brief sessions that we are hard pressed to explain. She can be calm one minute, straightening out her arms and legs the next, and then act very agitated and frantic later in the day. None of these activities is regular or predictable. We hope that repeating the MRI and EEG will give us some clues. No dates for those tests yet.

Anna seems unaffected, overall, by these blips on the radar. They give us pause, however. It is amazing how quickly things can change, is it not? Enough for now. We will begin work soon on a follow up letter to Anna's Friends. Look for it in your mail boxes some time in June.

Take care. Love,
Anna's mom

UNITED MITOCHONDRIAL DISEASE FOUNDATION

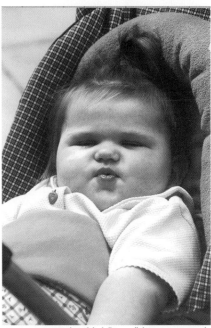

We never sent the third "Anna" letter. We made several drafts, but as we completed each draft we would decide that we wanted to include some event that was coming up in the next couple of weeks, so it would be put off again. At the end of August we had a completed draft ready to go. We just never sent it.

To keep Anna from getting bored, we took her to Festival 2000. Festival is an annual arts festival that takes over downtown Grand Rapids for a weekend at the beginning of summer. Festival proved to be another comforting event. We just pulled off to the side and watched the thousands of celebrants go by. It was important to us to be a part of the world around us rather than separating ourselves from it.

Thursday, June 1, 2000, 12:53 p.m.
From: Anna's Dad
Subject: It's me again

Well, today is A-day. My first real day with Anna as a stay-at-home dad. Of course, there have been other days along the way where I played that role, but now it is my career. To be honest, I must confess some trepidation about this career shift. Perhaps it is a guy thing, but it is hard to describe who you are without describing what you do for a living. Although I know taking care of Anna is a noble calling, it is certainly a very different calling than the one I was pursuing up until today.

To help me get used to my new duties, I would appreciate it if all of you could let me know what you do during the day with your kids and how you schedule the housework you have to do around taking care of a baby. I can tell you that so far we are doing well, but I think Anna is getting bored with me.

Anna's Dad

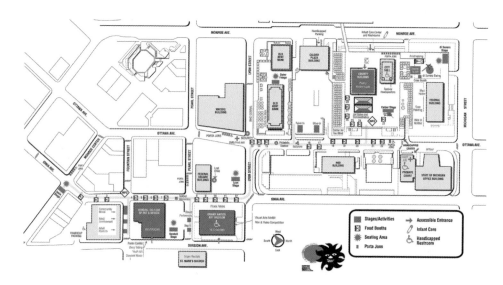

We are now about a week into this grand experiment. So far so good. Last weekend we traveled to Cleveland to attend a seminar put on by the United Mitochondrial Disease Foundation. We did not learn a lot of new stuff, but we did get the opportunity to meet many other people whose lives have been touched by mitochondrial disease. That alone was worth the trip. On Sunday, Anna made an appearance on the Children's Miracle Network Telethon, at least on the local part of it. She was, as usual, a star. We are starting to establish a routine. It feels pretty comfortable. Thank you all for your tips. Anna is doing well. Right now she is complaining that I should spend some time with her rather than the computer. I will comply.

Anna's Dad

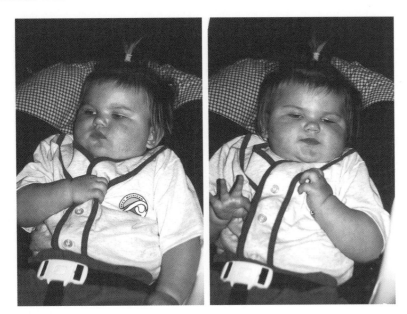

Dr. Squires, Kathleen, Anna and I told Brian Sterling of WOOD TV-8 about Anna. During the Children's Miracle Network telethon, they tend to focus on kids that get better. But, those kids are not the only miracles. It meant a lot to us to show the world that Anna was a miracle too, even if she was not going to get better.

Sunday, June 4, 2001, 2:00 p.m.
Children's Miracle Network Telethon Interview Excerpt

BRIAN STERLING: Joining us now is pediatric neurologist Dr. Liza Squires, Judge Kathleen Feeney, and John and Anna Stuive. We would like to welcome all of you here today. . . . Now Kathleen and John, how did DeVos Children's Hospital ease the pain and confusion for you when you heard the news that Anna had Leigh's Syndrome?

KATHLEEN: We had one particular nurse, Laura Wagner, down in the radiology department. She knew what was going on behind the scenes, even before we knew. Even though I had just met her that day, she stayed with us long after she went off the clock that evening. She stayed with us for three or four hours and came up to the room with us. When we couldn't even think straight she wrote out a list of things that we could say to people on the phone--an actual script that we could speak over the phone to people and say this is what is going on. Without that, we couldn't have made it through the first 24 hours.

BRIAN STERLING: Because too many things were going on?

KATHLEEN: Yes. When you find out that your daughter isn't going to have a normal life, there is nothing else that you can think about. Without the caring and understanding of Dr. Squires and Laura that first day, those first few days, we never would have made it.

BRIAN STERLING: I understand that you have a message that you want to pass along to the viewers at home?

KATHLEEN: We ask all parents to think about how wonderful it is that their children can walk and talk and smile. Anna cannot do those things. Think about what that smile is worth, and then call in and make a pledge. On behalf of Anna, and everyone who has supported us, we are pleased to present this check to Children's Miracle Network.

BRIAN STERLING: And I am very pleased to accept it. Thank you very much for sharing your story.

Well, it has been a busy weekend. Anna did a lot of shopping, went to a parade, a carnival, and Lake Michigan. Now she is sitting on Oma's lap playing with her balloons. The judge is busy judging; she is doing homework signing the dozens of proposed orders that pile up. All in all, it has been a very good weekend for Anna. She looks so sweet right now. I am just enjoying it.

Anna's Dad.

Anna's favorite toys were balloons, but when you are outside or driving around balloons are not the easiest toy to handle. Accordingly, Anna's second favorite toys were ribbons. She would comb her fingers through ribbons for hours. Here, she is holding a pom-pon of mylar ribbon.

Friday, June 16, 2000, 10:51 a.m.
From: Anna's Dad
Subject: Friday-prelude to Dad's Day

Opa and Anna in Opa's garden.

This photo gives you some sense for the mechanics of feeding Anna, although here we do not have the aid of the feeding chair.

It is only two days until Father's Day. I have been reminding Anna every day. She seems a little indifferent. Actually yesterday she was quite grumpy. From about 2:00 p.m. until she went to bed she basically just whined and complained. Since she woke up today, however, she has been in excellent spirits.

We have a list of tasks to accomplish today (as we do every day) and she is anxious to get going. There are many things running through my mind as I contemplate Father's Day. Rather than putting those thoughts into words, I want to paint a picture for you that kind of sums up all of the thoughts.

Last night Opa and Oma stopped over. Their excuse for stopping by was to drop off some of their homegrown strawberries, but Anna and I know they just wanted to see Anna. In fact, I have never seen the alleged strawberry plants that supposedly produced these strawberries. They could be buying them at Meijer for all we know. Either way, the strawberries and the company are always welcome.

Because it was feeding time shortly after they dropped in, they agreed to feed Anna. Standard procedure to feed Anna is to hook up the tube to her button and then hook up a 2 ounce syringe to the tube. Then, you pour some formula into the syringe and wait as gravity takes it in little by little. As the syringe empties, you fill it up again until the contents of the bottle are all in Anna's stomach.

We do not put a top on the syringe while we feed Anna. That has led to many spills but we have not come up with a top to put on the syringe that permits the formula to flow. Opa and Oma were sitting on the couch as they fed Anna who was in her reclining high chair. Opa held the syringe while Oma controlled the flow and filled the syringe.

Ruby and Jasper were trading off chomping on a rawhide; thus, they were not particularly interested in anyone or anything else. Ultimately, Ruby and Jasper started to quarrel about who had the bigger piece of bone. In the interests of peace I took the bone away and told them to just lay down and be quiet.

Once the rawhide was gone, everything else in the world moved up one notch on the Jasper priority list. After rawhides, typically, Jasper's first priority is Opa. Unfortunately, Opa was busy feeding Anna. In the hope that he could interest Opa in some roughhousing, Jasper was pleased to show Opa a new trick. Jasper snuck over to Opa's side and laid his head peacefully on Anna's high chair. Realizing that the syringe was consuming too much of Opa's attention, Jasper snuck his nose under the bottom of the vertical syringe and flipped it quickly up into the air.

It is a credit to my father that the syringe never actually left his hand. Because of the rapid movement, however, it was unavoidable that a lot of formula left the syringe. Although the formula splattered the walls, the couch, and the pillows (a couple of drops even landed on Anna), most of the formula landed directly on Opa's head. It must have landed right in the middle of the top of his head because it seemed to flow evenly in all directions. That is the picture I want you to see, my dad with what looked like a cap made of viscous yellow formula dripping down his face. I provide you that picture not because it was comical (even though it definitely was comical), but because of what came next.

In the midst of formula dripping off everything, barking and jumping dogs, and parents rushing in with towels, Opa's concern was only for Anna. He quickly determined to the milliliter exactly how much formula had escaped and with formula dripping off his face asked how we could replace that amount of formula.

I think that is lot of what it means to be a Dad. No matter how silly you look or what level of chaos you have descended to, your first concern is always for your child (or grandchild).

Thanks Dad. Happy Father's day.
Anna's Dad

Oma and Opa visiting with Anna.

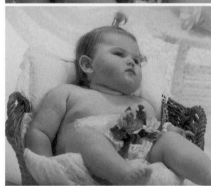

Monday, June 19, 2000, 11:03 a.m.
From: Anna's Dad
Subject: Monday

Whew, it is finally Monday. I know that sounds a little strange, but for Anna and I Mondays are pretty pleasant. We kind of meander our way through the week at Anna's pace. Anna's pace includes a lot of appointments and such, but other than that it is a pretty easy pace.

On weekends, on the other hand, we all move at Kathleen's pace. Kathleen's pace is very fast and moves in many different directions at the same time. That is not a criticism. That is part of what makes Kathleen Kathleen. So rather than having the "Sunday dreads" and the "Monday blues," Anna and I have the "Sunday tireds" and the "Monday laid backs."

This weekend included an extended photo session with a photographer in Rockford. It was kind of a combined Father's day/Kathleen's birthday present. We have to wait two weeks for the pictures. It is quite possible Kathleen's head will pop off if we actually have to wait that long. We also did a lot of shopping, a lot of yard work, painted windows on the house, made a bunch of strawberry jam, and attended two graduation open houses.

Today, Anna and I are perfectly content to just look at each other and wonder where Mom gets all of that energy. Fortunately, the next weekend is five days away.
Anna's Dad

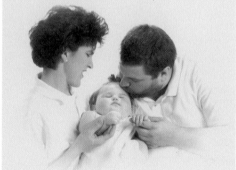

Thursday, June 22, 2000, 2:32 p.m.
From: Anna's Dad
Subject: Thursday-softball

In my new routine, Thursday is the day I finish the laundry that I could not finish on Wednesday. Thus, Thursday is pretty much a stay at home day. Yesterday was Kathleen's birthday. We celebrated by getting quotes for replacing our roof, which is shot. What fun.

Today is the traditional charity softball game between the local women lawyers and the local judges. For years, Kathleen has been a mainstay on the side of the women lawyers. This year, she will move to the other team. In the interests of justice, however, and based on the precedent set by Judge Sara Smolenski, Kathleen will play the first half of the game for the lawyers and the second half for the judges. If you would like to see Kathleen betray her teammates, the game is at Riverside Park at 6:00 p.m.

Anna is doing well. She is just starting to stretch after her post lunch nap (that is nap 3 on her usual 6-a-day nap schedule; it is a short one usually lasting about five minutes). As she awakes she is kind of whining that I am not immediately available to satisfy her need to complain face-to-face about the poor service she gets now that Aunt Lauran is not taking care of her anymore. I think I will let her stew in her own juices for a minute while I finish this post.

Again, Anna is doing well. I am almost afraid to say it, but we are settling into a routine of expecting things to be this good for a long time. We seem to be over the infections that troubled us in May and the beginning of this month. We are looking at almost a month before any doctor appointments, although we continue with regular physical therapy and occupational therapy.

We are also having a good drawn out battle in Blue Cross's internal appeal procedures because they absolutely refuse to pay for speech therapy, occupational therapy, or physical therapy. According to them, because Anna has no meaningful hope for improvement it is incredibly wasteful to pursue those therapies. Our doctors say otherwise. I almost cannot wait to sue them after we exhaust their internal appellate procedures. I plan to make the entire procedure very personal.

Anna's mom at bat for the judges' team.

There are no words to describe the frustration in having someone at your insurance company tell you that procedures and therapies essential to your child's care, comfort, and health are not covered basically because your child is not going to live very long. So, your child is dying and your insurance company is denying coverage as a result. You just want to scream and attack them through the telephone lines. That of course is pointless. We learned that it is best to speak calmly and rationally. Eventually you get to the right person.

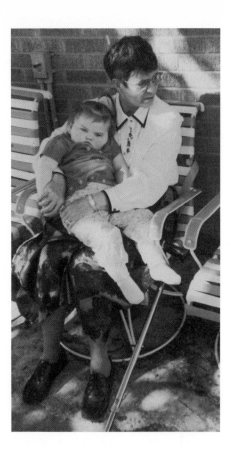

On a lighter note, we had some work done on the windows in our home over the past few months. The contractor finished on Tuesday. To prepare for the last task, we had to paint the trim on five windows. Over the weekend we diligently taped and painted the windows. It took several coats because we were putting a light color over a dark color. Each time we did a coat, we had to open and close the paint can. Even though we did five coats, there was still a lot of paint left because it was only used for trim on five windows.

After the fourth coat, Kathleen showed me a neat trick for closing the paint can tight. You just stand on it. After the fifth and final coat, I thought I would try this trick. Guess what, although a gallon paint can will hold the weight of one Circuit Court Judge, it will not hold the weight of her husband. As I stood in the puddle of latex paint created by the disintegrated paint can, I realized that I truly am a man of substance. I know Anna thinks so.

Anna's Dad

Friday, June 30, 2000, 10:06 a.m.
From: Anna's Dad
Subject: Friday-independence

Ah, Friday morning before the Fourth of July. The beginning of a holiday weekend always holds a lot of promise. In the spirit of the season, Anna and I have been watching a series of shows on the American Revolution. Although I am amazed at the sacrifice our forefathers (and foremothers) were willing to make in the name of freedom, Anna remains unimpressed.

Right now, Anna is fighting hard to stay awake. It is a battle she fights every morning after she eats. That is usually when I work on the computer. I pull her chair over to the computer. She watches the screen for a couple of minutes and then her eyelids start to flutter. Then, she begins to smack her arms around and grunt and groan a little. It is apparent that she wants to hang out and work on the computer with me.

Though the spirit is willing, the flesh is weak. Her eyes pop open and she kicks her legs in the hope of beating it back, but eventually her breathing gets very even, her eyes fall shut, and she settles into a very peaceful place. This cycle repeats two or three times until she is gone for good.

Once she is sleeping soundly, I feel a little better about focusing on something other than her for a little while. Even though my focus shifts, I am compelled to turn back to her every couple of minutes because she looks so content while she sleeps.

Ruby usually curls up at my feet while I work on the computer. She is definitely an inside dog. Actually, she does not think she is a dog at all. That is why she looks so forlorn when she has to go outside with that dog, Jasper. Jasper, on the other hand, can only stand being inside for a little bit in the morning. After about an hour of peaceful behavior or until our neighbor, John Kolenbrander, walks his Pekinese, Suki, down the lane, Jasper becomes adamant about going outside. Once outside, he barks a couple of times to let the neighborhood know that he is on sentry duty, then he lays down and stands guard for the balance of the morning.

These folks are our neighbors John and Mary Jane Kolenbrander. Because Anna's Great-Grandparents were all in heaven, John and Mary Jane agreed to fill that role on earth. You could not ask for better Great-Grandparents or neighbors.

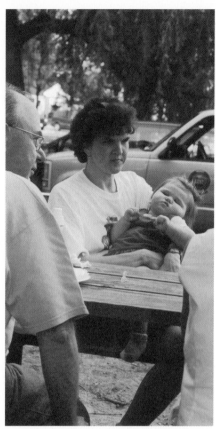
Anna and her mom at the court picnic.

When Ruby is outside, she always complains until we let her back in. When Jasper is outside, he is working and, apparently, it is work he enjoys.

Anna is in a pretty deep sleep now. She must dream, because she clenches and unclenches her fists and kicks her feet. I imagine she is in the middle of a fist fight with someone at Blue Cross Blue Shield. I am betting she will win.

Happy Fourth of July to all of you. Happy birthday to my judge.

Anna's Dad

Anna is snoring away, so I have a couple of minutes to write. If you saw my refrigerator you would cry.

As with most refrigerators, ours is covered with magnets and photos and notes except for the bottom couple of feet (which we are all too lazy to reach and which dog tails clean off on a regular basis). Not surprisingly, our refrigerator is a shrine to our family. Of course the prime spots on the freezer door and the refrigerator door are dedicated to Anna, but Ruby and Jasper are also well represented.

Many of you have already seen the thank you magnets we made with Anna's pictures printed on them. There are at least thirty different magnet/pictures in addition to the dozens of pictures that are held on by separate magnets acquired from God-knows-where over our lifetimes.

It is hard to just walk by our refrigerator without spending a couple of minutes tracing our past through the pictures on the fridge. In that way, our refrigerator satisfies the same need that prompted our ancient ancestors to make cave paintings. I have no doubt that your refrigerator serves the same purpose.

But today, our refrigerator is different. Today I finished a project I have been working on for a few weeks. Since about the beginning of June, I have been scanning the 6x6 tiles that friends and family painted at Anna's first birthday party. They scanned beautifully, just like photos. The scans were the first step towards my goal of making a poster so more people could see the tiles. (They are otherwise displayed in the office of the Honorable Kathleen A. Feeney. But if you are like me, the less time you spend in a family law judge's office the better, so not many have had a chance to see the display.)

Because there are more than one hundred tiles, I wanted an opportunity to see how different arrangements of the tiles would look before committing to a particular arrangement in the poster. Doing that with the tiles themselves is a little cumbersome; they are heavy, somewhat fragile, and take up more than 25 square feet when laid out together. Accordingly, I printed the scans in color on magnetic

paper, about 1/4 scale, and cut each one out. I finished printing and cutting today and then realized I needed a surface to work on. Of course, the fridge.

I cleared the refrigerator door by squeezing everything else onto the freezer and the sides of the box. Then I started laying out my mini-magnetic tiles. They now cover nearly the entire door, they even encroach onto no-man's land at the bottom. Let me assure you we now have the most beautiful refrigerator in the world. The only way to see these tiles and the love they represent is to see them all together. It is stunning. It is our version of the ceiling of the Sistine Chapel.

If you saw my refrigerator you would cry. I did.
Anna's Dad

Thursday, July 20, 2000, 10:21 a.m.
From: Anna's Dad
Subject: Thursday-peanuts and crackerjack

Well, I haven't posted for a while. In this instance, no news is good news. Things have been very quiet around here. Anna is doing well. Ruby is doing well. Jasper is doing well. Kathleen is doing well. I am doing well.

We found out this week that my insurance is going to pay at least a substantial portion of the occupational therapy and physical therapy charges starting in January of this year. That takes a little bit of pressure off in that Kath's insurance had denied benefits for those charges since last November. There will still be some to pay (assuming we do not win our fight with Kath's insurance) but it will be less.

Our preparations for our next trip to San Diego are underway. We are leaving August 5 and returning August 12. To avoid some of the tests there, we are doing them here before we go. Anna will undergo her MRI, MRS and LP on the 26th of this month and an EEG on the 30th.

I continue to learn what it means to be a stay-at-home dad. This week's most exciting event was a poopy diaper which I attempted to change in the parking lot of a local retail store. Halfway through I ran out of wipes. I am not going to tell you what I used instead. I am sure all of you moms are shuddering just thinking of the possibilities.

This stay-at-home thing has led to some startling changes in my outlook on life. First, although it used to be no big deal if the dishes got done tomorrow, now it is incredibly stupid to leave them even twenty minutes after a meal. Second, I now measure Kathleen's dedication to the family by how much time she spends working. The longer she works, the less dedicated she is to her family, obviously. If she really cared, she would be home promptly at 5:15 and she would not bring work home. I know that is not at all fair but I find myself thinking it anyway. Oh well, at least she is a good provider.

At Anna's first baseball game we sat between home plate and first base. Anna sat in her blue chair on the bleachers. She insisted on buying a Whitecaps jersey. She wore it all the time, even though they did not win that night. This jersey and her baseball pants constituted her favorite pajamas.

Anna went to her first baseball game last Saturday. We think she liked it. Normally in crowd situations she just shuts down: she closes her eyes and goes to sleep. She was up for nearly the whole game. She even saw part of it from the Mika, Meyers, Beckett & Jones skybox. Now that she has attended a sporting event without incident, I think we will try football next.

Anna's Dad

	R	H	E
Silver Hawks	8	9	1
Whitecaps	3	6	2

Thursday, July 20, 2000, 11:42 p.m.
From: Anna's Mom
Subject: Thursday

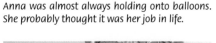

Anna was almost always holding onto balloons.
She probably thought it was her job in life.

Anna's Dad's provider here. Just wanted to let you know that I am busy providing, getting people divorced with as little conflict as possible, and trying to prevent young offenders from becoming adult offenders. It is all in a day's work. On the flip side, Anna's Dad has made tremendous strides at home and has turned out to be quite the homemaker. I am so proud of him! He still has not discovered day-time soaps and I hope he never does. Again, thanks for the prayers.

We are getting a bit anxious about the tests next week but we are very glad that we can have these tests performed here in Grand Rapids. We are in good hands in every way.

Anna is calling from the bedroom where Dad has fallen asleep but she is still ready to play. I must intervene.

Anna sends chubby-cheeked kisses to all her friends.

Always,
Anna's Mom

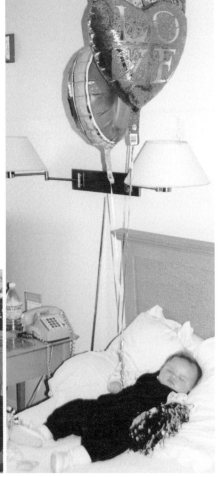

On the night of the 20th I went to my parents' church with Anna to talk to the Vacation Bible School kids. The VBS kids had adopted Anna as one of their projects. They brought in pennies for her, thousands and thousands of pennies.

The kids were fascinated by Anna. They all wanted to see her button. While I was talking, one of the people from the audience came up and approached Anna and me. She was a participant in the church's Friendship Ministry which is directed to developmentally disabled adults. This woman walked up to us and touched Anna on the face. Then, she handed me a fistful of crumpled dollar bills and change. It must have been everything she had. I do not know if she understood Anna's story, but she gave nonetheless. It was another one of the unbelievably generous gifts we received. The kids as a group raised nearly six hundred dollars in pennies, but they gave us so much more than that.

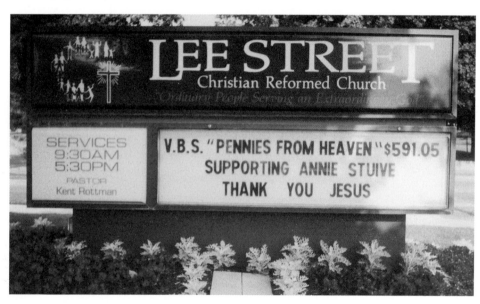

Sunday, July 23, 2000, 7:29 p.m.
From: Anna's Mom
Subject: Sunday–just relaxing

Anna and Dad are relaxing in their big chair playing with balloons and enjoying what is left of our Sunday. It has been a wonderfully lazy day. We watched Tiger Woods make golf history while we did chores around the house. We ran errands and took the family for a walk in the park. We stopped for Buster Bars at Dairy Queen. As I said, it has been a wonderfully lazy day!

I am beginning to think forward (something I try not to do) and contemplate what will happen on Wednesday when we take Anna to the hospital at 6:00 a.m. The tests may take the better part of the day and Anna will be anesthetized during all three procedures (lumbar puncture, MRI and MRS, the latter being the Magnetic Resonance Spectroscopy). We do not know how she will respond to the extended anesthesia but we know and trust Anna's anesthesiologist and that is a comfort.

The thought of going to San Diego in two weeks is also somewhat overwhelming. First, where has the summer gone? Second, has Anna been on the DCA for six months already? Third, what will the new DCA dosage do for Anna? The questions go on and on. Maybe I am just being reflective because it is Sunday night. Who knows. I need to hold and kiss my sweet baby, so I will sign off now.

Keep up the good work and prayers!

Much love,

Anna's Mom

This is Dr. Dan Visser, Anna's anesthesiologist. He stayed with Anna every step of the way when she underwent the tests during the summer of 2000. He would talk to Anna and kiss her on the cheek as if she were his own daughter. We do not doubt for a minute that Dr. Visser loved Anna. Dr. Visser really understood the special needs of his pediatric patients and their families. Although we were always concerned when Anna had to be knocked out for a procedure, we always knew she was in good hands with Dr. Visser.

Wednesday, July 26, 2000, 9:39 p.m.
From: Anna's Dad
Subject: A long day

I will start with the end of the story. Anna's tests went well. It took her a long time to wake up, but other than that it was an uneventful experience.

The MRI results are interesting. A comparison between today's images and those taken last September reveal some improvements in the areas that previously showed "signal changes." Put simply, Anna's brain is in better shape today than it was several months ago. It appears that this is attributable to the experimental drug, the DCA. That is good news.

Anna's lumbar puncture revealed a lactic acid of 2.7 which is just above the normal range and an improvement over the levels her cerebrospinal fluid has shown in the past. It is much higher, however, than the levels that have been in her blood.

This day started at 5:00 a.m. There has been a lot of "hurry up and wait." We are glad it is over. Next up is an EEG and a Brainstem Auditory Evoked Response test on Monday. Thanks again for your thoughts and prayers and keep us in mind again on Monday.

Anna's Dad

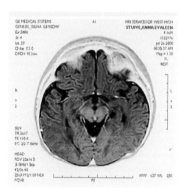 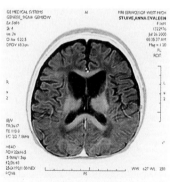 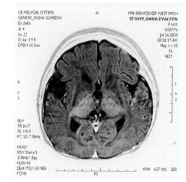 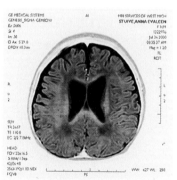

We have had an interesting weekend and there are certainly stories to tell, but that does not feel right. Sunday nights conjure up such mixed feelings. A little bit of sadness that the fun of the weekend is over and a little bit of sadness that work starts again the next day. Actually, those feelings are not mixed at all. Sunday nights are always kind of sad. Tonight is no exception.

We had so many things to get done this weekend. We did not finish them all, in large part because the weather did not cooperate. It was a rainy and dreary day. So there is a feeling of failure in the air.

We also watched a sad movie tonight, *The Green Mile*. We did not know much about the film. It was very good, but it was a movie about living and dying. Sometimes movies like that are hard to assimilate into our day-to-day struggle with those topics.

And, Anna had a seizure today. The first in a long time. Thus, it is kind of a sad night.

Anna is having an EEG tomorrow. If she is starting to have new seizure problems, we should see it on the EEG. The test is, therefore, certainly timely. We will keep you posted.

Anna's Dad

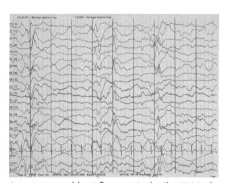

Poor Anna could not figure out why the EEG technicians wanted to make red marks with a pencil all over her head and then put paste in her hair. She had at least three of these procedures during her life, and she never seemed to get used to them. When her head was wrapped tightly with the gauze to keep the electrodes in place, she looked irresistibly cute.

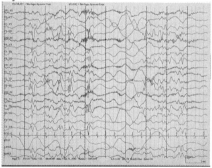

Monday, July 31, 2000, 3:16 p.m.
From: Anna's Dad
Subject: Monday

It is 3:00 p.m. and it has already been a long day. We got up early to get Anna to the hospital for her EEG and BAER (Brainstem Auditory Evoked Response) test. We tried to do both without sedation because Anna has such a hard time with most sedatives. Instead, we waited for her to fall into a deep sleep.

They got Anna all hooked up with about 30 electrodes on her head and then they wrapped her head like a mummy with gauze so she would not pull the electrodes off. All you could see was her angelic face.

Anna, however, decided this morning was not the morning to be an angel. If we wanted her to sleep she wanted to be awake. We sat for almost two hours singing lullabies and stroking her face and arms and wrapping her tight in a blanket and curling up next to her on the bed. We tried everything, but she would not sleep. She was rocking and rolling.

Finally, she tired herself out and she drifted off. They were able to complete the EEG, but every time they gave her the auditory stimulus for the BAER test, she would wake up. Eventually, we decided we would be willing to try sedation, but by then we were running so late they could not spend any more time on us. Oh well. At least it is one test we do not have to do in San Diego.

Anna has now had a quick shampoo to get the electrode goop out of her hair and she is once again ready to play. Thanks for your prayers. Monday feels a lot better than Sunday did.

Anna's Dad

We were just discharged from the Metabolic and Mitochondrial Disease Center at the University of California, San Diego this evening. Our first order of business was to drive directly to the local Kinko's in order to let all of you know that we are doing well.

Our trip out here was uneventful. Finding a hotel room in a town that is known for its August conventions was another story. John reported feelings of homelessness as he and Anna sat in the airport while I called 50+ hotels trying to find an available room for one night. Ever persistent, I found a room in Chula Vista, which is in the US but on the way to Tijuana. As we ate Dutch Apple pie and drank root beers in our newly-found room at 1:30 a.m., we gave thanks!

Anna checked into the MMDC on Monday morning and participated in her developmental evaluation with the neuropsychologist. No positive changes during her DCA treatment to report. We spent the rest of the day at the San Diego Wild Animal Park and had a spectacular time. The sunshine and wonderful breezes (and lack of crowds) made the experience very enjoyable.

Because we checked in on Monday, the MMDC staff was able to schedule Anna for her EMG and nerve conduction studies. These tests involve a hand-held probe that sends a little shock to the skin and the muscular or sensory responses are recorded by the same probe. It is uncomfortable (they tried it on me) but not painful. So, we have learned that when we get to the MMDC early (they did not expect us until Wednesday), you get to undergo more tests. Lesson learned.

On Wednesday, we checked into the MMDC for glucose and fructose tolerance tests, multiple blood draws, urine bags and the works. We stayed overnight and completed the 8 hour DCA testing plus an EKG.

Best of all, we celebrated Anna's 17 month birthday with the staff! We were here for her 9 and 11 month birthdays, so the staff are starting to expect cake and ice cream when Anna comes to town.

Anna loved her bumble bee balloon. It accompanied her everywhere she went in and around the hospital. Before we left, she decided to give it to another little boy suffering from a different form of Leigh's syndrome. Even though he was in pain and suffering from uncontrolled fevers, you could see his excitement over his new floating friend.

These tolerance tests required the insertion of a "hep lock," which is a good-sized tube inserted into her vein that can be tapped time and time again to draw multiple blood samples. Heparin is inserted into the tube in between draws to prevent the tube from clogging. While this seemed more humane than sticking her every few hours, we learned that inserting the hep lock was very challenging with little veins. One nurse, Gloria, became the chosen one for this task. She accomplished it with greater ease than anyone we encountered in all of our hospital stays.

There is a saying, I believe it is from the Koran, that goes something like this: "I cried because I had no shoes until I met a man who had no feet." Whenever we felt particularly down about Anna's situation, we would play a game where we conjured up even worse situations. After we met Baruch and his mother in San Diego, we stopped playing that game.

We also met a mother and her 19-month-old son from New York. The boy has been diagnosed with Leigh's Syndrome and has lost the ability to walk and talk. He has beautiful dark eyes and a winning smile. He is severely affected by infection, fevers, and other problems. Seeing him and meeting his mother were true gifts for us, and we will keep them in our prayers. Once again, God helps us to realize that we are blessed in so many ways. I must end, so Anna's dad can say hi.

Love to all.

Anna's Mom

Kathleen has certainly captured the events of this trip. I can tell you there is no more helpless feeling than arriving in a city far from home and finding out there is no room at the inn. I was figuring we would have to go with stables and mangers. Fortunately, Kathleen is more persistent than I am.

The rest of our trip has been pretty enjoyable. I think I enjoyed one of the greatest moments of the year on Tuesday. We finished our outpatient stuff and then headed for Sea World. Sea World has little to offer to us now. We have been there three times in less than a year (we bought annual passes to save money so we feel obligated to go).

Although nothing is new there, at one point, in a fit of heat and crowd frustration we pulled Anna's stroller on to a grassy hillside under a tree. We just laid in the shade for over an hour. Anna laid between Kath and I. She pulled the grass up in her hands and dug her heels into the ground so deep her socks were soaked. Imagine laying in the shade on a sunny Southern California day watching the madding crowd go by and then watching your daughter pull up grass as if it is the greatest thing on earth.

I cannot begin to explain why I was so content at that moment.

We will be home soon.

Anna's Dad.

You can enjoy the Wild Animal Park in a lot of different ways. You can walk and walk and walk and see a diverse collection of flora and fauna, or you can ride the train around the park. The train ride takes about an hour. It is like going on a safari; actually, it is like going on a lot of different safaris. The park has vast enclosures where animals live together.

Anna liked the train best (she and John can be seen riding the train on the left side of the page), but she also liked walking around. We spent a long time in the hummingbird aviary and in the lorikeet aviary. Anna really responded to these brightly colored birds. We think she liked them so much because they had the same bright colors as her dolly.

Because the Bannister House was not available even after the first night, we ended up in a nice hotel downtown. Using the hotel's down pillows and comforters, we built a nest in the window seat overlooking downtown San Diego. Judging from her long naps, Anna thought her nest in the window was the finest sleeping arrangement yet. Anna also enjoyed a pleasant lunch watching the sailboats and a view of downtown from the Cabrillo National Monument. She got her feet wet in the Pacific Ocean. She was certainly the belle of the beach.

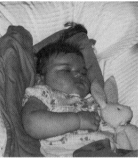

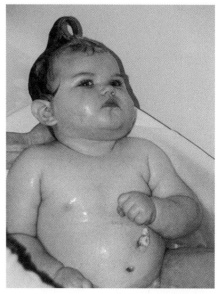

Sunday night is winding down and we are gearing up for the new week. Ruby is enjoying a night at home without Jasper, who will be arriving home from his "vacation" tomorrow. Anna has been sleeping most of the day and we are betting that she will be partying until about 3:00 a.m. (she was still going strong at 3:30 a.m. this morning).

She continues to experience a few seizures each day. This is not unexpected as we are getting her used to the new anti-seizure med and taking her off the old med. Transitions are never simple. The seizures only seem to make her sleepy. Thus, it may take her a while to get over her jet lag. If we look a bit tired over the next few days, you will know why.

Time for the angel's bath. I love spending this time with her and I think she likes to see how wet she can get me by time we are done. I cannot think of a better way to end a busy and exciting week.

Thanks for all the extra prayers, too.
Much love,
Anna's Mom

Anna loved her bath and afterwards she always smelled like heaven. Sometimes, it was the only way to calm Anna down. If you look carefully at the picture above, you can see Anna's button, just like a beach ball.

Bathing Anna was no simple task. It required the right equipment. Because she was hypotonic and could not sit up, we had to find the biggest baby bathtub available. To prevent her from sliding down toward the foot of the tub, she sat on a big bath sponge. We also put a big bath sponge underneath the foot of the tub as it rested in our bathtub to keep Anna in a properly reclined position.

To keep Kathleen comfortable as she bathed Anna, we would fold up a large towel on the edge of our bathtub. Kathleen would rest her chest on that towel, hold Anna with her left hand, and wash and rinse Anna with her right hand. Baths became quite an event and Anna became an expert splasher.

The switch from Phenobarbitol to Topomax was one of the products of our trip to San Diego. Dr. Haas and Dr. Squires collaborated on the appropriate next step to take in attempting to overcome Anna's seizures. We were lucky that our many doctors all worked well together. We think it was Anna's influence.

Sorry I have not written for a while. Between the trip to San Diego and Anna's unwillingness to sleep at night it has been a tiring couple of weeks. Yes, you heard right, our angel who has always slept through the night has decided that it might be fun to get her parents up in the middle of the night to spend a little quality time with her. We are not sure if this is a product of the medication changes, a slow readjustment to this time zone, or a precursor of the terrible twos. No matter what the cause, it is exhausting.

Last night at about 2:00 a.m., Anna started complaining about being left alone in her room. After listening to ten minutes of increasingly strenuous objections to her plight, I got up to see if I could help. I changed her and held her but she would not stop. We journeyed to the living room and turned on the television to see what Ron Popeil is selling at 2 in the morning. After about a half hour of infomercials Anna drifted off. I gave her another fifteen minutes to make sure she was serious about sleeping and then dumped her back in the crib.

As I climbed into bed, she started the cycle again. This time, by the time we got to the living room, she was already asleep. Apparently, she did not object so much to sleeping as to sleeping all by herself. So I sat with her until about 4:00 and then again returned her to her crib. She started complaining again, but either her heart was not in it anymore or I was just too tired to care.

When I talked to Kath this morning, she told me she got up with Anna at 4:45 and played the same game. It is the third time this week Anna has played this game. Then, to make sure she is prepared to play again the next night, she has taken to sleeping most of the day. I know, I know, we should just keep her up during the day. Let me tell you, that is easier said than done.

Hopefully, this is part of switching from Phenobarbitol to Topomax and, when the switch is complete in a couple of weeks, sleep patterns will return to normal.

Anna continues to have seizures, about five or six episodes a day, each consisting of a few ten second seizures. It is not pleasant to endure these episodes, but our physicians remind us that finding the right anti-seizure medication is a process, not an event. In the meantime, we may appear a bit bleary-eyed, but we are still hanging in there.

Anna's Dad

Anna's seizures were not always the same. Indeed, they varied significantly in frequency, intensity, and scope; but, they did share some common characteristics. Typically, Anna would get very still. Her eyes would open wide and she would stare blankly straight ahead. Her arms and/or legs would stiffen until they were fully extended. After a while, Anna would relax and begin to move freely. Then you knew the seizure was over.

As the roofers hammer on the roof, Anna and I decided we should share it with you: "pound pound pound pound pound pound pound pound pound pound pound pound pound pound pound."

We are still working on the change in seizure meds. Although we are farther up the Topomax ramp and farther down the Phenobarb ramp, we have still not seen any significant change in her seizures. Nonetheless, we remain patient. Okay, we are actually getting impatient, but we will continue to ride this out.

Anna's sleep pattern is still disturbed. Fortunately, the disturbance is falling into a pattern too. Usually, we get one night of sleep and then the next night she either will not go to sleep until 3 or 4 in the morning or she gets up at 3 or 4 in the morning. The only real problem is that I do not like what is on television at that time. We are going to start renting videos for wee hour viewing.

I am pleased that Anna is awake right now because it bodes well for tonight. She is displeased that I am banging on this machine as she would prefer to go outside and watch the roofers. I think she has a crush on one of them.

We are still working on the poster of the tiles. Hopefully it will be available by the end of September.

Thank you all for listening.

Anna's Dad

Monday, August 28, 2000, 4:45 p.m.
From: Anna's Dad
Subject: Monday

Well, last night we did not get up with Anna. That does not mean she slept. To the contrary, she was grousing almost all night long. Instead of getting up with her, we just turned off the monitor, closed her bedroom door, and waited it out. This may sound like old hat stuff to most of you parents, but for us this is new territory. Anna always slept through the night. Now, she sleeps through the day and complains all night. So, once again, I turn to you all for advice. How do you keep your child awake during the day if you are trying to shift her sleep time. I have tried many things (stopping short of putting ice cubes in her diaper) but nothing seems to help.

Other than that all is well. Anna's seizures seem to be decreasing in frequency. We have to wait longer to know for sure. We will keep in touch.

Anna's Dad

We took Anna to the beach at Grand Haven in the hope we would tire her out. We walked her and the dogs for a very long way, including all the way out on the pier. We were tired, the dogs were tired, Anna was not.

We found it unsettling to wait for over a month to get Anna up to the full therapeutic dose of her new seizure medication. In the past, it had taken a week at the most to get her seizures under control. Now, they were happening even while she was on the new medication. We wanted immediate results. We did not get what we wanted.

Thursday, August 31, 2000, 2:44 p.m.
From: Anna's Dad
Subject: Thursday-list shifting

I got an e-mail from Marianne Becktel today. She is the creator of this mailing list. As you may remember, we initially started out on Onelist which got swallowed by E-groups which is about to be swallowed by Yahoo. Marianne tells me this newest merger might not be what the Anna's friends list needs. So, she is contemplating finding a new home for the list. We will keep you posted on that.

I mention all of this because Marianne reminded me that we will have to harvest the archives off of the existing group site. We have not spent a lot of time looking back in the last year, but when Marianne mentioned the archives, I decided to look back. After reading a few posts, it became very apparent to me how far we have come with all of your help. When you spend your days living in the moment, you kind of lose the past and the future. Someday, I will look back over all of this and I hope to then recognize where this journey has taken us. Right now, living in this moment, all you see are today's trees.

Anna is still doing ok. Her sleep patterns are starting to return to normal. If she makes it through the night tonight, it will be two nights in a row. We think she is adjusting well to the new seizure med, Topomax, although we recently discovered that we are only halfway to the final dose even after three weeks. It will probably be at least another couple of weeks before we get to the full dose. Until then, we are stuck with the seizures.

She is getting back to her old self in terms of her talkativeness. Right now she is yelling at me for spending time talking to you. It is good to hear that kind of communication from her. It has been sparse the last few weeks.

We are preparing for a Labor Day weekend at home, cleaning the basement. Hope your weekend is more exciting.

Anna's Dad

Thursday, September 7, 2000, 11:14 a.m.
From: Anna's Dad
Subject: Thursday–back to work

Well, it's Thursday again. The holiday has really thrown us off stride. It is amazing how one day's difference throws the routine into a tailspin. For example, I am doing laundry today. Normally, that is a Tuesday job. Somehow doing laundry today just does not feel right.

The change in routine is aggravated by the fact that Anna has a cold. Now that might not sound like too big a deal, but anytime her respiratory system is in distress it always causes us great concern. Right now she is coughing and sneezing almost constantly. Because she does not have a lot of muscle tone, it takes every fiber of her being to cough or sneeze. She sounds awful, but it is probably harder on us than on her. After listening to her gurgle and cough, it makes *us* cough in the hope it will help *her* clear her throat.

Fortunately, her favorite way of dealing with her cold is to be held and then to snuggle deep in your arms. That is good for both of us, but it makes doing laundry that much more of a hassle.

The weekend was certainly productive (even though it killed my routine). We completed the cleanup of the front half of the basement. For a $2 dollar fee, we are willing to show you that part of the basement while it is clean. Act now, it probably will not stay clean long. We also managed to make a lot of peach jam out of grampie's peaches. I anticipate the peach jam will last longer than the clean basement.

Anna's illness is our main focus for the near future. Yesterday we attempted to access the medical services establishment to determine whether we could do anything to help Anna. After a few phone calls, we determined the pulmonologist would not be able to see us, so we tried the pediatrician. After another series of phone calls, we were able to get in for an afternoon appointment.

As I sat in the examination room with Anna, before the doctor was available, she fell into a deep and calm sleep in my arms. This presented a strange dilemma for me. On the one hand, of course, I was overjoyed that Anna could enjoy some true peace for a few minutes. On the other hand, I wanted to make sure that the

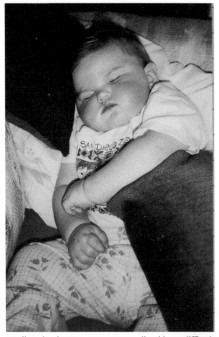

Until we had Anna, we never realized how difficult it was to get projects accomplished. We typically work best on projects, such as cleaning the basement or building our shed, when we work together. When one of us has to keep Anna company, it takes more than twice as long to complete our task. This is one of those things that they do not teach you in parenting classes. Although cleaning and organizing the basement may seem like a very small task, it was a tremendous accomplishment for us. Doing "normal" things like this helped us to feel like all was right with the world.

doctor saw her at her worst for two reasons: first, so that he could realistically evaluate her symptoms to determine the appropriate treatment, and second so that they would take us seriously when we call claiming an emergency.

That second reason may sound silly, but sometimes doctors think parents are overvigilant. When that happens, they can be a little patronizing. If you push the panic button too often, no one will take you seriously.

These are the kind of crummy thoughts that go through your head while you wait. Anna stayed sleeping, but the doctor was thorough in his examination and I am confident that we got a meaningful evaluation of Anna's condition.

It looks like the best treatment is just holding her close. That we will do gladly.

Anna's Dad

Sunday, September 17, 2000, 9:56 p.m.
From: Anna's Dad
Subject: Sunday

Sorry it has been so long since we posted. We have, as a family, been struggling with a cold. I cannot remember the last time when we were not coughing. What wimps we are.

It appears that we are all on the recovery side of things. Anna has slept through the night two nights in a row. We think that is the first time in seven weeks. We are hoping for three tonight. Once the sleep thing falls into place, we will fall easily into the old routine.

The last couple of days have been consumed by television coverage of the Olympics (unless there is football on at the same time, of course). There is something pure about Olympic competition that makes it impossible to ignore. On the other hand, there is something vile about the way the network covers the Olympics that makes it hard to watch. Oh well.

As we continue to slowly increase Anna's seizure medication, the seizures appear to be decreasing in number. In fact, although I almost hate to even write this, she has not had a seizure today. If that continues until bedtime that will make two days in the last week where she has been seizure-free. Although the seizures are less frequent, the few she has have become more pronounced. It is difficult to watch. There is simply nothing you can do other than tell her that you are there with her. We look forward to reaching the final dose. That should happen by the end of this month.

We are approaching some significant milestones. Kathleen has been sitting on the bench now for almost six months. She is working very hard and so far the reviews have been consistently positive. Although no one is running against her in the election, I am thinking of mounting a write-in campaign. That way, we can have a big party on election eve when Kathleen beats me. If you are in Kent County and a registered voter, think about writing me in.

We are also a week away from the first anniversary of Anna's diagnosis. That is a big deal for a strange reason. No one can say how the disease will cause Anna's health to decline, but everyone knows the mortality statistics. Fifty percent of the

We would talk to Anna, almost coaching her through the seizure. In hindsight it is apparent that we were just talking ourselves through the fear and angst.

Chapter 8: The Summer 243

children with Anna's diagnosis die in the first year after diagnosis. Dr. Naviaux told us that when onset is as early as it was with Anna, the first year mortality rate is even higher. Somehow passing that artificial hurdle means that we are beating the disease and that we can keep going forever.

Initially, we were going to have a big party to celebrate making it through the year. With the recent health problems, the cold and the seizures, it seemed a little presumptuous to plan a party. Rather than tempt fate, we decided to just say a prayer of thanks. So, on Saturday the 23rd, say a joyful prayer for Anna. We figure it will be a little like crossing the equator. You can't see it but you know you are in a very different place.

Kathleen just walked in with Anna fresh from her bath. There is no sweeter smell than a clean Anna. I think we are all looking forward to a fresh start.

Anna's Dad

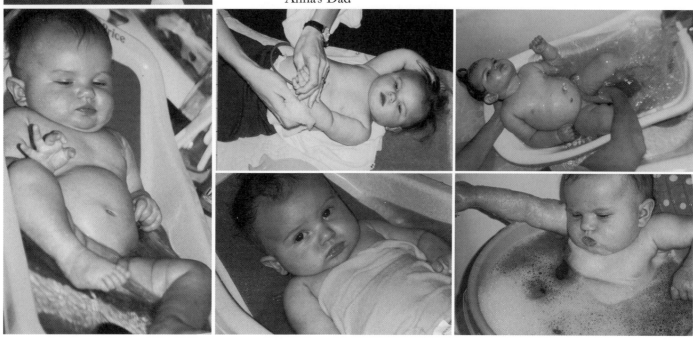

Thursday, September 21, 2000, 11:24 a.m.
From: Anna's Dad
Subject: Thursday-new med

Well, if you could see Anna right now, you would see the brightest little girl ever. She is on day two of her new seizure med, Vigabatrin. So far no seizures. She slept through the night last night. That is four out of the last five nights. She still has not made three in a row, but tonight could be the night.

Yesterday was an odd day, lots of highs and lows. We obtained the Vigabatrin from a family in Jenison. It is not available in the U.S. We thought we would have to travel to Windsor, Ontario, but this family was ending the use of the drug for their daughter and had some left over. It was generous of them to offer it to us. I met the mom and dad at their place of employment. They were anxious to meet Anna. They told me a wonderful story of how this drug had essentially saved their daughter's life. It was kind of difficult to explain to them that this drug was not going to save Anna; at best, it would make her more comfortable. I do not know if they understood or not. It was kind of hard to deal with.

Anna and I also went to physical therapy. Kathleen met us there. Anna is demonstrating more muscle tone as of late. We do not know why, but we are not complaining. At the end of the session, Anna's physical therapist and Kathleen put Anna in a standing position with their support. To see my baby standing up made me see her as a little girl for the first time. She is a very pretty little girl. In my head now, I can see her running around. I could not see that before. It was an epiphany. I do not think I will ever see her as a baby again.

After PT, we went out to the car. We were parked in a handicapped spot and our handicapped tag was prominently displayed on the rearview mirror. Nonetheless, a volunteer enforcement person had ticketed us for unlawfully parking in handicapped. Imagine trying to convince a city employee that your handicapped tag was prominently displayed.

Yesterday was definitely an up and down day. Sometimes I think the days that Anna and I spend at home are the easiest. Listen carefully tomorrow morning. If you hear a shout for joy, it means we made three in a row.

Anna's Dad

The Vigabatrin was a godsend. It is not approved by the FDA, however, due to its detrimental effects on the patient's eyesight. Because Anna's eyesight was already compromised, we did not hesitate to pursue this course of treatment for her myoclonic seizures. After Anna's death, we passed along her extra Vigabatrin to another family whose child was suffering from similar seizures.

We always thought of Anna as very long, not tall. Seeing her stand revealed the truth. Even though we have thousands of photos of Anna, we do not have one that shows her standing.

Sunday, September 24, 2000, 9:53 p.m.
From: Anna's Dad
Subject: Sunday-one year and counting

Well, our anniversary weekend is over. We had plenty of time to look back and forward this weekend. That is what we wanted. Weather kept us from a dog show in Howell on Saturday. Instead, we spent a good chunk of the day in bed watching Olympics and football.

Saturday night we went out for a fancy dinner. I say fancy because I had to wear a tie. This constituted the main part of our anniversary celebration. Perhaps it is better to say "recognition" than "celebration." We spent a little bit of time reliving the events of one year ago. Those are not fond memories. We spent a little time thinking about the things that have happened in the last year. It seems that the events of our day-to-day lives are dictated more by things that have happened in the last year than the first thirty-five years of our lives. There has been joy and despair over the past year, often at the same time.

We spent most of our "celebration" thinking of the future. What would things be like this Christmas, next spring, a year from now, or even five years from now? Projecting too far into the future is hard because it inevitably means plans that do not include Anna. We got that far a couple of times, but we just could not stay there. We will probably go out for a fancy dinner on September 23 for the rest of our lives just to remind ourselves how quickly things can change.

Sunday afforded time for introspection and retrospection as well. Anna slept through the night. We took a long walk with the dogs on a crisp, clear fall day. This time of year is my favorite. I am always working to convince Kathleen that fall is better than summer. A day like today makes it easier to persuade her. Football, church, grilled cheese and chili for dinner, and now kicking back and mentally preparing for another week. For me that means one last football game. For Kathleen, it is signing orders while Anna sleeps on her lap.

Although I am sure it is good to spend time navel gazing now and then (a life unexamined is not worth living, right?), I am glad we do not have to do this every day. Tomorrow I am going back to living in the moment, it seems to be safer there.

Anna's Dad

Wednesday, September 27, 2000, 9:25 a.m.
From: Anna's Dad
Subject: Wednesday-Anna's new ride

Anna is putting on quite a show this morning. She is sitting in her high chair holding on to four mylar balloons, two silver, one blue, and one orange. She is sitting in front of the picture window and the early morning sun is streaming in. When the sunshine hits the balloons it casts spiky ribbons of color and light on the walls and ceiling. Anna is absolutely transfixed by the fiery display.

Every few minutes the balloons will spin and no longer cast the ribbons of light on the wall that she can easily see. When that happens she vigorously jerks the balloon strings until the light comes back. I am sure in her mind, the balloon strings represent some kind of on/off switch for the pretty lights. When the light comes back on she grunts. For me, it is the absolute height of entertainment.

Anna has her new "stroller." Actually, it is her wheelchair. It is called a Kid Kart. It looks really cool. It gives her the support she needs. Because the support is so much better, she can sit in the new stroller in a much more upright position. Based on her reaction, I think she likes looking forward a lot more than looking up. She looks like a little princess on a fancy wheeled throne.

The sun has now risen high enough that the light no longer strikes the balloons directly. She is pulling her on/off switch for all she is worth but it is not working. I am going to take the balloons away so she does not lose faith in the light.

Today will be a quiet day. Anna seems to be coming down with a cold again. Hopefully not. We saw the otolaryngologist yesterday--Anna's first new "ologist" in a long time. He said she has gotten over her ear infection. Anna still has not made three nights of sleep in a row. Last night she decided the hours of one to two a.m. should be spent with me rather than the three thousand stuffed animals in her crib. Once she got her hour of attention, she was willing to go back to bed.

Sleepily,
Anna's Dad

Anna's Chair

We moved heaven and earth to get that wheelchair once we decided to go forward. It took us a while to get to that point. Seeing Anna in a stroller just meant she was a big baby. We thought that if she were in a wheelchair, we might not see her the same way. Maybe then she would be "handicapped." We were so wrong.

Once we decided to get the chair, however, we were told it might take six months. As I am sure you can imagine, we had a hard time seeing six months down the road. To wait that long for a chair was just unbearable.

The process is a long one. First you need to get fitted for the chair and pick the model you want. That task is performed by physical and occupational therapists. Then they submit their recommendations to the doctor to get a prescription for the chair. The prescription goes to the medical equipment supplier. The supplier generates a price quote. That is submitted to the insurers.

The insurers then consider the matter to decide whether they will cover the chair. If they do, then the supplier will order it. Then you wait for delivery and try to schedule an appointment for the final fitting; that must usually be set a couple of months in advance. After delivery and the final fitting, you get the chair. It is not unusual for a child to outgrow his or her chair by the time it is delivered.

We could not wait out that process. I begged and whined and cajoled and threat-

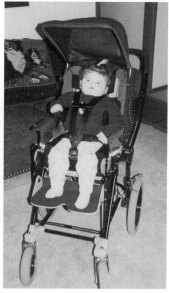

ened and guilted. I even made people cry. But we went from our initial fitting to prescription to quote to insurance approval to delivery to final fitting in one month. I think we beat the previous record by a matter of months. I am so grateful to all of the people who put up with me and made that happen. The end result was certainly worth it.

The first time that Anna sat in her chair in our living room, you could see her look around the room at the chairs and furniture. She was clearly amazed that we had all of this stuff in the house. Given that she spent most of her time looking up at the ceiling or leaning back in someone's arms, it is understandable that she enjoyed her new perspective. Seeing

how comfortable she was and how well the chair supported her also convinced us that she was much more comfortable in her chair than she was in the strollers. In hindsight, we wish we would have overcome our fears about the chair much earlier. Anna only used the chair for two weeks, but they were an outstanding two weeks for her.

That chair brought us a lot of joy. It is hopefully doing the same for others today. We donated the chair to the hospital and it is our understanding that another little girl suffering from a rare metabolic illness is tooling around in the purple and teal Kid Kart that Anna loved.

Chapter 9
The Fall

The parallel between Anna's condition and the season continued through the Fall. The change from Summer to Fall is typically a gradual one. It went a little quicker for Anna.

I was taking a little poetic license in this post when I suggested I was "alone." Kathleen and I spoke by telephone several times about Anna's apparent seizures. Nonetheless, I maintain there is a significant difference between telephone presence and physical presence, significant enough to qualify me as being "alone" under these circumstances.

Thursday, October 5, 2000, 8:45 p.m.
From: Anna's Dad
Subject: Thursday again

We are on day two of life without Mom. We dropped her off yesterday at a conference at the Grand Traverse Resort. When we left, the lobby was packed with hundreds of judges all in their robes. Keep in mind each one of those black robes gets to decide how things are going to go in their world every day. Anna and I were expecting arguments to break out. They did not—at least not before we left.

Anna and I got back last night. For two weeks (or since she started taking the Vigabatrin) Anna did not have any seizures. In fact, this past weekend she had some of her brightest days in recent memory. Perhaps Anna burned a little too brightly because she has been sleeping almost non-stop since Monday morning.

Starting Tuesday, Kath and I noticed that Anna's chin was quivering strangely every now and then. It would only last a few seconds and then she would drool profusely. On Wednesday, the seizures increased in frequency to the point they were coming every few minutes. I increased her Vigabatrin dose and hoped it would have the same immediate effect as when she started the drug. So far no immediate effect, but the doctor says the first time was unusual and we should expect results within forty-eight hours. Even if that does not work, we still have room to increase her main seizure meds.

Next week we are scheduled for an EEG and maybe that will tell us what is going on. But, right now, she is still sleeping. It could be the meds, it could be the seizures. Either way, it is hard to feel good about it.

One funny thing I have realized is how different it is to handle all of this stuff alone. Every time there is something new or different in Anna's condition, we always wonder whether we are perched on the brink of a downward spiral. When we are together, it is easy to get some perspective and convince each other otherwise. When you are alone its harder to push yourself back from that brink.

I do not believe we are on that brink right now, but I still wish Kath was here to convince me. Time to feed Anna.

Good night.
Anna's Dad

I am sitting here at the internet station in the Grand Traverse Resort with several colleagues showing off the beautiful pictures of Anna that we have posted to the Anna's Friends list site, and I could not help but read John's latest post. This is the first time in 27 months (yes, I included the gestational period) that I have been away from Anna for any length of time and I am having severe withdrawals.

I have also discovered that being away is more difficult when things are uncertain on the home front. It made me feel better to get on-line and read about my angel and to see her beautiful face plastered across my monitor, but it also makes me yearn to be home comforting her during her seizures and sharing the uncertainty with John. I echo his thoughts on facing all of this while separated from each other. I find myself daydreaming during some of the conferences and wondering what my two favorite people are doing. It will be a very long time before we are separated like this again, I can assure you.

On a lighter note, I got to see my sister-in-law and twin nieces at the girls' tennis lesson this evening. When you are five and one-half and you have a racquet in your hands, it can be a lethal weapon. Fortunately, no one was seriously injured during the hour-long lesson. Spending dinner this evening with my parents and brother also helped to ease my mind, although we spent a lot of time talking about Anna. It is hard to explain how the physical manifestation of the seizures changes our entire outlook—even when we know that the seizure activity is occurring almost constantly but silently. We long for her "bright" days and will try to be patient as the Vigabatrin hopefully starts working.

I have gone on long enough and must sign off now. I cannot tell you how wonderful it is to be able to reach out and touch all of you even when I am far from home and the ones I love.

Take care and good night.

Anna's Mom

It was so hard for me to be away, even for a three-day conference. I had never spent time away from her except during the few nights when she was in the hospital that John convinced me to go home and try to get a good night's sleep. I do not know why things had to change while I was gone. Once I returned from the conference I resolved to never leave her again.

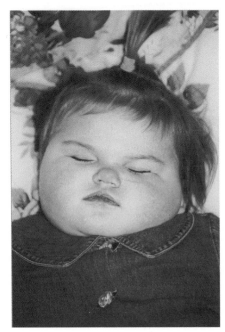

Sunday, October 8, 2000, 3:21 a.m.
From: Anna's Dad
Subject: Sunday-a long night

It has already been a long weekend and it is time that we updated you as to Anna's situation.

For the last two weeks of September, Anna was seizure free on the Vigabatrin. On Monday last week, Anna started to have chin tremors. They would only last a few seconds and when it was over, she would drool profusely. Also, Anna was very sleepy. In fact, on Monday, she slept almost all day. She was a little perkier on Tuesday, but the chin tremors continued, just a few that day. On Wednesday, she was again very sleepy and the tremors started coming more often. Sometimes, they would also be more intense involving her arms or her legs twitching in time with her chin. We increased her medication. Thursday was about the same.

By Friday night, the seizures were coming quite fast and interfering with her breathing. As the seizure would start, Anna would stop breathing. By the time it ended, her mouth would be full of saliva and it was very difficult for her to take a breath. Although we could watch and help her during the day, we were afraid we would miss the problem at night, so we hooked her up to the pulse/ox monitor. In the first twenty minutes, the monitor alarm went off three times.

Around 11:00 p.m., we decided we should take some action, but we were not sure what direction to go. I called my sister Lauran, the hospice nurse, and she came over to help figure it out. We decided we wanted to get her into the hospital but we wanted to get a doctor to admit her rather than deal with the wait (and the doctors who are not familiar with her condition) in the ER. Because Anna's problem was with breathing, we tried to admit her through the pulmonologist.

We spoke with the pulmonologist, but he was not inclined to admit her unless we were willing to authorize intubating Anna. Based on our description of the problem, he believed it was a neural rather than a pulmonary problem. We did not want to put Anna on a ventilator so we turned elsewhere.

As an alternative, we thought we might get into the hospital through hospice. We spoke with the hospice representative (keep in mind that by now it is 2:00 a.m.). In speaking with the hospice rep at length it finally dawned on us that we

The seizures made Anna look like she was gulping something, but drool was running out of her mouth and her lips turned blue. Her arms and legs would often stiffen rhythmically. Her eyes were open sometimes but she was not seeing anything. All we could do is hold her and urge her to take a breath. As we watched her seize time after time after time, it felt like we were losing her.

were at the point where we had to make hard decisions as to how aggressively we were going to pursue medical treatment for Anna. We began to realize that almost all of the treatment options available to deal with the immediate problem were going to be as hard for Anna as the immediate problem. We also realized that although we were extremely troubled by Anna's seizures, she was not. Her face was calm; she was not struggling. Finally, we determined that the only treatment that would really help Anna was to stop the seizures. We were already on the best course of treatment to achieve that end.

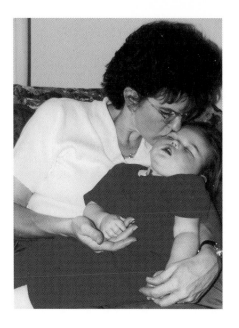

I can record these realizations in a few sentences, but coming to each one was like climbing a wall. By 3:00 a.m. when we stopped talking to people and sent my sister home, we felt like we had travelled a thousand miles.

Our neurologist dropped in yesterday. Although Anna conveniently decided to just sleep quietly the entire time she was here, we did show her some seizures on videotape. An EEG on Monday will confirm for sure, but the neurologist anticipates that the irregular electrical activity that previously led to the seizures over her cortex has moved deeper into Anna's brain stem. It will be difficult to treat this problem. The medication course we are pursuing now is as good a treatment as any.

We still can increase the meds a couple of times before we are at maximum doses. If this does not work, the only courses of treatment available to us carry some big downsides so it is not likely we will pursue them. On the other hand, the seizures might stop with no treatment. All we can do is wait.

For the last several days Anna has been pretty much sleeping full time. Her eyes open when she is having a seizure but we do not think she is really seeing anything. She will carry on her version of conversations with us while she is sleeping and she appears to be happiest when we are holding and talking to her. That is what we will be doing while we wait.

Sometimes Anna can go several hours without a seizure; sometimes they come every five minutes. Anna does not appear to be in any immediate danger. Although she is having problems breathing during the seizures, they do not last too long (not as long as they did on Friday) and she is able to breathe when they are finished.

She is still the fat, sassy, and healthy looking girl you know. Please keep us in your prayers in the coming days.

Anna's Dad

Tuesday, Oct 10, 2000, 8:46 a.m.
From: Anna's Dad
Subject: Tuesday

Anna had much quieter days on Sunday and Monday, fewer and much less severe seizures. She is still sleeping. Last night at about 3:45 a.m., Anna started having the big seizures again. She has only had a few. Now she is sleeping peacefully. She had an EEG yesterday. We still have not heard anything regarding that. Although she is always sleeping, she does coo and cluck in her sleep. We have carried on many conversations that way. We will keep you posted.

Anna's Dad

Anna's blissful quiet on October 11 did not continue long past the time I posted that message. The events of the next couple of hours were very troubling. As I sat with Anna, she started to have more seizures--severe seizures. As with her earlier seizures, they would start with tremors in her chin and she stopped breathing. These, however, spread beyond that. Her legs and arms would convulse rhythmically and, at the end, her arms and legs would stiffen. And, then, she would scream.

I could not get in touch with anyone who could help. I could not give her any more medication. I was completely helpless as my daughter, who had done nothing but coo and babble for over a year, sat and screamed. I prayed, I held her, I tried to comfort her, but in the end all I could do was scream with her. That is what I did.

That was the worst time of my entire life. I imagine that is what hell is like. I am sitting here crying as I write about it. The experience made it much easier to pursue more aggressive drug therapies to stop the seizures, even if that meant Anna would sleep even more.

Wednesday, October 11, 2000, 10:47 a.m.
From: Anna's Dad
Subject: Wednesday-waiting

Anna is sleeping very peacefully right now. She had a few big seizures starting at about 4:00 a.m., but the last couple of hours have been blissfully quiet. We are getting together with Anna's neurologist this afternoon to discuss Anna's EEG. We will keep you posted.

Anna's Dad

Wednesday, October 11, 2000, 7:34 p.m.
From: Anna's Dad
Subject: Wednesday-getting the news

Our visit to the neurologist this afternoon confirmed what Kath and I already knew in our hearts. Anna's time with us is drawing to an end.

Although it is impossible to estimate exactly how much time is left, it appears to be no more than a few weeks and perhaps as short as a week or two. Kathleen has taken a leave of absence from work so we can just hold Anna together for the time we have left.

The neurologist was very clear in stating that Anna is not in any pain. It is our goal to keep her comfortable. Anna has been sleeping for the past week and we anticipate she will continue to do so. We plan to make sure she is sleeping in the arms of someone who loves her from now on.

We have appreciated your support so far and we will need it even more in the coming weeks. We are still working out exactly what we can tell you when you ask how you can help. Rest assured we will come up with stuff but it might take a couple of days.

We are trying to get our families taken care of first but we anticipate the next weeks will be essentially an open house so that you can all get a chance to say good-bye. We will let you know the hours.

In the meantime, keep us all in your prayers.

Anna's Dad

When John called me at work and told me that we had an appointment at Dr. Squires' office, I could feel my heart break. I think we both knew that the news would be bad. The question was exactly how bad.

On the way to the appointment, I ran into a friend whose husband had recently died; he, too, had struggled with a rare disease. For months we had walked similar paths. For months we frankly discussed our journeys to the end of life. I cried as I told her that we could not stop Anna's seizures, and we both knew that the end was near without saying it. Even now, when I pass by the spot where we embraced and cried, I cannot help but remember that moment.

We met with Dr. Squires that afternoon to discuss the results of the EEG. We were anxious about the results. We desperately wanted the EEG to tell us what was going on in Anna's brain when she was having a seizure. But, she did not have any seizures during the EEG test. For that reason, we were initially concerned that the EEG might not tell us what we needed to know.

Once we got to Dr. Squires' office our fears that the EEG might have been fruitless were quickly dispelled. The EEG showed that Anna's brain was now very limited in its ability to function and simply could not continue to keep her going for long. We sat in Liza's office for almost 3 hours. We talked and cried with Liza and her staff who had become like extended family to us. I called my work and confirmed all the details of my leave of absence before we left her office. It all seemed surreal. It was nothing like I imagined it would be. Everyone took turns holding Anna. It calmed everyone down just to hug and kiss her as she slept in our arms. She had that effect on people.

We began using Diastat for Anna's seizures; it is essentially a gel form of Valium that is injected rectally. We would use the Diastat whenever Anna started to have seizures. It proved effective for a while in giving her relief.

Although we had our first contact with Hospice of Michigan when Anna was first in the hospital during September of 1999, we did not sign up for hospice services until this day. We were so blessed to have had their input from the very start. We learned so much from them about how to spend the time between diagnosis and death. Having that information early was essential for us. It proved an invaluable guide in our decision-making process through Anna's entire life. Now that the end was near, however, we required their assistance even more and we got everything that we needed: equipment, medications, a willing ear, and expertise that is simply not available anywhere else. Thank God for hospice.

This is our hospice team, from left to right, Marion Schaefer, Dan Hendricksen, Lauran Bittinger, Dr. Colleen Talen, and Ruth Merrill. These folks were with us in the hospital in September of 1999 and, in one capacity or another, they were with us again during the Fall of 2000. The only member we do not have a picture of is Kim Oberst, but she was with us during the Fall as well.

Thursday, October 12, 2000, 10:38 p.m.
From: Anna's Dad
Subject: Thursday–home together

Anna has had a very good day. It is taking us a little time to get the hang of using the new medications, but Anna has not had any seizures for the last seven hours. We think we have it figured out so that she will sleep quietly through the night. Hopefully so will we.

We have once again received an incredible outpouring of support. Thank you.
Anna's Dad

Friday, October 13, 2000, 8:31 p.m.
From: Anna's Dad
Subject: Friday-planning ahead

Anna has enjoyed another quiet day. Kath and I had a chance to look at plots in the cemetery just down the road from our house. It is already a special place for us as we have often walked through that cemetery with the dogs. We picked out a spot under some trees and we plan to plant roses all around.

We had many guests today. Anna certainly appreciated the opportunity to be held. She has not had a big seizure all day. Last night was the most sleep we have had in a long time. Other than getting up once to give her some more medication at about 4:00 a.m., it was clear sleeping. We think we have the seizure cycle figured out well enough to get a solid night tonight.

With or without a good night's sleep, we have found ourselves in a general state of fatigue. It is somewhat humorous. Yesterday, the first weekday that we have both been home to take care of Anna, we forgot to feed her in a timely fashion on three occasions.

To make sure we have some time for ourselves and to take naps, we are limiting the open house hours next week to Monday, Wednesday and Friday, noon to four and then seven to nine p.m. We will figure out the weekend when we see how the week is going. It is impossible for us to coordinate a schedule so that everyone can have a specific time to hold Anna. If you call before you come out, we can let you know if it is already a full house. Most of those times one or both of us will be here; if we need time out, we have "trained" some other folks to take care of Anna.

We have also found that we are having a hard time concentrating on our own meals. If you have the time to prepare a meal for us, it would be greatly appreciated. Once again, Sheri Leisman has volunteered to coordinate that effort. We usually number about four people at suppertime. Also, if you want to bring something to munch on during open house times, that is always welcome.

If you have never been out to Anna's house, we live at 6132 Rogue Lane NE in Belmont. That is a dirt road that runs north off of Rogue River Drive.

Anna, who is snoring loudly just like her mother, sends her love.
Anna's Dad

After talking with other parents in our situation, it appears that we were in the minority who took care of details like cemetery plots before our child died. We knew that we would not be able to function after she left us. And, for some reason, looking for her plot made us feel like we were doing something when otherwise we could do nothing but wait. While we were home with Anna, we were effectively waiting for her to die. I think John understood this then, but it was only many months after her death that this realization hit me.

Among those "trained" to watch Anna were Nancy Haynes and her husband Bryan Bickford. Bryan and Nancy were with us every step of the way with Anna. They came to our house several evenings every week and many weekends. They held Anna while we ate, they cleaned our house, they helped us make the plaster hand and foot casts of Anna's pudgy extremities, and they paid attention to Ruby and Jasper. They did the same for Anna when she was in the hospital. Words cannot describe what this meant to us and Anna.

Here, Anna is wearing a dress that Nancy's mom made for her to match a doll that Nancy's mom also made for her. We called that doll Anna's "Nancy doll."

Once we started reading the Narnia books to Anna, we were afraid she would die before we finished them. This led to several marathon reading sesssions. Our choice of reading material was divine providence. We knew we had to fit a lifetime's worth of books into a very short time. When we chose the Chronicles of Narnia, we thought we were giving Anna the best. The Chronicles certainly helped us to see the absolute joy that was awaiting Anna when she left us. It was just another gift that she (with the help of C.S. Lewis) gave us.

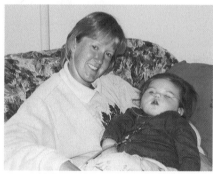

Anna with her godmother, Angie Jansen. In this picture you can see that Anna is sporting a nasal cannula. The cannula supplied oxygen to Anna to make sure she got the most out of every breath.

Tuesday, October 17, 2000, 00:41 a.m.
From: Anna's Dad & Mom
Subject: Monday-episodes

Anna has had a relatively quiet weekend. On Saturday, my Uncle Paul came over and took some family pictures for us. They are beautiful.

We had lots of visitors and ate lots of good food. We were able to make some preliminary decisions regarding funeral stuff. It may sound a little macabre to do that now, but we believe we will be able to think through some of those issues more thoroughly now rather than later. Anna also received the sacrament of Confirmation on Saturday.

Until this weekend, we had Anna sleep with us. Kath would hold her hands as she slept between us. If she had a seizure, we would wake up and deal with the medications. Now that we have the seizures under control, there is really nothing to let us know if she is in distress. Accordingly, we have started the night watch. On Saturday night, my sister Lauran and Kath's brother Patrick stood watch. Last night, my sister and I did the first half of the night and she and Kath did the second half. The night watch added a whole new layer to watching Anna and it will take some time to adjust.

Sunday night, we read aloud to Anna the C.S. Lewis book *The Lion, The Witch, and The Wardrobe*. It took about five hours. She enjoyed it very much.

It's about 5:30 p.m. on Monday and Anna is awake and talking in the arms of her Godmother, Angie Jansen. It is amazing to see her looking around and making noises at us like she used to! This is as awake as she has been in weeks and we're thrilled to see our baby's eyes and hear her voice. She had been stealing looks at us for short periods during the past two days, but she has been awake and alert for at least 15-25 minutes now. What a thrill!

On Sunday night, Anna had an episode where she stopped breathing for what seemed a very long time. Monday night the same type of episode occured three times, each a little longer than the last. Each time it happens we hold her tight and let her know it is ok for her to go, but each time she eventually draws a deep breath and comes back to be with us again. I think it is in part because she wanted to watch Monday Night Football with me one last time.

It was kind of a lousy game tonight, but I told her the Lions/Buccaneers game on Thursday might be better. We will have to see if she thinks it is worth waiting around for.

Anna had lots of guests all weekend and on Monday. She was very gracious in permitting almost everyone a shot at holding her.

We have been eating like kings thanks to the largesse of Anna's Friends. Right now sleeping like kings sounds even better. Because Anna's hardest times seem to be in the evening, we are planning to drop the evening session of the open house for Wednesday. The afternoon session will go forward as planned, God and Anna willing.

Thank you again for your support. You are all holding us up right now and we really feel it.

Anna's Dad & Mom

This is my Uncle Paul De Boode with Anna. The shots he took of us with Anna in the backyard (including the pictures below) are some of our favorites.

You can get some idea of how big Anna was at this time. The last measurements we have show that she was 33 inches tall and 32 pounds. John used to say that she was almost square.

Wednesday, October 18, 2000, 12:51 p.m.
From: Anna's Dad
Subject: Wednesday-changes again

It appears that Anna is anxious to see the Lions Thursday night because she has gone thirty-six hours without any seizures or other episodes where she has stopped breathing. What seemed so close Monday night now seems far away.

We have changed the way we give Anna the anti-seizure meds. Instead of waiting for the seizures to give her the heavy meds, we have started giving her some every six hours. It appears to steady her condition. She still has some congestion, but she is breathing steadily.

We have had many guests yesterday and already today. The open house will close tonight at 7:00 p.m. We are taking tonight and all day tomorrow to just sit and look at each other. Although it has been wonderful to see Anna in the arms of so many, it will also be nice to have some quiet time. We will reopen Friday at noon.

Last night Kath and I were both able to sleep the whole night through. Today seems a lot easier to handle.

Keep the faith.

Anna's Dad

These are but a few of our many open house guests.

Friday, October 20, 2000, 11:17 a.m.
From: Anna's Dad
Subject: Friday-time outside

Our quiet day yesterday was a welcome respite. We were able to sit outside on the swing under the maple and the big white pine. Anna always loves to sit on that swing and watch the sunlight filter through the foliage. Yesterday she slept while we were in the swing, but she really seemed to enjoy the change of pace. It was the first time she had been outside since last Saturday.

Anna also very much enjoyed watching the Lions beat up on the Buccaneers. She did miss the first part of the second half because Kathleen and Nancy wanted to watch ER. Anna was willing to humor them even though she really wanted to watch the football game.

We have spent a significant part of the last couple of weeks looking out the picture window in the living room. If you have been to our home, you know that the window provides a panoramic view of the backyard and the river that lies about twenty feet below the bluff on which our house is situated. It has been a joy to watch autumn progress.

Typically, if we were working, we would catch a glimpse of the seasonal colors as we drove to work and then another glimpse on the way home. That in itself is a pleasure, but this year we get to live Fall. We have seen dozens of trees shift from completely green to red, orange, yellow, and brown (the oaks). Just seeing the vibrant colors is enough of a treat, but to see the entire process from green to yellow to red to the gradual release of the leaves, then to bare branches is a moving experience.

It is hard to ignore the parallel between watching the leaves fall and watching Anna's condition. It is also reassuring to realize that even though we are losing the beautiful leaves, it ultimately gives us a better view of the river.

Although Anna's condition sort of stabilized on Tuesday and Wednesday, yesterday she again began to experience episodes where she simply stopped breathing. This morning, she went ten minutes taking only three breaths.

You can see how the light dapples the swing and the swingers. That was Anna's favorite part.

Because Anna stopped breathing so often and breathed in a very shallow manner, we kept her on oxygen around the clock. As a result, we spent almost every moment of every day inside. We did, however, sneak outside for a few minutes on one or two beautiful afternoons. This was one of those days. Friends came to visit this afternoon and spent time with us on the swing and in the Adirondack chairs under the big maple and white pine trees in the front yard.

We are so glad that we opened our home to all of Anna's friends. We drew immeasurable comfort and strength from the outpouring of love during the open houses. Our visitors took away something as well. Many have told us how grateful they were that we gave them the opportunity to hold, kiss and say good-bye to Anna in their own way. It made us realize that our little girl deeply touched many people. Amazingly, these visits were not sad times; they were filled with as many laughs as tears, they were marked by love rather than pity.

Please remember that these are not difficult for Anna. She is very peaceful and does not struggle at all. She just stops breathing, like she has somehow forgotten about it. Then, after a minute or a few minutes, she remembers again. When she stops breathing we hold her and tell her we love her and that she can go when she is ready even though we will miss her. So far, she has always come back.

We are open for business again today. Doors open at noon and we will probably kick everyone out at about seven p.m. Saturday is another day for taking inventory, another quiet day. Anna and I are planning to watch some football and Kathleen has already laid out her U of M and MSU outfits for the big game. Anna will support one team one half and then the other the next. Deep down, I know she is a Michigan fan and she is just humoring her mother.

The doors open again on Sunday, noon to seven p.m. We have greatly enjoyed the visitors over the last few days. I think Anna has already entertained more than one hundred guests. She is the consummate hostess. We are very pleased with the balance we have achieved with one day open and the next closed, so do not fear coming to the open houses because we have set aside enough times for ourselves when the doors are closed.

Thanks again for your support.

Anna's parents

Monday, October 23, 2000, 12:18 p.m.
From: Anna's Dad
Subject: Monday–the race

Well, the weekend is over. It is Monday and Kathleen and I are running on a complete night's sleep. It feels delicious. It looks good for another full night tonight and maybe tomorrow night. Getting a full night's sleep depends on whether we can get qualified people in to watch Anna during the night. For a few nights preceding last night, the qualified people were Kathleen and I. We would hook Anna up to an apnea monitor that was set to go off if she stopped breathing for more than thirty seconds. Unfortunately, the monitor also alarms if there is a loose connection. We were getting a lot of false alarms every night, even though Anna was in no particular distress.

Last night, we went back to the way we were doing it before: just having people stay up holding Anna all night. Last night my sister and nurse Ruth watched Anna. There were no incidents severe enough to justify waking us up so we enjoyed a full night's sleep. It feels great.

Kathleen has suggested that the current state of affairs is like running a race when you do not know the length of the race. Initially, we were pretty sure it was going to be a sprint, so we were running really fast. Now, it is starting to feel more like at least a 10K and maybe a marathon, so we are trying to pace ourselves a little more. (I know what you are thinking, where does Stuive get off using a running analogy, the only running he ever does is running out for lunch. Of course you are right. But, keep in mind two things: first, it is Kathleen's analogy, and second, I just watched the Olympics so I am pretty educated on running stuff right now.)

To help us slow the pace a little, we have decided to take a couple of days to ourselves. The next open house will be Wednesday and Thursday, noon to seven. Monday and Tuesday we are just going to hang out with Anna on our own.

Anna still seems pretty stable. Some little seizures are starting to sneak over the medication wall. They are not very severe; we are increasing the frequency of the meds to address them. I guess this may indicate continued deterioration but it really does not look or feel like Anna is deteriorating.

Taking care of Anna at night was tough. You would think that we could catch a few winks when Anna napped, but because she would stop breathing at any time without warning, someone always had to be awake watching her. Considering how snuggly Anna was and how warm she felt in your arms, it was often hard to keep your eyes open as you held this napping child. Eventually fatigue forced us to get help.

This is Ruth with Anna. We met Ruth for the first time the day after Anna was diagnosed. Ruth was part of the pediatric hospice team that helped acclimate us to living with a child with a terminal diagnosis. Ruth would arrive at about 11:00 p.m. and crash in the guest room for a few hours. I would hit the sack when she arrived. Kathleen would stay up and hold Anna until about 2:00 a.m. Then Kath would wake Ruth and she would hold Anna from 2:00 to 7:00 a.m. I would take over at 7:00. Ruth would wake us up if Anna had an episode or if she needed anything by using the cordless phone as an intercom.

She is still giving us a little bit of awake time every day although she is almost always sleeping. That's ok. I do not think I am ever as happy as when I am sitting in my big chair cuddled up with Anna; her warmth and weight are the ultimate comfort.

Right now Kathleen has that comfort. She is close to finishing another Narnia book. I think Anna wants to hear them all.

We will see you on Wednesday. If you are coming for open house, you do not need to bring munchies anymore, we have enough munchies to last until the Super Bowl.

I am the king of pie.

Anna's Dad

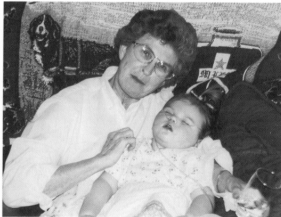

Tuesday, October 24, 2000, 2:35 p.m.
From: Anna's Dad
Subject: Tuesday-the art of crafts

Anna is again sleeping peacefully. She had a little bit of a tough night, coughing and sputtering for the first few hours. Our night watch did not come together last night so Anna slept with Kath and me. She did not set off the monitors at all, which was nice, but she was pretty congested. The night watch is set for tonight so we are hoping for a full night's sleep.

Last night we created a special keepsake. We made a plaster cast of Anna's hand. Thank you Kelly for the kit; it was incredibly entertaining to make the cast and the results are fantastic. Anna had been sleeping calmly all day yesterday when we dipped her hand in the goo to make the mold. She immediately decided that that was the time to make a fist. She would not let go and time was limited.

With a lot of coaxing Anna agreed to relax and let her hand stay in the goo. We pulled her hand out and the goo set with an almost perfect impression of her hand, including almost all the way around her fingers. We then poured the plaster over the goo. We let it dry a while and then pulled out the goo. We were left with a beautiful plaster sculpture of Anna's hand. It is reaching right out of the plaster. You can see all the way around her fingers, including her fingernails. She even got her fat little wrist into the picture.

Yesterday and today have been really pleasant for all of us. We feel we can use one more day, so it will not be open house until Thursday. We are sorry if that interferes with anyone's plans, but we needed this time more than we realized. We will be sure to leave a lot of open house time this weekend to make it up.

Thanks for understanding.
Anna's Dad

Believe it or not, this project took four adults to complete: one to hold Anna, one to hold Anna's hand still in the goo, one to mix and pour the goo and one to time everything. It was a moment of levity during a time of uncertainty. It gave John, Bryan, Nancy and me a chance to laugh and marvel over the beautiful intricacies of a baby's hand: the pudgy fingers, the perfect finger nails, and the "rubber band wrist." The project also helped us deal with a fear, a fear that we would not be able to remember what Anna looked like. We spent a lot of time during the last few weeks just staring at her trying to memorize every detail with precision.

We switched Anna from the Diastat to Ativan, an oral medication, when we could no longer control her seizures proactively. We started with the lowest possible theraputic dose and gradually increased it. We quickly decided that having Anna sleep all the time as a result of the drug was worth the price of stopping her seizures which also made her sleep all the time. It was a constant balancing act.

Medication amounts changed almost daily. We took educated guesses, but they were all guesses. We just tried to follow Anna's lead. It got to the point where we had to give Anna her Ativan every two hours. This made sleep impossible if just the two of us were caring for Anna. We often tried setting the alarm to wake us every two hours, and then we would trade off holding her half way through the night. The few winks we would get in between alarms did not exactly qualify as sleep.

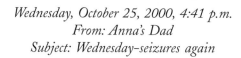

Wednesday, October 25, 2000, 4:41 p.m.
From: Anna's Dad
Subject: Wednesday-seizures again

It has been a busy day. Starting this morning, Anna was having seizures quite frequently. Although they were not long or as severe as they were a couple of weeks ago, the frequency, despite her medications, was troubling. Anna is not suffering with these seizures. She remains calm even during the seizures. We have stepped up Anna's medications and she has now gone a couple of hours without any.

It is difficult to say what this new round of seizures means. It may be in part that her body is growing accustomed to the medications. It may be that she is having more irregular activity in her brain. We anticipate that it also means we are one step closer.

Although we want to share all of this with you, we are not completely comfortable having guests when we are working to stabilize Anna's condition or holding her and saying goodbye because we think it might be the end. For that reason, we are not having open house tomorrow, Thursday, either. We will let you know when the doors will be open again.

Through all of this, we have enjoyed great peace. Our doctors and the hospice people have always been there to answer our questions. Know that we feel your support as well.

Anna's Dad

Friday, October 27, 2000, 4:26 p.m.
From: Anna's Dad
Subject: Friday-sleepy parents

Anna is sleeping peacefully in Uncle Patrick's arms. Today has been fairly quiet. Anna did some unusual things this morning, but they did not last long and were not severe. More importantly, they did not last past this morning. I am not completely sure whether they really happened or whether they were just the imaginings of a very tired Dad.

Kath and I did the switch-off-baby-hold again last night. Anna had a quiet night (only periodic suctioning) but we still have to get up every two hours because she now needs her meds that frequently. We have napped our way through last night's fatigue and are looking forward to this weekend; we have coverage every night and we may get three nights of sleep in a row.

Because Anna seems pretty stable and because we will probably be stable as well after a good night's sleep, we will have open house from noon to five p.m. on Saturday. Be warned, however, that Anna feels pretty strongly about watching college football and she may not give you her undivided attention.

Anna's Dad

Suctioning was not pleasant for Anna or for us. Anna would often struggle handling her secretions; sometimes her secretions would make it difficult for her to breathe. Other times they would just make her annoyingly gurgly. To address those problems you would use a suction machine.

The suction machine was a vacuum pump with an extension that had a catheter at the end. We would put the catheter in Anna's mouth to suction out her mouth and throat. Anna did not like that and she would frequently deny access by clamping her mouth shut tight. The only option then was to go down her nose. She hated that even more, but she could not stop that.

Even when Anna was really out of it, she would react to that damned suction machine. What choice did we have?

As the body shuts down it sends liquids it no longer needs to different places. For Anna, it was all secretions. We tried drying her out with medications, but it just thickened the secretions making them harder for her to handle and impossible to suction.

Can you stop giving liquids altogether? Her body did not need as much. Before October, Anna was getting 30 to 40 ounces of formula and free water per day. We gradually decreased that amount as she was needing and using fewer nutrients. She got noticeably skinnier.

So, how do you want your child to go: starvation and dehydration or would you prefer she choke on her own secretions? We would go back and forth on these issues and, correspondingly, how much liquid Anna got. Kath and I did not always agree. You muddle through anyway.

Near the end, Anna was getting only an ounce or two of formula and water a day. Really, it was just enough to flush her meds down the g-tube. Near the end we did not have to suction her at all and at the very end she was able to sleep peacefully.

Because we were always holding Anna, it was easy to tell when she was not breathing. You could feel the rhythm change. When you looked down at her you could watch the color drain out of her face.

When the episodes first started we would try to help. We would suction her out and change her position hoping that it would help her, but it never did. Then, all you could do was wait; one minute, two minutes, three minutes, four minutes, five minutes, sometimes longer. We would actually watch the clock tick away the seconds. By that time her face would be completely ashen and her lips and the area around her eyes would be blue.

And then, right when you were sure Anna was gone, she would take a single deep breath, not a labored breath, just a big gulp. The color would slowly return to her face, first around her nose and mouth and then her cheeks. It would only return for a few seconds though, because she would only take one breath. The color would drain again, you would tell her you loved her, sing to her, tell her it was ok to go, hold her tight . . . a second breath, a little quicker this time.

Eventually, after about fifteen minutes, the breaths would be coming frequently enough that you would say she was breathing normally, as if nothing had happened. We were always sure she was gone--she always came back.

Saturday, October 28, 2000, 9:23 a.m.
From: Anna's Dad
Subject: Saturday-one more breath

Last night we had another episode where we thought Anna might be gone. She stopped breathing for minutes at a time. We held her close and said goodbye, but she decided not to leave. She did it again this morning for a shorter period of time. Under the circumstances, we have decided to cancel today's open house. If you know anyone who was planning on coming and who might not get this message, please let them know for us. We are sorry for the inconvenience but it is so hard to endure one of those episodes when others are here.

Anna's Dad

Well, we are coming to the close of another day. Anna enjoyed watching football all day.

When the Ohio State/Purdue game was over, she stopped breathing again. Once again we held her close and said our goodbyes; once again after about fifteen minutes she was okay. We have certainly struggled to figure out what we are supposed to learn from these brushes with death. Hopefully we will gain some benefit. Right now, it just seems hard. Maybe Anna wants to see the Lions one more time.

Anna's Dad

Although John always avoided asking "why," after going through these near-death experiences a few times, I started to ask God why He was putting us through this torture. I tried hard not to ask God many "why" questions. I believed that there was a plan that I could not comprehend. But when I was exhausted, my child was dying, and I kept getting these false alarms, the emotional drain became unbearable. There had to be an easier way to prepare us for the end.

Sunday, October 29, 2000, 10:01 p.m.
From: Anna's Dad
Subject: Sunday-open eyes

The hospice people let us know early on that even though Anna's death was imminent it did not mean that Anna's condition would follow an inevitable linear path downward. Instead, there would be instances when death would be very close and other times when death would not be so close.

Every time death was close we had to decide how much to "intervene." When Anna would stop breathing we had to decide whether to simply hold her or to take action to try to bring her back. Every time we suctioned her out during these episodes or massaged her chest in the hopes of stimulating her to breathe, we were possibly changing the path that Anna was leading us down. We could have been prolonging an existence that for her was undesirable.

For Kathleen the choice was always simple. She could not sit there and do nothing as Anna stopped breathing. She did get to a point, however, that once she had tried suctioning and massage for a few minutes, she could just sit with her and hold her. It was easier for me to do nothing but hold her.

In the end, it made no difference. It did not appear that the suctioning or massage ever brought her back or that failing to do them interfered with her coming back. Trying to balance these considerations was unbelieveably difficult. No matter what we did, every decision we made regarding Anna's care had significant consequences.

It has been a wakeful day. Starting at 4:00 a.m. Anna decided to wake up. She stayed up with her eyes open, talking for about an hour. Although we missed the sleep a little, it was really nice to talk to her again. She was pretty much awake for an hour this evening too.

She did have one more episode this morning. Several minutes without breathing and then finally the first breath. Eventually, she was breathing again. We have become so accustomed to the episodes that it just does not seem to be that big a deal. Do not misunderstand, we know that each of these episodes takes us to the brink of death. We are just getting more accustomed to being there.

Because she had one Friday night and then Saturday night and then Sunday morning, we thought it might be an escalation. But it has been a quiet day for Anna. We will enjoy her company as long as she wants to hang out with us.

Anna's Dad

Tuesday, October 31, 2000, 1:34 p.m.
From: Anna's Dad
Subject: Tuesday–being together

Good afternoon. Sorry we have not posted, but the last couple of days have been so peaceful that we have not turned on the computer.

Anna has not had any long episodes of not breathing since Sunday morning. Given the increasing frequency of those episodes, this respite is rather unexpected.

Anna has also been awake more frequently lately despite taking enough Ativan to render me unconscious around the clock. It is hard to figure the how or the why of any of this; we are just trying to get better at rolling with the punches. It is pretty easy to roll with the present punches.

Yesterday was also one of the first days that Kath and I and Anna spent alone together all day. We read some more, we worked on funeral stuff, and we just acted like a family. It was very nice. We are going to keep going like that for a while. I am sure we will have an open house again eventually, but right now it feels good to just be bored with each other.

We have now made multiple castings of Anna's hands and feet. If this goes long enough, we may be able to make an entire plaster statue of Anna.

The end seemed very close last weekend, now it seems far away. It is not clear to us which is better, even though we are certainly enjoying our time with Anna.

Anna's Dad

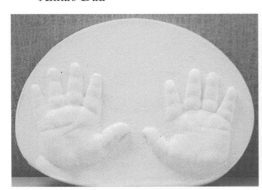 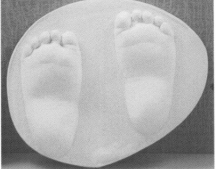

Anna was taking enough Ativan to keep her comatose indefinitely. It was amazing to see how her little body could use the Ativan where it was needed most and free the rest of her brain so she could wake up and chat with us. These moments were beyond precious.

Our description of the power of Ativan was no exaggeration. We obtained the Ativan from the hospice pharmacy, but we would always seem to run out on the weekend when the hospice pharmacy was closed. When that happened we would contact the hospice "on-call" person who would phone in the prescription to a local 24 hour pharmacy.

One time, when I went to pick up such a prescription, the clerk would not give it to me. Instead, she called the pharmacist over. He asked if Anna's birthdate, 3/9/99, meant she was born in 1899. When I said no, he said he did not think he should give this medication in that dosage to a twenty month old baby. According to him, the dose was enough to keep ME comatose 24 hours a day.

He was not going to give me the meds. Although I did not feel like explaining, and he was ultimately sorry he made me explain, I explained the circumstances and he let me have the drugs. The incident, however, made us marvel that Anna could be awake at all.

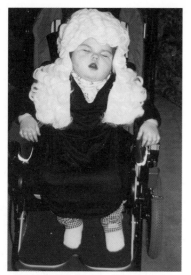

We never posted the pictures of Judge Anna, probably because she looked so out of it. She did wake up a little bit for Brian and Nancy. They made and decorated Halloween cookies for Anna.

Not much to report. Anna had one episode Wednesday morning where she did not breathe for a while, but it seems to be the exception rather than the rule right now. Anna dressed up as a judge for Halloween. It was sort of impromptu. When we cut off the raggedy ends on the arms and the bottom of a witches outfit, it was very clearly a judge's robe. I told Kathleen it was interesting how little effort it took to make a witch into a judge, but she did not think it was funny. We also added a judge's wig, you know, the old English wigs that go way down their shoulders. Anna slept through the robing ceremony and her whole time on the "bench" (her wheelchair with the tray on it).

We are starting to get a little more used to the idea that Anna might still hang around for a while. Maybe not, but maybe so. We continue to feast every evening on fine meals. We continue to work our way through the Narnia stories; we are on book six. We continue to enjoy our time with Anna and we continue to work on the little details that we will have to attend to in the coming days.

We also continue to thank you for your support.

Anna's Dad

Friday, November 3, 2000, 5:16 p.m.
From: Anna's Dad
Subject: Friday

Help, we are suffering an infestation of five year old Feeneys. Other than this pestilence, all is well.

Anna's Dad

Saturday, November 4, 2000, 11:20 p.m.
From: Anna's Mom
Subject: Saturday-peeking

Anna has been a bit gurgly today but is resting comfortably. She had a wonderful time with her cousins yesterday and was "peeking" at many of her visitors. Actually, she is peeking at me right now—it is always a wonderful event.

This morning, our friends from Mika Meyers made quick work of the leaves on our lawn for the second year in a row. It is a wonderful sight to see the green grass again, although we miss the color we saw a few weeks ago.

It has been a quiet day except for the shouting that we did while watching the football games. Anna keeps reminding us that we have not read to her in two days. Perhaps tonight we will have the chance—our friend has the night off so Anna is stuck with the two of us all night. We think she is looking forward to it.

Time to hold the baby.

Anna's Mom

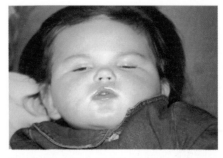

Sometimes, even though it might have been to Anna's detriment, we would exact a promise from the person on Anna-duty to not read to Anna from the <u>Chronicles of Narnia</u> because we did not want to miss anything while we slept or were otherwise out of earshot. The ultimate luxury was to just relax with your eyes closed to better picture the words or with your eyes open to gaze out the picture window at the fall colors. It was as if the listener was taking in every word, every sight, and every sound, for Anna while she slept.

You may have noticed that you have not heard much about Ruby and Jasper during the fall season. They were there. They were very happy because we were at home with them 24/7. Each day I would take one or the other for a walk in a nearby park. I kept a cell phone handy so Kathleen could reach me if necessary.

After the first couple of weeks, I would really look forward to having some time by myself each day, away from the house and away from Anna. When I was walking the dogs I could let my mind wander on other things for a while. Kathleen never took time like that. In fact, she left the house only two times during those last weeks with Anna, once to look at cemetery plots and once to look at headstones. I do not know how she did it. She certainly has more stamina than I do.

Sunday, November 5, 2000, 10:27 p.m.
From: Anna's Dad
Subject: Sunday

Another quiet day. Last night Kath and I were on our own, so we were a little tired today. (Our fatigue is compounded by the fact that we both seem to be coming down with colds).

Anna had some problems handling secretions all day. We are struggling to find the right combination of meds and fluids and suction to help her out, but we are not having a lot of luck.

Since about 7:30 p.m. (around three hours ago) she has been sleeping very calmly. We needed that very badly. Now we are fighting to stay awake until the cavalry arrives.

Actually, we do not need to stay awake. It works just fine to fall asleep with her in our arms, we just need to wake up every two hours to do meds.

It has been several days since Anna had an episode where she stopped breathing. It is possible we have hit a plateau. Only time will tell. Big help, huh?

Anna's Dad

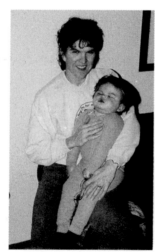
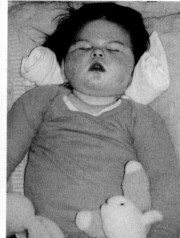

Monday, November 6, 2000, 9:23 p.m.
From: Anna's Mom
Subject: Monday-fighting colds

Anna and her Dad are in their usual spot watching Monday Night Football. Anna smells wonderful after her bath, but Dad looks like he could use some help.

Yes, both Dad and I have decided to come down with colds. Great timing was never our forte, but we will cope. We have lots of food in the fridge, so we are feeding our colds (or is it starve a cold?).

Anna continues to gurgle, so we are experimenting to see whether it is (a) the formula itself, (b) the amount of liquid, or (c) a combination of the two that is making it so difficult for Anna to handle her secretions. We wanted to poll a representative cross-section of the voting public, but all the pollsters are busy. Wonder why.

We will rejoice on Wednesday when all the political ads will cease. Please do not forget to vote and, for those of you in Kent County, be sure to put your mark next to my name.

Time to feed Anna and take a nap until my shift begins tonight.

Much love,

Anna's Mom

Even a slight increase or decrease in Anna's fluid intake--a few cc's one direction or another--seemed to have wildly varying effects on Anna's ability to breathe. At first we tried to ensure that she was receiving nutrition. As her ability to handle any fluids decreased, we changed priorities and focused on the total amount of secretions she would create. It was amazing to see how she could function on so little fluid. Even when she was only on microscopic amounts of fluid, I still gave her at least one small dose of formula. It was a futile gesture but, as a mother, I could not starve my child. In that situation, I had to follow my heart rather than my head.

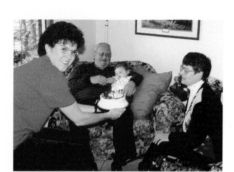

Of course, we celebrated Anna's 20 month "birthday" on November 9.

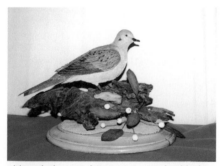

Although the open houses were over by this time, Anna still welcomed guests and she received many special gifts. One such gift, pictured above, was a hand carved mourning dove. It was created by Geoff Schram.

Wednesday, November 8, 2000, 10:00 p.m.
From: Anna's Dad
Subject: Wednesday

Anna is greatly enjoying her first presidential election and, as with other things, Anna is stretching it out to get the maximum enjoyment. If we were sleep deprived before, now we are double deprived.

Anna has slept very soundly the last couple of days with very few wakeful periods. She has also been very congested. We are working hard to figure out the right volume and content of her liquid intake to minimize the congestion.

We are pleased to announce that Kathleen garnered her fair share of the vote. We are glad to have the first election behind us.

Anna made it through our wedding anniversary; it was our eighth on Tuesday. It is my birthday on Friday. We are hoping to get past that as well. Of course it should not make a difference, but it would be awful if Anna decided to leave on a day like that.

Thanks again for your support.

Anna's Dad

Thursday, November 9, 2000, 9:52 p.m.
From: Anna's Dad
Subject: Thursday

Today has been a study in contrasts. Right now Anna is awake, as awake as she has been in weeks. She is looking around, making lots of facial expressions, and talking to her mom. She has been this way for one to two hours at a stretch three times today.

On the other hand, when Anna has been sleepy today, she has been very sleepy, almost completely out of it, taking very shallow breaths. We are also getting some indication that Anna's digestive system is slowing and may be shutting down. We are keeping a close watch on this.

But right now, she is just our very awake little girl.

Anna's Dad

We used much of this time to play with her, give her a bath, sing with her, massage her, read to her, and show Anna her favorite V-Tech toys so she could play some songs for us. It was as if we were trying to live a thousand moments in every minute that she was awake. More than anything, we just wanted her to know how much we loved her and that we would be right here if she fell asleep again- -and we would still be here if she woke up again.

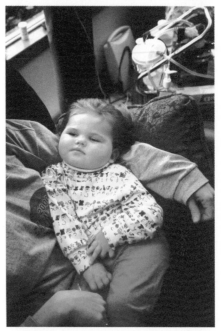

Anna awake. This picture, one of the last we have of Anna awake, shows how truly at peace Anna was at this time. We treasure this picture because it represents the best part of those last weeks with Anna. On the other hand, you can also see the accursed suction machine in the background.

It is impossible to convey what it was like for us to live twenty-four hours every day. Every moment was consumed with all things Anna. We drank her in and tried to savor each moment. We would sit with Anna for four to six hours at a stretch. We kept track of time by the number of Ativan doses she received while we held her. We reluctantly handed her over to the next care-giver when our shift ended. We then prepared her medications, tended to the needs of the immediate care-giver, and waited.

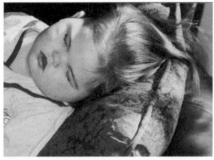

We never cut Anna's hair. When she was born it was dark brown. As she got older, it became a sandy blonde. In the sun it shone like gold. Kathleen loved to wash it, brush it, and play with it. The color, shine, and sweet aroma of Anna's hair are firmly stamped in our memories.

Saturday, November 11, 2000, 8:24 p.m.
From: Anna's Dad
Subject: Saturday–homebound

It has been a remarkably lazy day. Both Kath and I are still under the weather with our colds. I think we have slept more than Anna did today. Fortunately, Anna could watch football while we slept.

With our colds and everything, we have been pretty much homebound for several days. In a way, this house is starting to feel like a coccoon. Hopefully, we will emerge more beautiful than when we came in.

Anna has continued her wakeful ways. She has been awake and alert again today for an extended period. Given Anna's EEG results and her heavy load of medications, it is kind of hard to explain how she could be this way. Do not get me wrong, we are not complaining. It is fun to talk to her again. She seems to have a lot to say and she is quite unhappy if you are not giving her your full attention.

We are still struggling with the amount of formula to give Anna, if any. Each time we try, she gets very congested and uncomfortable. It appears that her digestive system is calling it quits. We are told that Anna will lead us to the right decisions on matters like this, but sometimes it is hard to hear and sometimes it is hard to listen to what she has to say.

She is fast asleep now on Kath's lap, her mouth open, and snoring loudly. I think I will join her.

Anna's Dad

Monday, November 13, 2000, 7:47 p.m.
From: Anna's Mom
Subject: Monday–a quiet day

Not much new to report. Anna is still sleeping soundly. She has been more sleepy the last couple of days. She had a nice bath this evening and she has been cooing happily since. We will be in touch.

Anna's Mom

In some ways it felt like we were stuck in Summer a long way into Fall. Now, it feels like we are caught in between Fall and Winter. Weather becomes a big deal when you spend your days looking out of windows.

Anna is doing okay. She is weaker. Her breaths are shallow. She is also more peaceful. Her coughs are milder and less frequent so it just seems like she is sleeping quietly.

A week ago we were contemplating that she might be at a plateau and that she might be there for a while. Now it seems clear that she is still declining. It has been two weeks since Anna had an episode where she stopped breathing for an extended period of time. No one has explained why such a problem would come and then go, but we are glad to see it go.

For our latest project, we painted Anna's hands and feet with fabric paint in primary colors and then pressed them onto a pillowcase. We plan to do some more pillowcases and some sweatshirts. Anna does not mind recording her footsteps in paint, but she does resist a little when it comes to her hands. I think she just does not want to be fingerprinted.

Anna's Dad

Even though Anna remained sleeping while we painted her hands and feet and pressed them on white pillow cases, she was still able to express her dissatisfaction with the entire process. Poor Nancy was the designated baby holder during these procedures. She often apologized to Anna while we completed our works of art.

Anna is quite relieved that the Wolverines survived the Ohio State game. As this is her second Michigan/Ohio State game she really is starting to gain an understanding of the importance of the rivalry. Anna has become quite an astute college football fan.

You will have to forgive me for this focus on football, but it was always my dream to have a child and then hold that child on my lap as we both drifted in and out of sleep while we watched football on Saturday and Sunday afternoons. Anna seems to really enjoy this as well.

Although roses were not at issue today for the Wolverines, Kathleen did get the last rose of the season off the rose bushes today. It was very striking to see this beautiful rosebud bending under the weight of the snow. We now have several inches on the ground.

Anna has been sleeping peacefully pretty much all day. That is okay.

Anna's Dad

Nancy and her nieces, Clare and Elizabeth, watched Anna while Kathleen and I looked at headstones.

Monday, November 20, 2000, 6:37 p.m.
From: Anna's Mom
Subject: Monday–meeting Drew

Snowy day. Anna had an episode at about three this morning where she stopped breathing for quite a while. She came out of it. That was the first such episode in almost three weeks. Other than that, today has been uneventful.

Anna very much enjoyed meeting her cousin Drew yesterday. Drew thought her hair was especially fun and tried to take some back to Oma and Opa's house with him. Drew and Anna are looking forward to lots more meetings.

Anna's Mom

The view out the back window shifted from green to white.

Drew is my nephew, the son of my sister Lisa and her husband Ron who live in Seattle. Ron and Lisa met Anna when she was baptized in June of 1999 and then again after Anna was diagnosed in September of 1999. This day, however, was the first time that Kathleen, Anna and I met Drew.

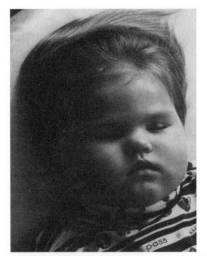

That Wednesday, Anna spent a very quiet day with us. We hardly used the suction machine. We watched the musical Fiddler on the Roof. We sang all the songs to Anna. Kathleen made a quadruple batch of stuffing for our Thanksgiving meal. It was not a noteworthy day; we were just preparing for Thanksgiving.

Wednesday, November 22, 2000, 12:55 p.m.
From: Anna's Dad
Subject: Wednesday–Anna's new friend

Happy early Thanksgiving. Anna is all geared up for turkey and football tomorrow and she says she is thankful for many things. I know we are.

Although Sunday and Monday nights were kind of rough, last night was very calm. We have decreased her fluids again in the hope that it will help decrease her congestion and secretions. It appears to be helping.

Last night Anna had some visitors, including a nine week old yorkshire terrier/toy poodle cross. This teeny puppy was just Anna's size and enjoyed some quality time snoozing with Anna.

It was hard to believe that such a tiny creature could be the same kind of critter as Jasper and Ruby. Jasper fell madly in love with the puppy, but he simply could not find a way to relate to it because of its size. The best he could do was lick her, giving her a complete bath with one swipe of his tongue.

Among the things we are thankful for this Thanksgiving is this list and its members. Thanks for listening, it makes a big difference.

Anna's Dad

The puppy came along with part of our hospice team, Dan Hendrickson and Dr. Colleen Talen. They were part of a group of people who met with us on Tuesday night. As a group we were planning to set up an organization that would provide services to the families of children with terminal or life-limiting diagnoses. We will tell you more about that later.

Chapter 10
The Winter

284   *Anna's Friends*

It is very early on Thanksgiving morning as we write this. We will send it a little later on.

At about 3:00 a.m. this morning, Anna went back to heaven. It was so peaceful. Aunt Lauran had first watch tonight. During that watch, Anna's breathing just started to slow down. She would take four or five breaths a minute. It was very different than all the other times she stopped breathing; this time everything just slowed down.

I got up at about 1:30 a.m. and held her for an hour. Her breathing became slower and slower and she was very warm.

Kath got up at 2:30 a.m. and took Anna's temp. It was very high. Kath held her for the next half hour wiping her forehead and arms with a cool cloth.

At 3:00 a.m. Anna got very heavy, she took another breath, and then she was gone.

The changes Anna had in her breathing and temperature indicate that her brain had finally had enough and could not handle even the autonomic functions of respiration and temperature control. There was clearly no pain for Anna. Her face was so angelic.

There is a strange combination of pain and peace for us. We are certainly happy that Anna can now run and laugh. We know she is with friends and family. We give thanks for that. We also give thanks for every minute and second we had with Anna. We give thanks for answered prayers.

There are volumes of words in our hearts that we wish we could share but it is hard to even organize our thoughts. Instead, we have attached the obituary that we started writing a few weeks ago and completed this morning:

"Anna was born on March 9, 1999. She returned to heaven on Thursday, November 23, 2000. Thus, Anna stayed with us for one year, eight months, fifteen days, one hour and forty-four minutes. Every minute was an incredible gift.

We spent a lot of time thinking about when Anna could not die. She could not die before our entire families saw her for one last time. She could not die before our friends had a chance to say goodbye. She could not die while one of us was out of the house. It was not until John and I sat in bed together on the eve of Thanksgiving that we determined we had gotten past all of the "could nots." We finally said to each other that it would be okay if Anna returned to heaven. It was only 3 hours later that Lauran let us know that Anna's breathing had slowed dramatically.

Rather than jump out of bed, as I usually did, I stayed in bed while John took stock of the situation. Even after he came back and told me what was happening, I asked for just one more hour of sleep. I think that the agreement we reached--that we were ready to let her go--helped me to be at peace even though I knew the end was near.

Anna spent time with each of us in the darkness of those early morning hours, giving each of us the closeness and peace that we sought. There is no doubt that Anna stayed with us exactly as long as she was supposed to stay on earth in our care. She left us quietly, without pain. One would expect some notice. All I perceived was a sudden heaviness as I held Anna, as if someone had thrown ten pounds onto my lap with Anna.

All of the false alarms that we survived when Anna stopped breathing prepared us to appreciate the sanctity of the moment she died. It was almost as if we could feel her soul leave her body and God's presence in our living room as He held her in one arm and wrapped His other arm around us. Thinking of that moment of quiet holiness brings tears to my eyes. I pray that all parents who lose their children experience that peace of heart and mind at that moment.

After Anna died in our arms, we just sat as a family in one of our oversized chairs by the big picture window, hugging, crying, touching her fair skin, talking to her, saying good-bye, and loving each other. It was quiet. Peaceful. Sorrowful. We sang her favorite songs to her. We took turns holding her in our arms, feeling the familiar weight and sensing a difference in the way she felt. After a while, we gave her a bath. She loved her baths. We massaged her with baby lotion as always. We dressed her and dried her hair, leaving her long tresses combed to the side rather than pulled up in a whale spout. I pulled together the outfits (yes, more than one) that she would need for the visitations. Looking back, it all felt seamless, like we had rehearsed this ritual many times before. There was no confusion. Only calm.

This may not seem like a long time to live but it was exactly as long as Anna was supposed to live because the amino acids were mixed up in the mitochondrial DNA of Anna's cells. The "mix-up" has been described to us as a defect, a mutation, or a disease. But, to us, because it was written into her cells from the moment she was conceived, it was as much a part of Anna as her blue eyes or her pudgy fingers.

Even though Anna did not live very long, she lived very well. She loved her dolly, her balloons, and ribbons. She loved to watch the sunlight filter through the leaves of the big maple tree in the front yard. She loved to be sung to, read to, and she loved to be held. Anna especially loved to be held while she watched football games on television.

As much as Anna loved to be held, she loved to hold others. She would always be sure to firmly grasp the fingers of anyone holding her, to let them know that being held was a two-way street. During July of 1999, Anna learned to laugh. She forgot how to laugh a month later, but for that one month Anna loved to make people laugh by laughing first.

Anna also loved her family: her parents, John C. Stuive, Esq., and the Hon. Kathleen A. Feeney of Belmont, her grandparents Johanna and John Stuive of Wyoming, and Delores and Verne Feeney of Traverse City, and her aunts and uncles Lauran and Oscar Bittinger of Grand Rapids, Dr. Ronald and Lisa DeVries of Seattle, WA, Dr. Brian and Crystal Feeney of Traverse City, and Patrick Feeney of Traverse City, her cousins Kaitlin and Kenzie Feeney of Traverse City and Drew DeVries of Seattle, and her Bernese Mountain Dogs, Ruby and Jasper.

Anna brought all who knew her indescribable joy. Anna never walked, she never talked, she could not hold her head up, and for the last year of her life she could not even smile; nonetheless, she spoke volumes to us, she taught us many lessons, and she touched an entire lifetime's worth of people. We thank God for giving us Anna and we thank you all for your prayers and support.

Visitation will be held at the Pederson Funeral Home in Rockford on Monday, November 27, 2000, from 2:00 p.m. to 4:00 p.m. and from 7:00 p.m. to 9:00 p.m., and Tuesday from 2:00 p.m. to 4:00 p.m. and 6:00 to 9:00 p.m. On Tuesday starting at 8:00 p.m., a Remembrance Service will be held at the funeral home so Anna's friends can share their special memories of Anna with those who love her. The Funeral Mass will be held at Assumption of the Blessed Virgin Mary Church in Belmont at 10:00 a.m. on Wednesday, November 29, to be followed by interment at the Plainfield Township Cemetery and a luncheon at the church. Memorial contributions may be sent to The Anna's Friends Foundation, at 6132 Rogue Lane NE, Belmont, Michigan 49306. The foundation funds research, education, and services for children who have been diagnosed with terminal or life-altering illnesses."

We will write again when we are better at putting words together. Anna's Mom & Dad

Later, we contacted our families and told them that Anna had returned to heaven. A call to our parish priest was next on the list. I then went to church with an entire box of kleenex. Most of our friends who attended John's RCIA classes were there. It was more than I could take when Father Bozung announced to the congregation that Anna had left us Thanksgiving morning. The love that I felt and the hugs I received at the end of church would lift me up repeatedly over the next week. It all helped me to realize that there had to be a tremendous celebration in heaven that day as Anna greeted all of our dearly departed family and friends for the first time. I could only imagine her holding her dolly as she sat in the arms of her great-grandparents.

Friday, November 24, 2000, 11:10 a.m.
From: Anna's Dad
Subject: Friday–new things

Our next door neighbors later told us that they knew Anna had died on Thanksgiving because they saw us turn out the lights in our living room that night for the first time since early October. For them, the light shining in the dark was synonymous with Anna's continued presence on earth. How true.

Anna had lots of stuffed animals, but her favorites were her green bunny, . .

. . her glowworm, . .

. . . and her dolly.

There are so many new things. Last night we turned off the lights at night for the first time in seven weeks. No one was on watch, trying to stay awake. We do not need to keep track of time, there are no meds to keep up with every two hours or three hours or four hours or twice a day. There are a lot of phone calls to make and errands to run; now we can go together.

It was impossible to watch football yesterday without Anna. (I have this vision of Anna napping in God's arms as they watched the games. I wonder if God has a big recliner too.) We are in a constant state of feeling like we have forgotten something because there were so many more things to remember two days ago. I do not mean to convey that we are somehow in a constant state of confusion or agony. Sometimes it is overwhelming, but most of the time we are just fine. I think that was a big part of Anna's gift to us. She gave us enough time to prepare.

Anna's Dad

Wednesday, November 29, 2000, 11:27 p.m.
From: Anna's Mom & Dad
Subject: Wednesday–the funeral

On the night Anna was born, after the epidural had kicked in but before Anna was ready to arrive, Kathleen and I sat and watched a "Law and Order" rerun on television. The television is on again tonight and that show is on. Although there is a symmetry in that, our hearts are just not into symmetry tonight.

The last few days have been a haze of hugs and tears. Once again we have enjoyed wonderful support from all our friends and family. We decorated the funeral home with hundreds of pictures of Anna, all of her birthday tiles (and a couple dozen of her birthday balloons), all of the plaster casts of her hands and feet, and the gifts Anna received from all of her friends, and lots and lots of flowers.

It was a celebration of Anna's life. The funeral home people were probably glad to see us go. Tuesday night's remembrance service was beautiful. The funeral was also beautiful. Again we are overwhelmed by how many people Anna touched.

We buried Anna in the cemetery right around the corner from our house. We have walked through that cemetery dozens of times and it feels very much like home to us. We buried Anna between two trees so that she can continue to enjoy the light as it filters through the leaves. I know that is silly; I know that Anna is not really there. But at least we will enjoy the sunlight as it filters through the leaves. I am sure we will be spending time there.

We talked the cemetery guys into planting a huge box of tulip, daffodil, and hyacinth bulbs as they filled in her grave. We have gone to the monument place to look at monuments for Anna. We plan to spend some time thinking and making it just right, so the bulbs will be Anna's monument for the time being.

Right now we feel a huge emptiness. We are going to go away for a couple of weeks, kind of a retreat. For a long time our every thought and action was geared towards Anna. We need to rediscover each other and figure out a new agenda.

Part of that agenda will be the development of a resource center for families with kids who have been diagnosed with a terminal disease as well as their doctors. Our experience has demonstrated some gaps in the available resources and we have discovered that others have had to try to leap those same gaps.

The people at Pederson's Funeral Home, especially Dave Pederson, made it clear that they were honored to participate in the celebration of Anna's life. We were certainly grateful that they were willing to let us redecorate the place for a few days.

The bulbs were a fitting monument for the short-term.

We have a group of pediatric specialists, hospice people, and parents who are excited to participate in developing this vision. We met for the first time on the Tuesday before Thanksgiving. We all passed Anna around as we shared our own experiences and discussed new and different ways to address some of the problems. Both Kathleen and I are confident that Anna heard all of this, decided that it was a good idea and that we should work hard on it. She wanted to make sure we had something else to do before she left. We do not plan to let her down.

Over the last few days we have talked to many of you who have listened to us through this list. Some have joined recently. If you are interested in looking back, all of the posts are archived on the Anna's Friends list page. Just go to www.onelist.com/ community/Annasfriends. I do not think any of you can understand how important this list has been for us. We are going to keep going with it, at least until Anna's second birthday in March, because we are not ready to give you up yet.

I will leave you tonight with a letter we wrote that Anna's Godfather, Neil Jansen, read for us at the funeral.

"Dear Family and Friends:

Thank you all for being here today and for celebrating Anna's life with us not only today but during every day that we were blessed with her presence.

Most of you have met Anna personally. You've kissed her chubby, silky soft cheeks, felt the weight of her as she nestled in your arms, felt the squeeze around your finger as she held you in return. You've seen the beautiful blue of her eyes. You've heard her coo. And you have smelled the heavenly aroma of Anna's freshly washed hair. Many of you can remember when she smiled and would start "laughing conversations" that would leave her with her mouth open wide in a silent but full-bodied belly laugh. You've seen her at her birthday party with balloons all around, ribbons in her hands, and roses on her cheeks—and her dolly not far away. These are the memories that we will keep alive in our hearts forever.

Although Anna's breathing had been labored and gurgly for a significant portion of the previous few weeks, her breathing was relaxed and clear during the few days before Thanksgiving. Maybe it was a harbinger that the end was coming, but that was contrary to everything we had been told or had read. We prefer to think that on Tuesday night, Anna wanted to hear every word as we discussed the Foundation and how we would help other families care for their terminally ill children.

Anna's Uncle Patrick and Uncle Ron read passages from the Bible at the funeral mass. We chose Ecclesiastes 3:1-15 and Romans 8:28, 31-32, 35-39 for our message to Anna's friends and family. It took us several weeks to agree on these two readings; I am glad that we did all of the preparation and made all of the important decisions before she died. Reviewing these passages gave us words to consider as our time with Anna drew to a close. There is a time and a season for all things: a time to live and a time to die, a time of joy and a time of sadness, a time to celebrate Anna's life and a time to mourn its end. We prayed that God would give us the peace which surpassed understanding.

Many of you have met Anna in your prayers, although never in person. Without ever meeting her and seeing how wonderful she was, you opened your hearts and minds to us. You blessed us on a daily basis with your prayers, cards and thoughts. Your children also joined in praying for "baby Anna," and we trust that the prayers **of** children **for** children must be the most blessed of all.

Merely saying thank you for all of your love and support seems insufficient; nonetheless, we thank you. We thank our parents and siblings for their unending love, understanding and prayers. We ask that you pray that God will give them comfort and strength as well. We thank all of our friends, co-workers, and colleagues who have prayed for us, delivered meals to us, sent cards to us, raked our leaves, cared for our dogs, given us time to be with Anna, and followed our journey through the Anna's Friends mailing list. You cannot begin to understand how you have helped us.

We were very fortunate to have known early on that we would have to live each day with Anna as if it were her last. Because of that Anna lived a very full life; she traveled to lots of places and saw lots of things. For the last seven weeks, however, Anna just stayed at home with us. We held her every minute of every day and that made her very happy.

We had always read books aloud to Anna, but once we knew that Anna's time with us was drawing to a close, we knew that we would have to fit a lifetime's worth of books into a short period of time. The first book that came to mind was C.S. Lewis' *The Lion, The Witch and The Wardrobe* from the seven-volume series known as *The Chronicles of Narnia*.

In *The Chronicles of Narnia*, C.S. Lewis weaves beautiful tapestries that reveal Biblical stories and Christian themes set in the land of Narnia, another world where animals talk, great battles are fought,

Melanie Vugteveen sent us another poem after Anna returned to heaven. Melanie prefaced her poem with the following: "No one can speak personally for Anna, but if Anna could talk, here are some things I'm sure she would say."

Thank you for...

Thanks Mom and Dad for loving me completely and unconditionally, for always giving of yourselves so unselfishly.

God couldn't have chosen better parents to love and care for me during my brief earthly stay. You really taught me (and others too) to make the very most of each and every day.

Thank you for going to great lengths to not only help me, but to help those that are still here. I lived through your strength and your incessant ability to persevere.

You both are an example of "there's nothing you can't do when you let God be your Guide." Your unfaltering faith has been a lesson of how all should abide.

I know you had to make difficult decisions on account of me. Thank you for all the hours of research and reading you did so willingly.

Thank you for sharing me with all your family and special friends. Your openness and willingness to share never seemed to end.

Mom and Dad, I know it must have been pretty hard to leave your jobs you worked so hard at. But I enjoyed and savored every minute we had....even when we just sat.

Thank you for the courage to keep life worth living. I experienced a lifetime through all of your giving.

I loved all of our special moments together. Watching football, reading, arts & crafts, ...and more that I will cherish forever.

My love for you goes beyond any measure. Your love for me is my greatest treasure.

I'll always be with you because those you love are never really gone, they live on forever in your heart. I'll be but an angel's wing away fulfilling my new guardian angel's part.

By Melanie Vugteveen, November 26, 2000

Through the efforts of Sister Rosemary, the elementary school at Assumption Church had adopted Anna as one of their own. They offered this tribute on their bulletin board after she was gone.

I once attended a funeral where we sang "hers" instead of "hymns" in honor of the woman who died. They were all wonderful old church songs that you knew whether you were Catholic or Protestant. At that funeral, we sang at the top of our lungs to make ourselves feel better and to share in the unity of the moment.

We wanted to have that same feeling at Anna's funeral mass. So, we sang some old and some new songs that touched our hearts: How Great Thou Art; The Prayer of St. Francis; When Peace Like A River; Shine Jesus Shine; Great Is Thy Faithfulness; and Ave Maria. Whenever we hear those songs now, we cannot help but cry remembering how much the words meant to us and the beauty of the melody sung in the packed church at Anna's funeral.

and where the Creator, Redeemer, Protector, and Provider is known as Aslan, the Great Lion.

Fearing that our time was very short, we read *The Lion, The Witch and The Wardrobe* aloud to Anna cover to cover in one night. Anna slept during most of the story but we are sure that she heard every word.

Our sense of urgency continued as we completed all seven books in the *Chronicles*. Little did we know that the last pages of the last book in the series would speak volumes to us.

At the end of the last book, titled *The Last Battle*, all of the human characters who have visited Narnia have died, although they do not know it yet. They find out, however, when Aslan, the Great Lion, tells them that, "The dream is ended: this is the morning." C. S. Lewis then writes "[T]he things that began to happen after that were so great and beautiful that I cannot write them. And for us this is the end of all the stories, and we can most truly say that they all lived happily ever after. But for them it was only the beginning of the real story. All their life in this world and all their adventures in Narnia had only been the cover and the title page: now at last they were beginning Chapter One of the Great Story which no one on earth has heard; which goes on forever; in which every chapter is better than the one before."

Lewis' words resonated with us. The story of Anna's life here with us has ended, but what a fabulous story it was—how a little child who could not speak, walk, or talk touched so many lives in so many ways, and how privileged we have been to witness God working through her. But even that fabulous story was only the title and cover page of the real story. Anna has begun Chapter One of the Great Story, the real story, which no one on earth has heard, which goes on forever, and in which every chapter is better than the one before. We look forward to the day when she will read that story to us.

Anna has always been our rose. She had a natural affinity for that most beautiful of flowers. We are sure you have seen many pictures of Anna and roses; they just went together. As you leave the church today, we ask that you take home one of the roses in the sacristy. Take it home and treasure it. Even though each rose will bloom and then die, you will be better off for having been blessed with its beauty, even if for only a short time.

That is the way it has been with our rose, Anna Evaleen. We are all better off for having lived in the light of her beauty even if only for a short time. We have all been a part of the most wonderful shared experience—God's sharing of Anna with all of us. She provided us with a glimpse of heaven, of the perfect peace, beauty, and joy that awaits all of us."

The last of the roses are gone, but next time you see one, please think of Anna. Thank you.
Anna's Mom & Dad

We buried Anna in a beautiful outfit: she wore a turtleneck with roses printed on it, a rose-embroidered white sweater with a matching headband, and rose-colored pants. She also wore white tennis shoes so she could run really fast in heaven. We let her take the blanket that Oma knitted for her, her dolly, her glow worm (it was the first thing that ever made her smile), a small stuffed bernese mountain dog, her favorite book, _Barnyard Dance_ by Sandra Boynton (we would sing the words to her to the tune of Turkey in the Straw), and pictures of all her family and Ruby and Jasper.

The day of the funeral was a gray cold day. As soon as the mass was over, it began to snow, big, fat, pure white, magical flakes of snow that drifted lazily to the ground. (We now call that kind of snow "Anna snow.")

At the cemetery, as we said goodbye, we sang the songs we sang to Anna every day. We sang our version of Edelweiss, where we would sing "Anna Evaleen" instead of "edelweiss, edelweiss." As the snow fell around us the words were very appropriate: "blossom of snow may you bloom and grow, bloom and grow forever. Anna Evaleen, bless our baby forever." We kept singing songs until almost everyone had left. We never even noticed they were leaving. It all seemed so beautiful and so perfect as we said goodbye for the last time.

Even months and months after Anna's death, we still had trouble sleeping. We resorted to prescription medications, over the counter sleep aids and other suggested methods in order to fall asleep. One would expect that the exhaustion would be sufficient to help you to sleep. Not true. A free mind is the enemy of a grieving parent.

Over the next few months, we began overscheduling ourselves so we were not left with free time. We had become very efficient at living so we could spend the majority of our time taking care of Anna. Now we needed to fill all that free time and keep our minds busy. It all added to our exhaustion. Maybe exhaustion should be one of the recognized stages of grieving.

Although John has dreamt of Anna, I have not. I long to dream of her, to see her face again in the reality of my dreams, and to tell her how much we love and miss her. When I wake up in the middle of the night, I wonder whether it is because Anna is there trying to reach me. I talk to her a lot as I lie in bed unable to sleep. I wonder if I will recognize her angel's voice. Every night, I write letters to her in a journal and read a short daily reading from a grief book that a friend gave us entitled Healing After Loss--Daily Meditations for Working Through Grief by Martha Whitmore Hickman. Even that does not help me sleep, but it is a very good book.

Friday, December 1, 2000, 6:35 a.m.
From: Anna's Dad
Subject: Friday-wandering

Yesterday we said goodbye to the last of our visiting family. We created a list of things we had to do before our retreat and started ticking off the things on the list. So long as we are busy with these things, it is not so hard.

The hard part comes at night, when we go to bed. Even if we can keep our minds away from Anna during the day, at night, before you go to sleep, you cannot stop your mind from wandering. As thoughts wander, they always seem to end up on the well-trod paths in our brains that think about Anna. At night, in the dark, as we walk these paths, there is no comfort.

Last night, after laying in bed for about an hour, we just gave up and turned on the television for distraction. Eventually, however, you have to turn it off again. Then you are back where you started. Inevitably you cry. Ruby or Jasper comes over to investigate and you pet them for a minute. After that, things do not seem so bad. Once things are not so bad, sleep catches up with you.

Thank God for the comfort of crying, Bernese Mountain Dogs, and sleep.

It is getting light again; I think I will start getting busy.

Anna's Dad

Saturday, December 2, 2000, 8:13 a.m.
From: Anna's Dad
Subject: Saturday

We are away. See you on the 20th.
Anna's Dad

Saturday, December 2, 2000, 8:41 a.m.
From: Anna's Mom
Subject: Prayers

Dear Friends:

We would like to ask all of you to say some extra-special prayers for two of Anna's favorite people—Bryan Bickford and Nancy Haynes. Bryan and Nancy helped us in countless ways throughout Anna's life, and she loved them very much. Nancy's father died Friday night. We know that Anna is with him and Nancy's family. We know that all of you, like us, will keep Nancy, Bryan and their family in your hearts and prayers during this difficult time.

Anna's Mom

Nancy and Bryan were always there for us. They were there the day after Anna was diagnosed. They were always at the hospital with us. They ran our household those last few weeks Anna was with us. They came with us to the funeral home on the Sunday before visitation to see Anna and hold our hands. They were there during visitation to help everyone feel at home. They were there at the funeral. Despite all this time we spent together, we never really sat and cried with them over Anna. Our hearts were all broken but we did not do it.

When Nancy and Bryan came to our house that morning to take us to the airport, however, the tears began to flow for them and for us.

Right after Anna died, we decided that we needed to leave the house for a while. We had spent the last eight weeks in the cocoon of our living room, but the thought of sitting there without Anna resting in our arms was unbearable. So we called a friend's travel agent, gave her only general instructions on potential get-aways, and picked up the itinerary she made for us a few days later. We are glad that we did not have to make any decisions about our retreat.

We retreated, but we could not escape the pain. We took that with us. This trip did not give us an opportunity to rediscover ourselves as much as it gave us time to sit and let reality sink in. We spent many days keeping busy and many dinners sitting in silence and staring at each other or the beautiful scenery. Still, it was good to be in a place surrounded by natural beauty (and not very many roses).

Tuesday, December 12, 2000, 9:06 a.m.
From: Anna's Dad
Subject: Tuesday

Aloha. Ok, guess where we ran away to? We spent a couple of days in San Francisco on our way to Maui. Now we are on Kuaui. We have seen some incredibly beautiful things. We have snorkeled amongst gorgeous tropical fish, stood atop the Haleakala crater 10,000 feet above sea level, driven through clouds, stood under waterfalls, and watched the surf pound cliffs of lava. We have had a lot of time to think about things. We are rediscovering each other, and setting our new agenda for day-to-day living when we return. We are mourning. We see Anna in every child we encounter and we think about her all the time. We still cannot seem to sleep through the night. Some of this is very hard; there is no avoiding that. Hard or not, this is what we needed. Thanks,

Anna's Dad

Tuesday, December 19, 2000, 4:07 p.m.
From: Anna's Dad
Subject: Tuesday (or is it still Monday continued)

We are home. At least I think it is home. Things seem a little sterile around here and it is not just the obvious, that Anna is not here. We have yet to pick up the dogs. They are still on their vacations. Without them it is very quiet.

Moreover, while we were away, the carpets were cleaned. If you were in our house any time over the last ten weeks, it took a beating. We were in and up all the time for the whole time. Because we were in and up the dogs were in and up (for the most part) as well. Between the dogs dirty feet, our dirty feet, spilled meals, spilled meds, and spilled formula, our off-white shag (not our choice, it came with the house) had traveled a long way off white. It was sort of a game to try to walk from the front door to the kitchen on existing stains. Now it is just plain off-white again, certainly more appealing to the eye, but just another indicator that things are different.

Our retreat is over. As I mentioned in the last post, we saw some incredibly beautiful things. As we meandered from spectacle to spectacle we would almost always say "Anna would love this," even though we knew in our hearts that Anna probably would have been just as happy looking at our back yard.

In many respects it was a very strange trip. Do not get me wrong, it was fantastic and most of the time it was like any vacation, but whether we were on the road, on a trail, in a pool, in the ocean, or in a restaurant, sometimes we would look at each other and realize we had not spoken for minutes and that our minds had just been drifting, wandering and wondering. At the end of that drift is just emptiness.

Although you might disagree, I think it was better to begin to come to grips with that emptiness in a place where we could be anonymous, just two people with no responsibilities.

As we anticipated, our retreat also gave us some time to set a new agenda. It was not like a meeting, where you would call things to order and proceed point by point to debate and decide the future. Instead, every once in a while we would just start talking about something important. If the other felt like it too, we would keep talking; if not, we just moved on to frivolous things.

The funny thing is, we reached consensus on almost every issue we discussed almost immediately. We talked about career plans, family plans, how we want to live our lives each day, what our priorities are going to be. I expected that because Anna had been our only focus for so long, that once she was gone we would be without direction. That was not the case. Either we always thought a particular way and we just fit Anna into it or Anna gave us a direction that transcends her time with us, but at least on "big picture" stuff, our discussions were not journeys of discovery or dramatic shifts; they were simple recognition of where we had been going for a while. Of course, the devil is in the day-to-day details. We will struggle with those.

This was also going to be our chance to rediscover each other. It turns out that Anna had already introduced us to ourselves pretty thoroughly, especially over the last two months. It was still nice to goof around, but nobody mistook us for newlyweds. Either we demonstrated sufficient disdain for each other that it was obviously a marriage of long-standing, or the different last names confused the issue.

Anyway, we are home. It is good to be here. We visited Anna's grave on the way home from the airport. We finished our plans for her monument while we were on the trip. We plan to proceed with that ASAP.

We picked up our mail. It took us two and a half hours to open the cards we received while we were gone. We cried a lot, but we have discovered that crying a lot seems to cut down on headaches. Try it.

Mahalo (thank you) for your support.

We will keep you posted on things.

Anna's Dad

This was the longest sustained cry that either of us had from the time when Anna was first diagnosed. Although we cried often, we never sat for hours and cried, at least not until we got home and opened the cards. Then, there was no holding back. It was a tremendous catharsis.

Monday, December 25, 2000, 10:07 a.m.
From: Anna's Mom
Subject: Merry Christmas

From our home to yours and our families to yours, we wish all of you a blessed and peaceful Christmas. We are thankful for God's gift of His Son and for so many things. Looking back to the message we posted one year ago reminds us of the great breadth of human experience. May you feel God's unending love and Anna's angelic presence today and every day.

Anna's Mom

Sitting in Church on Christmas Eve was difficult. All I could do was imagine Anna in her red velvet coat and hat with the white faux fur trim that she wore last year for Christmas. Every little child in church (and there were hundreds of them) made us think of Anna. During the mass, I distinctly felt a warmth and heaviness in my left arm--the arm where Anna usually rested. If I closed my eyes, I could actually see her resting there and feel her snuggle close to my body. It was reassuring and heartbreaking at the same time.

Tuesday, December 26, 2000, 7:24 p.m.
From: Anna's Dad
Subject: Tuesday-finding a new routine

Well Christmas is over. It was harder than we thought. Actually, all of this is more difficult than we anticipated. We got so good at living in the moment. Now, the moment is not always the most pleasant place to be and it is hard to see beyond it. It is hard to describe the feeling, it is emptiness and hollowness and it feels like we are just going through the motions. It will be nice when the holidays are over just so we can establish a new routine.

We have seen more movies together in the last couple of weeks than in the last couple of years. It is even enjoyable to go to a bad movie. We still have lots of details to attend to, lots of loose ends. Each day we make a list, each day we cross things off. Kathleen goes back to the bench next week. We will probably post less frequently for a while. We still would like to hear from all of you.

Anna's Dad

Even going to the movies reminded us of Anna. John and Anna attended several matinees and the three of us went to at least two movies together. Anna would watch the movie screen. She was drawn to the wall full of color.

On one occasion, we saw some friends as we were leaving the theater and decided to go with them to a local restaurant to grab a bite to eat. The piped-in music was almost drowned out by the din of the diners, but I could hear Billy Joel's "Goodnight My Angel" in the background. I could not bear it, and I began to sob, right there over dinner. Our friends fell silent and I felt bad for making the situation uncomfortable, but there was nothing I could do. When I regained my composure, we continued dinner.

Grief is just below the surface at all times. It erupts more easily on some occasions than others.

We spent a quiet New Year's Eve with Bryan and Nancy. We were all still reeling a little from our recent losses and, accordingly, we all had a hard time finding joy in any of the festivities.

Sunday, December 31, 2000, 3:42 p.m.
From: Anna's Mom
Subject: New Years Reflections

We look back to one year ago and the post we sent to all of you, and it amazes us to see how much living we have done in the past twelve months. It is equally surprising to realize that such a little child can leave such a large void in our lives.

We wish every one of you could experience the warmth and love of God that we have felt, particularly of late, as we humbly receive your cards, letters, and prayers. You are God's messengers, reminding us that neither He nor you are far from us. We can never repay all of you for the gifts you have given to us and to Anna. Nonetheless, please know that we thank God for Anna, for all of Anna's Friends, and for the memories that we will all keep alive in our hearts.

It is impossible to greet the New Year without reflecting on the year that has past, and there is no way to avoid the melancholy that comes with the empty yet heavy feeling in our arms and against our chests where Anna used to rest. We pray that with the start of the new millenium, we will feel Anna's presence in our lives without feeling the heartbreak of her absence.

Sending our love to all of you and our best wishes for a blessed 2001.

Always,
Anna's Mom

Thursday, January 4, 2001, 8:00p.m.
Subject: Thursday-a new rose

One of the wonderful gifts we received in Anna's memory and honor was a plant in a clear vase. Although we did not realize it at first, one of the children who visited us at the funeral home told us that there was a fish in there. He was right. We named the fish Rosie, because he was such a beautiful red hue.

When Kathleen and I retreated after the funeral, Rosie and the plant went to live with my sister. Rosie did fine, but the plant had a hard time of it. Unfortunately the plant was pretty important to Rosie, so we got a new one.

A new plant was not enough. Rosie was a sufficiently important part of our lives that I went out and bought a 30 gallon aquarium and all of the stuff to go with it. We decided that Rosie should be centrally located to participate in our daily lives. We chose the fireplace. We took out all of the fireplace stuff, plugged up the chimney with foam, and tore off the fireplace screen. We built a special stand and put it on appliance rollers so we could roll the aquarium in and out of the fireplace for cleanings. We bought a book about aquariums and read it from cover to cover. We put in rocks and gravel and filled the aquarium with water. We waited a couple of days before we were going to put Rosie in because we wanted to make sure the water was suitable (ignoring the fact that Rosie was in the same water in his vase).

After two days, we subjected the water to the six tests available in the test kit, we added chemicals to make it right. The next day we tried again, still no luck. The major problem was the water hardness. The book suggested diluting with deionized water, so we went to a water supplier and got some. We did not get enough. The next day we got more, and more rocks, and more fake plants.

We set it all up yesterday and tested the water today. Everything was fine. Rosie loves it. When you sit on the floor by the tank he faces the front of the tank and just looks at you. He also watches the dogs, but not as closely as Ruby watches him. The front of the tank is already covered with Ruby nose prints. She sees him and then lunges at the tank. I hope Rosie has a strong heart. Rosie is a welcome addition to our living room. I am sure Anna would be pleased.

Anna's Dad

We needed something to fill our time, and Rosie obviously provided a welcome diversion. As with most of our "projects," it took on a life of its own. Friends would e-mail almost daily to check on Rosie and the other fish that called our aquarium home. It gave them a way to check on how we were doing without coming right out and asking. It made it a bit easier for all of us.

Yesterday we picked up some friends for Rosie to play with, two dalmatian mollies, five red fin tetras, and ten neon tetras. Before we even put them in the tank, we named the mollies "spot and dot," the five red fins "huron, erie, ontario, michigan and superior," and the ten neons "wolverine, spartan, brutus buckeye, hoosier, boilermaker, chief illiniwac, wildcat, hawkeye, bucky badger, and golden gopher" (we decided not to name one "nittany lion" because we did not know what a nittany lion was).

Once we put the fish in the tank with Rosie, however, it was apparent that we had misnamed one of the neon tetras. Although nine of them hung out together, one just hung out by himself pretending somehow he was better than the others and refusing to play with them regularly. We renamed this one "fighting irish." Then, this morning, that one was floating at the top of the tank. We then renamed him "Michigan basketball." We held a memorial service in the bathroom.

Anna's Dad

It is Saturday night and we are enjoying a gourmet dinner of chicken pot pies. Not our usual fare, but these are not usual times. I have been gone to New Judges' School in Lansing all week (I came home on Tuesday night because I missed my family), and on Wednesday, John took the opportunity to throw his back out. I have been gone from home by myself only twice in the last three years or so. On the first occasion in October, Anna started having seizures. On the second occasion, John became immobilized. I will not be leaving again by myself for a long time.

The New Judges' School was just that: we went to classes from 8:30 a.m. until noon and from 1:00 p.m. until about 5:00 p.m. for five days. Fifty-two of us from all over the state gathered together, shared our stories, and learned from each other. Some had been on the bench for over a year. Others had only four days of judging under their belts. Some had not yet taken the bench.

It was a wonderful place to learn and make new friends. I met two other judges whose children had returned to heaven. Reid returned before his fourth birthday and Mariah was born three months early. Both left their families several years ago. We shed tears and promised to keep in touch as the process of grieving is continuous. We smiled upon realizing that Anna, Reid and Mariah were probably getting to know each other while we were sharing their stories. I will never forget this week or the new friends who let me grieve by sharing Anna's beautiful story with them.

It is time to ice John's back. Thanks for your continued love and prayers,
Anna's Mom

When a child predeceases the parent it is considered exceptional, but we were amazed to find out how many others had experienced that exceptional circumstance. We talk about Anna all the time. Once people hear about Anna, they often come to us in private and share their own story of their wonderful son or daughter who has also returned to heaven. The telling brings tears to eyes that appear happy to the rest of the world. It is in telling the story to another who has experienced the same pain that remembering becomes a holy and cherished event. We are now part of a group to which no one wants to belong; it is a close-knit group nonetheless. Its members openly embrace each other's grief, they neither diminish nor shy away from it. And that makes all the difference.

Taking all of this equipment to Dr. Squires' office was a difficult ttask. Giving up her much loved Kid Kart and her other things was like giving up a part of her; it did not even matter that she never used the feeder seat. We fought hard for it, and it was hers. Our hospice friends later said that they saw Anna's chair being put to good use. That made us feel a bit better. But the whole experience showed us that it would be almost impossible for us to give away anything that was Anna's. So we never have, except for these items and her unused medical supplies.

On Monday, Kathleen brought Anna's wheelchair, her feeder seat, and her bathseat to Anna's neurologist's office. We donated them to the hospital's foundation to be used at Dr. Squires' direction. She identified another little girl who could use them. Perhaps already by now, they are being used.

We certainly hope that someone else can get as much joy from that wheelchair as we did. It was surprising how emotionally attached to that chair we had become. Looking back, Anna used it for a couple of weeks; it only seems like a lot longer than that. Of course, those two weeks were two of her best, but I think the chair meant a lot more than just those two weeks.

Just getting the chair was a bit of a struggle against the medical establishment and the insurance industry. That triumph was an important symbol for us. On another level, the chair also symbolized a yielding, an acceptance of the fact that a plain old normal stroller was just not going to do it for Anna any more, that she needed something special. As long as she was in a stroller, no one knew right away that Anna was different. I think we both found some comfort in that. We both thought that putting Anna in a wheelchair would make it a little harder for everyone else and for us to see how normal Anna was.

We were wrong. It was not our view of Anna that changed; it was our view of wheelchairs that changed. The chair did not make Anna less normal; Anna made the chair normal. So, I suppose, giving up the chair was a little like giving up her clothes or her crib. In that context, the emotional attachment is probably a little easier to understand. Either way, we both hope the next parents grow as attached as we did.

Anna's Dad

Tuesday, January 23, 2001, 8:45 p.m.
From: Anna's Mom
Subject: Two months ago

Today has been an interesting day.

Two months ago today, Anna returned to heaven. When I think about how long it has been since we held her, November 23rd seems like an eternity ago. The emptiness seems brand new. We are keeping busy but it is impossible to keep thoughts of her pudgy cheeks and deep blue eyes suppressed for long. Even when you are not thinking about her, you realize that you are picturing her in your arms. I am anxious for it to be next January 23rd. I think it will be a better day than this.

We have been spending much of our free time at the movies. We have seen more movies in the last month than in the last two years. Our latest film, "Finding Forrester," featured a wonderful rendition of "Somewhere Over The Rainbow" and "What a Wonderful World" as performed by the late Hawaiian singing sensation Israel Kamakawiwo'ole, better known as "Iz." This musician tipped the scales at 700 pounds, yet he had a wonderful tenor's voice. This song, which is played over Forrester's closing credits, is the same song that E-Toys used on their TV commercials during the holidays to entice parents to buy erector sets and snorkeling gear for their children. The song is beautifully lyrical and wonderfully poignant. We have downloaded it and been playing it every day on the computer. I think we will add this to our repertoire of songs to sing to our children.

Anna's Mom

If you need more evidence that Anna changed everything for us, even the calendar is not the same. The 23rd of every month is a special day for us. It is the date she left us and the date of her diagnosis. Similarly the 9th is a special day, the date of her birth. We set aside these dates every month to remember Anna. Kathleen lights a candle in her office on those dates. Everyone there knows what it means when the candle is burning brightly. I usually visit the cemetery on those dates. Actually, I visit the cemetery several times a week, it is only half a mile from the house. But during my visits on the 9th and the 23rd I work especially hard at remembering how those dates have changed our lives.

During January and early February I completed a project we had conceived while we were on our retreat. We decided we needed to find a special way to recognize all of the health care professionals who had gone above and beyond the call of duty in helping us care for Anna. We decided to do this with cheesecakes.

For a couple of days each week, I would go to the Las Vegas Cheesecake Company in Grand Rapids (the best cheesecakes in the state as far as we are concerned) and pick up cheesecakes. Then, I would spend the day delivering them with a card which is reproduced below.

It was an emotional experience to go back to all the places where we had spent so much time with Anna and see all the people who were so important to us. That is why it took so long to complete the project. You just could not take the emotional drain two days in a row.

We even managed to get cheesecakes to our out-of-town health care providers through the delivery services of The Cheesecake Factory. In all, we distributed almost fifty cheesecakes.

Monday, January 29, 2001, 4:35 p.m.
From: Anna's Dad
Subject: Monday

Today I went back through the archived messages on the list, from September 1999 to January 2001. I did it so I could have them all in one word processing file rather than having them scattered across the list archives. I could not figure out a quick way to do it, so I just copied them one by one. Although I really did not intend to read each one, I could not help myself. It was a very interesting journey. The farther down the path I got the harder it got. I knew how it ended.

As I read the messages of last summer (blissful in their ignorance of the ending) I wanted to tell the writer to watch out, just like you want to tell the young girl in a horror movie not to answer the door. As I got through July and August, I was crying like crazy. I knew what was coming. The funny thing is that I was not afraid of Anna's impending death. The event I was afraid of was in October, on the eleventh, when we finally had no choice but to recognize that there was no hope.

Reliving the death of hope was harder than reliving those last few weeks with Anna after hope was gone. I do not know why.

Anna's Dad

On November 23, 2000, Anna Evaleen Stuive returned to heaven. She was with us for one year, eight months, fifteen days, one hour and forty-four minutes. Every minute was a gift.

Although all our time with Anna was precious, it was not always easy to meet the day-to-day challenges of caring for her. We were very fortunate to have a lot of help. Along the way, we encountered people who went above and beyond the call of duty in caring for Anna or in helping us care for her. You are one of those people.

We will never forget your kindness. We cannot adequately thank you for the gift you have given to us and to Anna. Please accept this cheesecake as an expression of our gratitude.
Thank You.
Kathleen A. Feeney & John C. Stuive

Monday, February 5, 2001, 5:59 p.m.
From: Anna's Dad
Subject: Monday-breakfasts and berners

We are coming off of an extremely busy week. Last Thursday we attended the National Prayer Breakfast in Washington D.C. at the invitation of our congressman, Representative Vern Ehlers. Typically, we would not accept an invite that took us so far away from home for such a short time. In this instance, however, we have so closely felt the power of prayer over the last two years that it seemed appropriate that we might participate in a national celebration of prayer.

On the one hand, it was impressive to see our nation's leaders all gathered to pray. On the other hand, it seemed a little political with applause at the right times for the right people. I was drifting a little towards being cynical until, at the end of the breakfast, Wintley Phipps sang "When Peace Like a River."

We sang that song at Anna's funeral. The minute I heard the first word my head dropped and I began to cry. The music moved right through me. Although I could not look up, I knew that Kathleen was crying too. When the song was over and I got my composure back, I looked up, a little embarassed, but no one was watching us. After that, I felt bad that I had let my cynicism get the better of me. All in all it was wonderful and meaningful trip.

Following our trip to DC, this weekend, we traveled to Bay City and then Mt. Pleasant for the annual pilgrimage to Berners on Ice. No, this is not some Disneyesque ice follies show; it is an annual gathering at the home of Ruby's breeders (who started this list, by the way) for all of the Bernese Mountain Dog people in the state. It is "on Ice" because Ruby's breeders live on Saginaw Bay which is frozen over at this time of year. After lunch we typically let the dogs (about thirty or so berners) run around on the ice where they can run long distances and still remain within sight.

After the day on ice, we retire to the home of Sherrie Start in Mt. Pleasant where we (this year four families and ten berners, one bichon frise and two cats) pretty much just sleep and eat very well for a day or so.

This is the pack (plus or minus a couple of dogs) that would travel to Sherrie's after Berners on Ice. As you can see, they traveled other places too.

This is our first time doing the Berners on Ice weekend since 1998. In 1999 Kathleen was very pregnant; in 2000 we were in between Anna's surgery and a trip to San Diego.

This group of dog people has gotten together as long as we have had Ruby and all of the dogs get along very well. You might have a hard time imagining ten big dogs running around inside your house but it is not uncommon at Sherrie's. The thing that is probably hardest for you to imagine is that traditionally it is very peaceful. This year was a little different. Since we had last made it for the weekend, two of the dogs had died and three new ones had come on board. One of the missing dogs was Taiga. Tai was a big beautiful male who clearly commanded the entire pack. If things ever got out of control Tai could put things back to normal with a single bark or even a look. Tai's second in command, Brady, also passed away the week after Anna did. They left very big paws to fill and none of the other dogs were quite ready to fill them.

It appears the heir apparent is Ike, a 120 pound whole male. Unfortunately, the only dog that Ike really needed to put in his place was Jasper who fell madly in love with Piper and simply would not leave her alone. Things were still pretty peaceful, but it was certainly different. Ruby and Jasper slept all the way home.

In a way, the differences in the pack this year reflect some of the unsettled feelings we get when we go back to things that we did before Anna. The faces are the same and we are doing the very same things we used to, but for some reason it is harder to find fulfillment in the very things that used to offer a lot of joy. Hopefully, in the same way the pack will settle into a new hierarchy, we too will find new ways to enjoy the old things. For the pack and for us, this weekend was a step in that direction.

Anna's Dad

This feeling has yet to go away completely. During the first months after Anna's death everything seemed hollow. It was like we were going through the motions of our lives, but getting nothing out of it. Happiness was impossible to find, even in those things that used to bring us so much pleasure, like the dogs. This feeling was compounded every time we had a "first," the first time we went to the beach without Anna, our first dog agility trial without Anna, our fist visit to our favorite special restaurant without Anna. The passage of time has certainly helped, but it has not healed all wounds.

Wednesday, February 7, 2001, 4:01 p.m.
From: Anna's Dad
Subject: Wednesday–vive la difference

I have been dreading today for about three weeks. Today was the day I would try to achieve a final reckoning with White & White (our medical equipment supplier) and Spectrum Health.

Between confusing billing practices, confusing insurance practices, and all the emotional baggage that comes from reducing illness to dollars and cents, it has been an uphill struggle to try to make sense of the documents that come in the mail every day. To try to simplify things I created a database that reflected every charge from Anna's care providers and how insurance resolved it. It is only through the reports I could generate with the database that I was able to get the big picture.

Unfortunately the big picture was not always a clear one: insurance would deny claims they should clearly pay, the care providers would bill and get paid twice, we had four different insurers over Anna's life, and the care providers do not bill to the customer everything that gets billed to the insurance company. Adding up all of these things meant confusion. Until today, every contact I had with the hospital or the equipment provider regarding these matters failed to resolve anything. In the hopes of wrapping things up, I set up today's face-to-face meetings.

The closer we got to today, the harder time I had sleeping. Medical billers are very entrenched in how they do things. Even when you know you are right it can be very difficult to convince the billers. Today was different and *vive la difference*. Today the billers did all of the things they had previously told me that they would not or could not do. Today we all talked the same language, today we all worked toward a common goal, and today we all left having resolved many uncertainties. Today I was able to give them answers and they were able to give me answers.

Within two weeks, we should have the accounts completely worked out with both institutions. I am certainly thankful that it all seemed to be different today. The best part: we do not owe anything. They owe us. It is not possible for me to convey the incredible sense of relief that comes from resolving these uncertainties.

Anna's Dad

We intend to use the lessons we learned in the process of resolving our problems with insurers and health care providers to help other families.

Although dollar-wise, most of Anna's medical bills related to hospital care and doctor's visits, a significant portion also related to medications and equipment. An entire cabinet in our kitchen was dedicated to Anna's medications and the means to dispense those medications.

When Anna was on oxygen, we had an oxygen concentrator backed up by tanks. In the end, we found the tanks to be as effective in delivering the oxygen and they were much quieter so the concentrator became the backup.

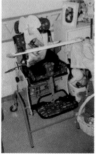

Anna's Kid Kart and her feeder seat (which she was never actually able to use) cost almost $5,000.

Wednesday, February 14, 2001, 5:00 p.m.
From: Anna's Dad
Subject: Wednesday–the good fight

Happy Valentine's Day. Today I met with Blue Cross/Blue Shield for our last level of internal appeal. Things do not look good. Apparently I confused you all last week with my positive news regarding my meetings with the hospital and medical equipment supplier. Those meetings went very well and we are on the same page with those folks. Our battle with insurance, however, continues.

In a way, it is very tempting to just drop it. She is gone. If BC/BS does not cover it, Children's Special Health Care will. We are probably not out any money either way. Still, it is so frustrating when the insurance company just denies coverage and provides no compelling reason. Today, they wanted additional information which, given their reason for denying coverage, is totally irrelevant. I will get it anyway. I will keep fighting. Maybe if we can make them see the light they will not do this to the next parent.

The most difficult thing to do is to remain civil when all you want to do is lash out and scream and yell and threaten. It makes me so tired to hold it in. If we fail at this step, I will not bother with the remaining steps in front of the insurance commissioner. Instead we will just file suit. Even that becomes an empty gesture. Although normal people fear the courts, insurance behemoths are very comfortable there. The BC/BS rep was quick to let me know today the name of the big law firm they use for their local matters.

I would pay handsomely if I could make this something we could settle with fists or by jousting or some physical way. Then, even if I lost, I could feel like I fought the good fight. There is simply no satisfaction in any of this.

Anna's Dad

I just finished reading the Anna's Friends "book" that the Muller family presented to us. For those of you who may not know, John's aunt, uncle and cousins extracted our messages from the list, set them in lovely type, and had them bound into a book for us. Although we have written almost all the posts to the list, only John has actually gone back and looked at all the posts in one sitting. I have not. It was unbelievable to see our heart-felt words organized and bound together so we could read them uninterrupted from start to finish.

I read the book in little bits, only an hour at a time. John read it cover to cover in one sitting. I just could not handle so much emotion all in one sitting. It has been a stressful week for both John and me. Stress and grief can take enormous tolls on the body, the emotions, and the psyche. Our exhaustion was quenched somewhat by 12+ hours of sleep last night. Too bad we cannot get that kind of reprieve every night.

I thoroughly enjoyed the beautiful red roses that John sent to me at work for Valentine's Day. Perched in the middle of this sea of red velvet was one beautiful white rose—from my beautiful Anna Evaleen. I have spent a lot of time wondering what color of roses we will plant at her grave site, but after seeing this beautiful arrangement, I am fairly certain that we will go with white roses.

As his Valentine's Day gift, John received a ukulele. He loves it. It was an easy decision after our trip to Hawaii and after realizing how deeply the song by Iz, the 700 pound Hawaiian singer, touched our hearts. John will have the song mastered in no time at all. I also have a renewed desire to pull my guitar out of hiding, so the two of us can learn together. The dogs are fascinated, kind of. We will see if they will sing with us.

We continue to marvel at how music can evoke immediate responses (typically tears) from us. John recently purchased the River of Dreams CD by Billy Joel because it contains the song "Goodnight My Angel" that I often sing to Anna. We put the CD in the tower of our computer hard drive and found three music videos

We are deeply indebted to John's Uncle Bruce and Aunt Cobie and his cousins Mike and Sheri and Chris and Leslie. The book they gave us inspired us to create this one.

Looking through the book from the Mullers permitted me to look at our entire life with Anna. Although I was consumed by my grief over losing her, I was not overcome by regrets. In fact, I have only two. First, I regret not getting Anna her wheelchair much earlier in the process. She really loved it and you could tell she was much more comfortable in it. And second, I regret not letting her squish around in her birthday cake on her first birthday. For some reason, we overlooked that rite of passage. These are not earth shattering regrets, but they are there.

It is funny that we do not at all avoid the music that causes us to remember. Instead, we embrace it. We have started building sort of a grief library of recordings. I think we like to listen to the music because it is a shortcut to the sort of meditative state where you can really feel things.

popping up on our monitor. One of the music videos was for "Good Night My Angel." It was in black and white and featured little children running in and out of scenes with white gowns on and big angel wings strapped on their backs. The tears were plentiful as we saw the vision that the lyrics had previously created in our minds. The tears feel good. In case you've never heard this song, I will include the lyrics after I sign off.

For now, we are doing okay, especially after our extended slumber. Enjoy the weekend. We will try to do the same.

Anna's Mom

Lullabye (Good Night My Angel)
by Billy Joel

John and Anna gave me a very special gavel when I took the bench. They inscribed the words from this song (You should always know-wherever you may go-no matter where you are-I never will be far away) on the top of the gavel box to remind me that no matter where I was, both of them would always be with me. The gavel sits on my bench so that I will never forget those words.

Good night my angel time to close your eyes
And save these questions for another day.
I think I know what you've been asking me
I think you know what I've been trying to say.

I promised I would never leave you
And you should always know
Wherever you may go
No matter where you are
I never will be far away.

Goodnight my angel now it's time to sleep
And still so many things I want to say
Remember all the songs you sang for me
When we went sailing on an emerald bay.

And like a boat out on the ocean
I'm rocking you to sleep
The water's dark and deep
Inside this ancient heart
You'll always be a part of me.

Good night my angel now it's time to dream
And dream how wonderful your life will be.
Someday your child may cry
And if you sing this lullaby
Then in your heart
There will always be a part of me.

Some day we'll all be gone
But lullabies go on and on
They never die
That's how you and I will be.

Monday, February 19, 2001, 8:57 p.m.
From: Anna's Dad
Subject: Monday

One of the things we learned from reading all of the Anna's Friends posts was that there were some gaps in the story. Some of those gaps we planned on leaving, others we wanted to fill in. Because we are getting down to the last few weeks before Anna's birthday (and the end of the list), we thought we should use the remaining time to fill those gaps.

Perhaps the most prominent gap occurred at the very beginning of this list. We never really told you anything about the day Anna was first diagnosed. I wanted to fill in that gap today but, I have sat in front of this computer for hours, typing and deleting, typing again and deleting again—for some reason, I just cannot do it. I can recount the chronology of that day, but I cannot really capture that day in words at all. So I am not going to try anymore.

Anna's Dad

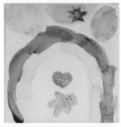

We celebrated Anna's second birthday at Clay Art Studios again. Although we will tell you more about that later, here is a preview of some of the second birthday tiles.

As we get closer to the end of the list, it gets harder to post. We have been working on pulling together all the resources we have that tell Anna's story. In addition to our posts and the letters we wrote, we have many pictures and some video. We recently obtained videotapes and audiotapes of a couple of interviews we did. We also have been reviewing our home videos.

The videos and audio interviews have offered us an unusual opportunity, a chance to bring Anna back. I know that sounds funny, but other than our initial participation, we had never seen or heard these things before. We had never reviewed some of our own home video. To see Anna again for the first time is a wonderful feeling. We saw the video of the Children's Miracle Network telethon from last summer. Anna made an appearance on the telethon, but we had never seen it. As we viewed the video, we had a new experience with Anna. Same with our home video. In fact, we have video from another interview that I have never seen. I am saving it for a time when I really need to be with her.

In a way I am trying to cheat death. When Anna died it seemingly brought to an end our opportunity to have new experiences with her. The little memorable moments, be they glances or cuddles or smiles or heavenly aromas or any shared experience, suddenly became a finite set. Now, I can add to them.

That brings me to my reason for posting today. If you have pictures or videos that include Anna or relate to Anna (pictures or videos that we did not give you, of course) please send them to me. I will make copies and send them back. We would be pleased to reimburse you for any postage.

Thanks.

Anna's Dad

We spent the better part of today doing some early spring cleaning. If you would like to come over and admire our freshly-scrubbed floors, just give us a call. We needed to clean up a bit because we are having our third meeting for "the foundation" tomorrow.

It's exciting to be on the ground floor of a project like this, but it is also a bit frightening. So many of these organizations barely get off the ground before they crash and burn for any number of reasons. We must succeed. I know that is quite an absolute thing to say, but it is true. We feel so strongly about this foundation because it is the continuation of Anna's legacy—she sat here with us two days before she died and listened quietly while we dreamed aloud about the foundation. We know it is a lot of pressure to put on a fledgling organization, but we are as sure about this project as we are about the fact that Anna was always meant to be our daughter. We will try to keep our expectations to a minimum, however, until we see whether our initial plans will take flight.

We are also feeling some trepidation as we approach Anna's 2nd birthday on Friday, March 9th. Last year's birthday party was such a wonderful celebration for her and for us—we watched the video last week and were amazed to see so many of you there painting tiles, writing on balloons, and sharing time with Anna. We cannot even imagine the birthday party that they will have in heaven for her this year. Anna will be running, laughing, and singing with the rest of the saints and angels! Be sure to think of her on Friday and remember how much happiness she brought into our world...and be sure to smile because we are confident that she will be smiling back at you.

Time to sign a few orders and head off to bed—hopefully to dream of Anna.
With all our love,
Anna's Mom

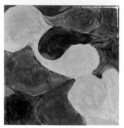

Just days before Blue Cross called, John told me that he was tired of this fight and willing to give it up. It just consumed too much of his emotional reserves. I was too busy with work to take on this battle, so we were really facing a dilemma. Thank God the matter was resolved before we gave up. By the way, they covered Anna's speech therapy expenses as well.

I am writing with tears in my eyes. I just got off the phone with a Blue Cross/ Blue Shield reprepresentative. They are going to cover Anna's physical and occupational therapy bills. We are still waiting to hear on the speech therapy, but I anticipate they will cover those as well. I am overwhelmed by a sense of relief. It will not make a difference to us dollar-wise, but it means so much to know that this will not end with an unjustified denial of a claim. More importantly, it means that it will end— no more fighting, no more phone tag, no more waiting on hold, no more pass the buck. We are certainly grateful to put that battle behind us. We can address all of the other challenges that we face with renewed vigor. Once again, prayers are answered.

Anna's Dad

Saturday, March 10, 2001, 4:23 p.m.
From: Anna's Mom & Dad
Subject: The end

From Anna's Mom:

3/9/01: I do not know how we can make it through a lifetime of March 9ths. I stopped at her grave this morning to give her some birthday balloons, to sing to her, and to wish her a happy birthday. Her first birthday in heaven. Can you imagine the celebration? I am sure it will be and is magnificent. I just wish we could be there to celebrate with her.

This was the first day since I have been back to work that I could not keep it all together at work. The 50 or so pictures of Anna that I have in my office all spoke to me of happier times. The dozens of tiles that were painted on her first birthday line the walls of my office like a living border; they remind me of the love of friends, family, and Anna. It was all too much to handle at times.

I kept a candle burning for her all day. Even the gentle scent of warm candle reminded me of Anna's heavenly smells. I just could not fathom that two years ago, we were waiting to see Anna's face for the first time. Now, two years later, we still yearn to see her face. A very good friend of ours who recently lost her spouse offered these words of comfort on Anna's birthday: "Above all I hope that it will not be too long before the sharp pain of your memories changes to a softer sorrow."

Right now, the pain is too great to even imagine that it will soften with time. I am so tired, tired of being strong, tired of having to understand that there is another plan that I cannot comprehend, tired of having empty arms, tired of trying to get on with life.

A part of me is gone. I cannot feel her when I need her most. The grief blinds my heart and prevents us (Anna and me) from reaching out to each other. Does she understand why we are sad even though we know that she is perfect and perfectly happy? Does she know how much we long to see her face, stroke her smooth skin, smell her freshly-washed hair, and kiss her velvety soft skin? Does she think of us as much as we think of her?

After reading this post, people approached me and said that they had no idea that I felt this kind of pain. Perhaps it is because I always try to maintain a positive attitude. Perhaps people see outward happiness and blinding grief as incapable of existing in one person at the same time. It can. Grieving is an energy consuming state of being. In some respects it is easier to simply go about your daily activities than it is to cry all day.

Whenever I feel really bad, I find myself focusing on or talking about the foundation. Maybe it is my living link to her. Maybe it is one of the greater goods behind God's plan for Anna and us; you know, there must be a good reason why God would put Anna and us through all this pain. The foundation might be that good reason. Maybe it is just my way of coping with the pain. I cannot tell.

I feel a tremendous weight on my shoulders—like the weight I felt at the hospital when we first received the news that Anna's time with us was not going to be measured in terms of years but in terms of months, weeks, or days. It is oppressive and smothering. I can only hope that with the passing of another day, and 364 more days to prepare for the next March 9th, I will be better prepared to handle her 3rd birthday.

I think Anna would have loved the remembrance we held for her at Clay Art Studio. She really loved her first birthday party there, and we felt very connected to her there tonight. Sometimes you just want to lose yourself in those moments. For tonight, however, I will only lose myself in the pain.

3/10/01: After a good night's sleep, I was tempted to erase all that I wrote last night after living through Anna's 2nd birthday. I decided that would not be a good idea. As John has told me, when words come from the heart, they are authentic and should not be tampered with. That is why, as we write our book about Anna's journey through life and death, we are using the words we wrote as we lived those events. From time to time, we feel compelled to drop a footnote to tell you more about the story behind the story. But for the most part, we rely on the words (and exclamation points) that came to us as we walked our short road with Anna.

Now that she is gone, we are still walking the road, but it is a different path—a fork that will hopefully link back up with the main path someday. Now, we are pursuing the path toward helping other families with terminally ill children reserve the precious little energy that they have at the beginning of each day to deal with their child's care. We want to protect those parents from energy-robbing experiences involving insurance, employment, and related problems. We want to care for the parents so they can care for their kids. Anna started us on this path, and we must see it through to the end. With your prayers and God's help, we will.

I agree with John that the pressure of ending the list is overwhelming. There is so much we want to say but words cannot describe how much we have relied on all of you for the prayers and support that helped us to survive each day since September of 1999. Just because the list will be discontinued does not mean that we must cease all communication. You are all welcome to contact us by e-mail or phone at any time.

You should all know, of course, that we will continue to keep all of Anna's Friends in our thoughts and prayers. We thank God for all of you. You were and are God's messengers coming to us and reminding us that God has not forgotten us throughout this journey. Yes, the journey continues one day at a time. Yes, we continue to need your thoughts and prayers. Yes, we will miss this link to all of you. But we are sure that we will always feel your love surrounding us and Anna.

We love you. Anna loves you. Remember to talk to her and smile when you think of her, because I am sure that she is smiling and laughing as she watches over all of us and all of the children who prayed for her.

The tears I cry now are tears of thanks. Not tears of good-bye.

Thank you Anna's Friends.

I leave you with the prayer that I used to say every night to Anna. I will continue to say it every night for all of us:

> May the Lord bless you and keep you. May the Lord let His face shine upon you and be gracious to you. May the Lord bless you and give you His peace. May His guardian angel watch over you and protect you from harm. May your eyes see clearly and your ears hear clearly, too. May you know how much we love you, and may you show that love in return. I pray that today was the happiest day of your life, and tomorrow will be happier than today. May you fall asleep quickly. May you have sweet, sweet dreams. And may God bring you back to us in the morning light.

Good night.

Love, Anna's Mom

From Anna's Dad:

The last post. I dread this because it means I will not have you to rely on anymore. Anna's birthday was a difficult day. Actually, it was not so much more difficult than the last few weeks. I have been working on a book about Anna. That means every day I have been reliving some part of Anna's life. The endeavor has made me smile a lot, but I have also cried a lot. I have cried more in the last two years than in the previous thirty-six. I have cried more in the last three and a half

This is a moment I will never forget. I only caught the end of the song as I came back into the room after my shower. Father and daughter were sharing a quiet moment together. It was so beautiful.

months than I ever thought I could. I sometimes wonder whether I will ever cry and then afterwards say to myself that it was my first cry in over a year. I doubt it.

The hardest part about Anna's birthday is that it brings back all of the hope we felt on the day she was born. I remember so well holding her in Kathleen's hospital room and singing her a song for over an hour. It was just a nonsense song, I sang to her about what it would be like to be one, and then two, and then three, and then what preschool and kindergarten would be like. I think we were somewhere in the high school years when we were interrupted by a visitor. As I look back, I realize how presumptuous that song was. I hope she is not mad at me for having misled her.

A few gathered at Clay Art Studio again, not so much to celebrate as to remember. We have an awful lot of wonderful memories. Without question, our days with Anna were the best days we have ever had. That is why the now is so hard. When I spent my days taking care of Anna, my calling was a noble one, I was consumed by love, I had a clear purpose. How can you ever top that?

Anna taught us a lot. She taught us to think and act like a family. She taught us that you better live today, this minute, right now. She taught us that everybody and every life is of inestimable value. She taught us that people who cannot walk or talk or do any of the other things that are considered normal are normal anyway. She taught us, in the words of Sister Felicia, that "just to be is a blessing." She taught us that the people you love are more important than anything. She taught us that it is ok to ask for help. She taught us not to be afraid of death. She taught us that worrying is just a big waste of time. She taught us more than you can possibly believe about our faith. She taught us to smile and laugh as often as you can. She taught us that the best thing, the very best thing, is to let someone hold you and to hold them in return. She taught us to just sit still for a while and watch and listen. She taught us that you can do anything.

Billions of people have lost loved ones. It makes me wonder why the world is not a better place.

Although we cannot ignore our sadness and our pain, it would be wrong to leave you with only that. You know the absolute joy and peace that Anna brought us. Do not forget that part of the deal. It is a shame (for us) that Anna cannot share her physical presence with us anymore. It would have been an absolute travesty if we had never enjoyed her physical presence at all. I think the gift that Anna was she always will be.

We will leave you with a poem written by Sister Felicia Bertaina. Sister Felicia taught the baptism class at Assumption Church, so she knew Anna almost right from the start. Then, I started RCIA classes led by Sister Felicia a couple of weeks before Anna was diagnosed. Anna came with us to almost every class.

Thank you so much. Keep the faith.

Anna's Dad

Just a Rose . . .

Anna, today you would be two . . .
    And you are.
You would walk and jump and run . . .
    And you do.
Your heart would beat so strong . . .
    And it does.

Your voice and laughter
    would ring so clear;
like sunshine your smile
    would fill the place;
like rose petals your hands
    would touch us with Love.

All that you would be . . .
    You are.
All that we long to see and hold . . .
    You are.
And more . . .

We see you and hold you
wrapped in mystery,
Embraced by Infinity.

Yes, just a rose . . .
So simple, so single, so tender . . .
A blossom hidden from sight,
    for a while,
    to grace forever . . .
our Garden our Home.

Chapter 11
The Monuments

The dictionary says that a monument is a lasting reminder of someone notable or great. Certainly Anna was sufficiently notable to be worthy of a monument. For Anna, one monument was simply not enough. We have worked to erect three monuments for Anna. But there is one more, the monument she left behind.

Anna stayed with us for one year, eight months, fifteen days, one hour and fourty-four minutes. Every minute was an incredible gift.

This may not seem like a long time to live but it was exactly as long as Anna was supposed to live because the amino acids were mixed up in the mitochondrial DNA of Anna's cells. The "mix-up" has been described to us as a defect, a mutation, or a disease. But, to us, because it was written into her cells from the moment she was conceived, it was as much a part of Anna as her blue eyes or her pudgy fingers.

Even though Anna did not live very long, she lived very well. She loved her dolly, her balloons, and ribbons. She loved her Bernese Mountain Dogs, Ruby and Jasper. She loved to watch the sunlight filter though the leaves of the big maple tree in the front yard. She loved to be sung to, read to, and she loved to be held. Anna especially loved to be held while she watched football games on television. As much as Anna loved to be held, she loved to hold others. She would always be sure to firmly grasp the fingers of anyone holding her, to let them know that being held was a two-way street. During July of 1999, Anna learned how to laugh. She forgot how to laugh a month later, but for that one month Anna loved to make people laugh by laughing first.

Anna brought all who knew her indescribable joy. Anna never walked, she never talked, she could not hold her head up, and for the last year of her life she could not even smile; nonetheless, she spoke volumes to us, she taught us many lessons, and she touched an entire lifetime's worth of people. We thank God for giving us Anna.

Anna's Parents

The Stone

Anna's first monument is a traditional one. It is a big black chunk of granite at her grave site. I encourage you to go see it because it really is beautiful. It certainly is "lasting." The monument company says it will last ten thousand years. It also certainly is a reminder of Anna. It features her picture, a few carved roses, some of the text from her obituary (kind of like an introduction to Anna), and, on the back, an artist etched a scene from our front yard with all the trees in full leaf and the gardens in bloom. Ruby and Jasper are there. I am in one of the Adirondack chairs and Kath is on the swing, holding Anna, as the sunlight filters through the leaves in the big maple. I can think of no more fitting reminder of Anna.

It took us 8 months to design, order and complete the stone. The wait was worthwhile because it is perfect. Her beautiful smiling face (one of the rose pictures taken when she was 6 months old) is laser etched on the stone's front. It is so good to see her gorgeous face smiling at us whenever we go to see her. It helps me to feel like I will never forget anything about her because I will always be able to see her smiling cherubic face.

We also put a bench between the pine and oak trees that shade Anna's grave. The bench carries a plaque that reads, "In Loving Memory of Anna Evaleen, Our Beautiful Rose." The stone beckons you to come and meet Anna, and the bench permits you to stay and visit for a while. Anna always loved visitors. We spend a lot of time there.

The Book

You are holding the second monument. This book is a lasting reminder of Anna and, from our perspective, it is the most important monument of all.

During the last few weeks of Anna's life, I wanted it all to be over. At the time, I could conceive of no purpose that was served by Anna being constantly asleep as we essentially waited for her to die. I often wished God would take her sooner rather than later so that we could move on to the next step. I know that sounds harsh, but it was the simple truth. Now, I see things a little differently. I see that hanging around those last few weeks gave Anna a chance to say goodbye to everyone and gave us a great and last opportunity to be a family. Nonetheless, I do not think that Anna or Kathleen or I could have continued that waiting much longer.

After Anna died, Kathleen gave her a bath and dressed her. Then we waited until it was light. It did not seem right to drive her to the funeral home while it was still dark, so we waited. After we arrived at the funeral home, we spent a long time talking to the funeral director as we held Anna. Eventually we realized that we were going to have to say goodbye. Right then, at that moment, I was struck by a crippling fear that I would forget what Anna looked like or the thoughts and feelings she inspired in me. That made it almost impossible to hug her for the last time and to say goodbye.

I still suffer from that fear, but simply putting pen to paper and compiling the materials that make up this book have significantly diminished it. When I open these pages, I remember.

Although I never asked "why," I would be lying if I said I did not have any questions during the last few weeks of Anna's life. Our parents blessed us by instilling in us a strong faith in God. Sometimes I wonder how I could have coped without that, without knowing that there was a heaven to receive Anna or a plan that she and we were serving (even if we could not understand it).

The Foundation

The third monument to Anna is The Anna's Friends Foundation, Inc. As you have already read, we established a foundation in the fall of 1999. That foundation was a trust solely for the benefit of Anna. The new foundation is a non-profit corporation for the benefit of families with terminally ill children. It is our attempt to do for others what so many did for us.

The purpose of the foundation is to support the parents of terminally ill children so that they may preserve their energy for the care of their children. With the help of other parents and medical professionals, we have identified a number of programs that we believe will lighten the load for parents. First and foremost, we want the foundation to be the one place parents can turn when they need help.

To let parents know we might be able to help, we are setting up a first contact group. With the cooperation of local hospitals, doctors, and clergy, parents will learn of Anna's Friends as soon as practicable after they first learn of their child's terminal diagnosis. If the family is interested, we will come and see them in the hospital. Our first contact groups will come equipped with a "stuff" bag with items that are useful when you on living on "hospital time," information regarding Anna's Friends, and open ears.

Those first few days actually do not offer as many opportunities to help as you might think. It takes some time for the news to sink in and for families to get used to the idea that their lives have dramatically changed. The mourning begins immediately. It will be a continuous process thereafter.

We hope to help families deal with that grief, but we are as concerned with the practical day-to-day challenges they will face. There are many new questions that follow a terminal diagnosis. Will insurance cover prescribed treatments? Will I be able to keep working? Where are we going to get the money to pay for extraordinary medical expenses? How do I fill out these forms? We are in the process of preparing informational brochures covering these and other topics to give parents some peace of mind.

For example, on the topic of insurance, with the assistance of parents, attorneys, and representatives of the insurance industry, we are preparing a brochure that instructs parents on how to compile the documents necessary to determine the scope of coverage, how to organize and record the information from explanation of benefit forms and medical bills, and how to handle disputes regarding coverage. We will also offer seminars on the topic and hands-on assistance from volunteer attorneys if it proves more than the parents can handle on their own. We plan to offer brochures, seminars, and volunteer attorneys ready to assist on other topics including employment, fund-raising, and special education requirements. In all these areas we are attempting to provide immediate assistance to answer the questions that can tear you up when you ought to be thinking about your child.

After Anna was first diagnosed, we found we were so consumed with her care that we let a lot of other things go. We missed a lot of meals, let the house degenerate into a mess, inside and out, and never got around to running a lot of errands that otherwise fill up the day. We were fortunate in that we had a wealth of friends and family that filled the gap. Every family with a terminally ill child needs that kind of support.

We do not anticipate that the foundation will be able to supply that kind of assistance to every family, nor is it our goal. Although we plan to coordinate volunteer assistance for some situations, we will instead focus on helping each family build its own community of support. Everyone has family, friends, colleagues, and neighbors. They are all looking for a way to cope with their own grief and they are all looking for a way to help the family. For the family, it is often very difficult to ask for and accept assistance. Sometimes, just taking the time to think of ways that family and friends can help is difficult. It is usually a question of organization and that is where we can help.

We also hope to serve as a library of sorts. Not so much a library of books, but a library of equipment. Terminally ill children need all sorts of special equipment. It is hard to know what you need or what works best unless you have an opportunity to see the equipment and actually try it out. We also hope to provide internet access for parents. The internet proved an invaluable source of information for us as well as a powerful point of connection to other parents and our friends and family.

If parents had an opportunity to learn about the helpful equipment that exists in today's marketplace, i.e., tumbleform chairs, bath seats, completely adjustable wheelchairs that do not look like wheelchairs, and the like, they would be much more inclined to seek out these aids for their terminally ill child. We received a feeding chair and bath seat for Anna that were wonderful, but they arrived too late. Had we known about them, we would have ordered them earlier. Information is power, and that is exactly what parents with terminally ill chidren need: power to help their children.

We hope to house our library in a facility, probably just a house. We envision a home where parents can come for a little respite, to talk about how things are going, and to learn. This may take some time, but we want to offer a safe place to go when things get overwhelming.

Finally, we hope to focus the voices of families in need so that they are heard by all. The health care system is geared towards healing. Sometimes, when that system is confronted with terminal illness, it does not know how to handle it. Therefore, we will work to educate doctors and nurses as to how they can meet the special needs of families with terminally ill children. Similarly, our federal, state and local governments need to know about the special needs of families with terminally ill children and how they can help these families.

That is Anna's third monument. It is my full time job. You have already helped the foundation by buying this book. A portion of the proceeds from the sale of each book goes directly to the foundation. If you want to help more, buy the book for a friend (an order form follows this chapter) or you can contribute directly to the foundation with a donation of time or money. Even if you cannot help the foundation, you can help families in need in your area. I promise, you will get more than you give and, in heaven, Anna will smile.

The Last Monument

The final lasting reminder of Anna is not something we did; it is something she did. Anna changed everyone who knew her irrevocably. We learned from her and we live differently now. That certainly fits the dictionary definition of a monument.

Perhaps you have already seen some of these lessons in the preceding pages. We believe the lessons she taught us have almost universal applicability, so we hope you will bear with us as we try to set them out in one place. We also hope that Anna's lessons will benefit you.

Lesson 1: Do Not Worry

After Anna was diagnosed, I was almost beside myself with worry. I would start thinking about her death and my mind could not let it go. I would imagine scenario after scenario, how it might happen and what I would do in response. I convinced myself that I was preparing myself. My incessant worrying was undoubtedly the reason I kept asking the question, "when is it going to happen?"

All that worrying accomplished nothing, but I had a hard time letting it go. I even asked other people, people whom I knew had lost loved ones to terminal illness, whether contemplating the end before it actually happened might not have helped them prepare for it. The answer was unanimously no.

Over time, several things worked together to free my mind of worries. First, eventually, I had to recognize the utter futility of worrying. There is simply no part of worrying that is positively reinforcing. Second, the immediate demands of caring for Anna simply did not permit a lot of time for cogitating on an uncertain future. It is difficult indeed to give your child the fullest life possible when all you are thinking about is the fact that life will be short. Third, and finally, every single time something came up, God gave us the grace to deal with it. After a while, we acquired some expertise at facing unexpected and frightening events. In fact, that leads me to Anna's second lesson.

"Do not be anxious about anything, but in everything, by prayer and petition, with thanksgiving, present your requests to God. And the peace of God, which transcends all understanding, will guard your hearts and your minds in Christ Jesus."

Phillipians 4:6-7, The Holy Bible, New International Version.

Another category of thought that is as futile as worrying is "why" or "why me" thinking. After Anna was diagnosed it took a little while to get beyond that focus. Until we did, however, we could not take control and be effective advocates for Anna.

LESSON 2: YOU CAN HANDLE IT

This lesson did not actually originate with Anna; it is straight from the Bible. Although there is some comfort in this lesson, it is not always immediately apparent. Whenever people would say, "God does not give you anything you cannot handle," we would wince inside. In fact, in our heads we would frequently respond with words often attributed to Mother Teresa, "I know God will not give me anything I cannot handle. I just wish He did not trust me so much."

No matter how hard it was to hear, the lesson was proven true again and again. We could handle it. We did handle it and so can you. In the hospital when Anna just would not wake up, as we reviewed the MRI films and found out how short her life would be, in the car on the way home from Thanksgiving while Anna gasped as if each breath were her last, in San Diego as Anna endured test after test, in the waiting room as we wondered whether Anna would return from surgery, at a Med-Center in Wisconsin as we felt so far from home, at home on a quiet Sunday as Anna had her first seizure in months, in San Diego again as the opthalmologist told us Anna could not see us, at home in the big green chair as Anna screamed, in the neurologist's office as we learned that Anna's time with us was drawing to a close, in the wee hours of the morning when Anna would stop breathing again and again, on Thanksgiving as Anna finally gave in, at the funeral home as we gave up our baby, in the narthex of the church as they closed the casket, at the cemetery as we said our final goodbye, we handled it. I do not mean that we simply closed our eyes and endured it or that we somehow managed to live through the experience. I mean that, at those dark times, right there in that moment, God gave us the grace and peace to cope. At those moments we were given everything we needed.

That is also a part of the biblical version of this lesson. After the assurance that we will not be tested beyond what we can bear, Paul explains: "[God] will also provide a way out so that you can stand up under it." 1 Corinthians 10:13, The Holy Bible, New International Version. He always did. Sometimes that "way out" was an overwhelming sense of peace that could have no other source. Sometimes that "way out" came in the form of the helping hands or kind words of someone else, but that is actually part of Lesson 3.

"And God is faithful; he will not let you be tempted beyond what you can bear."

1 Corinthians 10:13, The Holy Bible, New International Version.

If you are a parent, it is not only true that you can handle it, it is also true that you must. You see, no one knows your child better than you do. Doctors do not know your child as well. Nurses do not know your child as well. Therapists do not know your child as well. Trust your instincts. Persist in questioning until you get answers that satisfy you. You are your child's most effective advocate. You control the scope and nature of medical examinations, procedures, treatments, and therapies. If you do not, someone else will and it will be someone who does not know or understand your child as well as you do.

A grieving person's need for comfort is almost insatiable. Before Anna, I was not inclined to satisfy that need. At a funeral, I might offer a couple of platitudes, but thereafter, I would never broach the subject of loss with the grieving person. I would excuse myself to myself by claiming I just did not know what to say. I have since found that what you say beyond "I am so sorry" is not all that important. Listening is the key. Another thing I have discovered is that it is almost always acceptable to talk about the person who has died. Whatever you do, do not act uncomfortable and turn away. Death is not the exception, it is the rule. Someday it will be you with the insatiable need for comfort and a willing ear.

Lesson 3: Ask for Help When You Need It & Accept It Graciously

Although we could handle it, we could not handle it alone. It was difficult to learn to ask for help. Asking makes you vulnerable and dependent. That is not how we were brought up. That is contrary to the spirit of independence that lies at the foundation of our American culture. God helps those who help themselves, right?

Wrong. In fact, that message is contrary to biblical teachings and it was certainly contrary to our experience. It took some effort to ask for help, but once we did there could be no question it was the right thing to do. It was the right thing for Anna's sake and for ours. It was the right thing for all who came to our aid as well. People want to help; people need to help. You have to let them help.

As we mentioned in our first letter to Anna's Friends, sometimes the assistance we received from others was more than we could take with a dry eye. If you offered or provided assistance and we looked away for a moment, it was because we were crying tears of gratitude for the knowledge that we were not alone. Anna's Friends met our needs in every way you can imagine. They relieved us of the burden of work, at our jobs and at home, so we could spend time with Anna. They gave us money so we could care for Anna. They gave us food so we could eat. They held Anna so we could rest. They gave us strength through prayer. They renewed us and invigorated us. They comforted us. I cannot conceive of any need that remained unmet. Everything was given to us for the asking. For everyone's sake, do not try to keep warm alone.

Lesson 4: Provide Help in Your Community Whenever You Can

Lesson 4 is a necessary corollary of lesson 3. We received so much that we can never repay. Our response, in gratitude, is to try to do the same for others. That is what the Anna's Friends Foundation is all about. We now also keep our ears closely attuned to requests for help at church, at work, and in our neighborhood. We are compelled to support the community that supported us. That, in part, is what defines a community.

You do not have to be Mother Teresa to support your community. Simple things like neighborhood picnics or recycling or just patronizing local businesses will help. The important thing is to realize that you are part of a community and, then, to live that way.

LESSON 5: SET YOUR PRIORITIES AND LIVE THAT WAY, TODAY

This is a lesson Anna taught us in part when she was with us and in part after she was gone. As to setting priorities, when Anna was with us, we did not have to think about it. She effectively set them for us. Every day we would wake up and know that caring for Anna and giving her the fullest life possible was our number one priority. All the numbers after that were not that important. What she taught us while she was with us was the importance of living out our priorities right now, today.

I do not mean to suggest that before Anna we were simply muddling through our lives without purpose. We had goals and priorities, but they were poorly defined and not particularly challenging. They were often pushed to an unknown time in the future and it was hard to link them up to what we were doing that day.

In contrast, when Anna was with us, we had a clarity of purpose that animated every day. When Anna died we lost that and, in much the same way we wanted Anna back, we wanted that clarity of purpose and sense of fulfilled priorities back. The only way to get it back was to spend time thinking about it, talking about it, and resolving exactly what our priorities were going to be. We did some of that on our retreat. We continue to do it every day.

I will not bore you with the priorities and goals we have chosen. I will tell you, however, that it is easier to get up every day knowing those goals and priorities and it is easier to go to bed at night knowing how what we did that day fits within them. I wish you that same peace.

MORE LESSONS

There are more lessons that Anna left behind. Some are less weighty: take lots of pictures, laugh whenever you have a chance, cry whenever you have to, hold close the ones you love, and do not forget to sometimes just sit quietly, watch, and listen. Others require no explanation: just to be is a blessing, all life is sacred, and death is part of life and not to be feared. We value these lessons as well. We do not doubt that we will discover new lessons from Anna for the rest of our lives. And we also look forward to the lessons she will teach us when we get to see her again.

Thank you Anna's Friends.

Anna's Parents.

"Since no man knows the future, who can tell him what is to come?"

Ecclesiastes 8:7, The Holy Bible, New International Version.

There is a Dutch phrase that sort of describes what I am talking about: helder ogenblik. Roughly translated it means a moment of clarity. That is what we had when Anna was with us, a moment of clarity.

You already know Anna's story. Maybe you can help us.

The Anna's Friends Foundation

We support the parents
of children
who face terminal or life-
limiting diagnoses
by assisting them
in caring for their child
and by helping with the
tasks of daily life.

Anna's Friends can help

We asked many parents to identify the things that pulled at them, that drained their energy or otherwise kept them from being able to care for their child. Based on what they told us, we are developing a few programs to help.

1. Building communities of support.
2. Issue education for parents.
3. Equipment Library.
4. A helping hand in the hospital.
5. Education for medical professionals.

Maybe you can help us.

The Anna's Friends Foundation is always looking for new friends to help families in need. We offer a wide variety of volunteer opportunities. Whatever your abilities, we can use your help. The Anna's Friends Foundation also accepts financial contributions.

To learn more, or to let us know if you can help, just call or write to:
The Anna's Friends Foundation, Inc.
6132 Rogue Lane NE
Belmont, MI 49306
taffi@iserv.net
616-361-9478
We cannot wait to hear from you.

Of course, there are other ways to help. Please consider a contribution to either of the following:

 The Mitochondrial and Metabolic
Disease Center
c/o Dr. Robert Naviaux
UCSD School of Medicine
214 Dickinson St., CTF C-103
San Diego, CA 92103-8467

UNITED MITOCHONDRIAL DISEASE FOUNDATION
United Mitochondrial Disease Foundation
P.O. Box 1151
Monroeville, PA 15146-1151

Be sure to let them know that your contribution is in memory of Anna Evaleen Stuive.

 # Order Form

If you would like to obtain additional copies of *Anna's Friends*, please call or write us and provide the following information:

Name: _____

Address: _____

City: _____ State: _____ Zip: _____-____

Telephone: ___-___-____ e-mail address: _____

Payment

Please indicate the number of copies: ____

Each copy of *Anna's Friends* is $27.95.

There is a 10% discount for orders of 5 or more books.

Please include $4.00 shipping and handling for the first book, and an additional $2.00 for each additional book.

Please add 6% sales tax for books shipped to Michigan addresses.

Make checks payable to: Rogue River Books L.L.C.

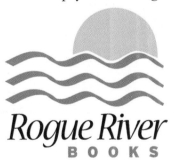

Rogue River Books L.L.C.
P.O. Box 253
Belmont, MI 49306-0253
(616)-364-1068
rrbooks@iserv.net

A portion of the proceeds from the sale of every copy of *Anna's Friends* will benefit the Anna's Friends Foundation p.s. these are some of the tiles that were created at Anna's third birthday party.